The Complete Films of
MARLENE DIETRICH

The Complete Films of

MARLENE DIETRICH

by HOMER DICKENS

Revised and updated by JERRY VERMILYE

A Citadel Press Book
Published by Carol Publishing Group

First Carol Publishing Group Edition 1992

A Citadel Press Book
Published by Carol Publishing Group
Citadel Press is a registered trademark of
Carol Communications, Inc.

Editorial Offices   Sales & Distribution Offices
600 Madison Avenue   120 Enterprise Avenue
New York, NY 10022   Secaucus, NJ 07094

In Canada: Canadian Manda Group
P.O. Box 920, Station U
Toronto, Ontario M8Z 5P9

Design: William Meinhardt

Manufactured in the United States of America
10 9 8 7 6 5 4 3 2 1

Carol Publishing Group books are available at special discounts
for bulk purchases, for sales promotions, fund raising, or
educational purposes. Special editions can also be created to
specifications. For details contact: Special Sales Department,
Carol Publishing Group, 120 Enterprise Ave., Secaucus, NJ 07094

Cataloging data for this title may be obtained from the
Library of Congress

ISBN 0-8065-1316-0

To

The memory of

AILEEN FRANCES DICKENS

1901 – 1961

always in my heart

ACKNOWLEDGEMENTS

The writer of any book must obviously and inevitably be indebted to a great many people—especially when the book is a pictorial one. The nature of this indebtedness is much too complex to be indicated below, but its full extent is most assuredly realized by the author.

THE INDIVIDUALS:

Alan G. Barbour	Al Kilgore	Ruth Nachtigall	Michael Sparks
Jean Barbour	Dolores Kilgore	James R. Parish, Jr.	Eberhard Spiess
Bob Board	Leni Kroul	Alfonso Pinto	Neil Sullivan
Manus Canning	John B. Kuiper	Gustav Postén	Romano Tozzi
Carlos Clarens	Gerhard Lamprecht	Mark Ricci	Charles Turner
John Cocchi	Wolfgang Längsfeld	Gene Ringgold	Lou Valentino
Lotte H. Eisner	Joseph Longo	Olle Rosberg	Katharine Vaughan
William K. Everson	Albert Lord	Michael Russ	Jerry Vermilye
E. M. Hacke-Baedeker	Cliff McCarty	Lillian Schwartz	James Watters
Elza Irbe	Dion McGregor	Robert Shaye	Jürg Zander

— *with special thanks to* —

Geoff N. Donaldson	Rudolf Leutner	Norman Miller	Jack Edmund Nolan

THE INSTITUTIONS:

Academy of Motion Picture Arts and Sciences (Los Angeles)
Cinémateque Française (Paris)
Cinémateque Royale du Belgique (Brussels)
Cineteca Italiana (Milan)
Det Danske Filmmuseum (Copenhagen)
Deutsche Kinemathek, e.V. (West Berlin)
Deutsches Institut Für Filmkunde (Wiesbaden-Biebrich)
Deutsches Institut Für Film und Fernsehen (Munich)
Filmhistoriska Samlingarna (Stockholm)
George Eastman House of Photography (Rochester)
Goethe House (New York City)
Institut Für Theaterwissenschaft der Universität Kölns Niessen Collection (Cologne)
Jugoslovenska Kinoteka (Belgrade)
Library of Congress (Washington, D.C.)
Memory Shop (New York City)
Museum of Modern Art Film and Still Library (New York City)
National Film Archive/British Film Institute (London)
New York Public Library's Theater Collection (New York City)
Osterreichische Gesellschaft Für Filmwissenschaft (Vienna)
Proszenium (Kemnath-Stadt)
Puritan Film Laboratories, Inc. (New York City)
Transit-Film Gesellschaft, G.m.b.H. (Frankfurt am Main)
United Press International (New York City/Los Angeles)

Contents

The Legend Lives On

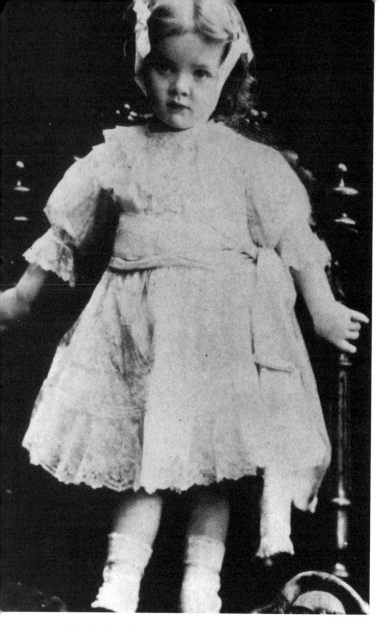

Maria Magdalene Dietrich at two

"She was one of those rarely gifted beings who cannot look or speak or even stir without waking up (and satisfying) some vague longing that lies dormant in the hearts of most of us."

— GEORGE DU MAURIER
Trilby

Marlene Dietrich is a woman. But don't let an apparently simple statement mislead you. It is a woman's nature to be complex and simple at will, whichever pleases her at the moment. Perhaps this is why they have fascinated men — and members of their own sex—since the beginning of time. There are no two alike.

Despite all you have read, heard, or thought about her, it is Dietrich the *woman* who today survives the golden age of Hollywood, a splendiferous era of star-making, the likes of which we shall never again see.

Nowadays, there are no shadows cast by great studios, and businessmen sit where once ruled men of creativeness and imagination. Yet, at a time when she makes very few film appearances, Marlene Dietrich still commands attention wherever she goes and whatever she does. What is it that can still a noisy room to utter silence? Certainly not just a glamorous appearance.

Few of her contemporaries possessed this *quality,* which has enabled Dietrich to appeal to the movie-goers of today as she did to those of yesterday. The future, too, seems to be hers, for the *quality* I speak of is not confined to any particular medium or time and thus it is twice as difficult to define — if, indeed, it can be defined at all!

Dietrich seems to possess an inner magic (for want of a better word) which she, as a woman, knows how to utilize to its fullest extent. This is coupled with a wisdom acquired over the years — from her acting, her associates, her friends, and a strong will to improve upon what she already has. Thus, she has become more than just a "body." She has become a mind *and* body. As a performer she senses what audiences need and want, knows just what of herself to give, and when to break off, leaving them not only enriched but longing for more.

This is why Dietrich the woman is stressed, not the actress, the entertainer, the chanteuse, the authoress — she is all of these and more, but they are only a small part of the *enigma* which was created solely for the movies and has confounded all by its infinite variety and seemingly endless longevity.

Upon her arrival in the United States in mid-1930, the publicity hawks at Paramount Studios began to veil her background in mystery and half-truths, thus hoping to create a "Paramount Garbo." (Her *creator,* Josef von Sternberg, undoubtedly commanded this campaign to satisfy his urge to be responsible for a sublime "creation"!) Comparisons between Garbo and Dietrich, to set the record straight, had actually begun in Germany as early as 1929. At first, Dietrich gave no interviews and would only be seen in the company of von Sternberg. It soon became apparent to studio executives that comparison to Metro's lady was absurd. Dietrich could hold her own — and did!

Although she disliked participating in publicity

of any kind, her mentor assured her this was a necessary evil and advised her to go along with the campaign as best she could. The public, he reminded her, determined whether or not a studio's player became a star. Soon she began admitting nothing — letting her publicity releases speak for themselves. And what a useless barrage of "facts" they were! Her birthplace was changed. Her father and stepfather changed places and sometimes merged into one. Dates ran together. Even her age—not that it really ever mattered—was never the same twice in a row! Anywhere between 1898 and 1904 was given, preferably the latter.

In 1964 Marlene Dietrich's birth certificate was reportedly located in an East Berlin registry and sent to West Berlin officials. Perhaps even this document's authenticity can be challenged. Who knows? But, anyway, this scrap of paper tells us that Maria Magdalene Dietrich was born on December 27, 1901, in the West Berlin district of Schöneberg. She was the second daughter born to Louis Erich Otto Dietrich, an officer in the Royal Prussian Police, and his wife, the former Wilhelmina Elisabeth Josephine Felsing, daughter of Conrad Felsing (then head of the famous Felsing jewelry firm in Berlin).

The Dietrichs maintained a strict German household. They were of that middle-class aristocracy whose ancestors had enjoyed not only wealth but position — leaving their decendants with a tradition to live up to. Little Maria Magdalene gained a tremendous self-discipline from the severity of this early upbringing, but at the same time a strong-willed nature was being nurtured. She and her older sister Elizabeth were taught proper etiquette and, from a governess, gained a workable knowledge of French and English.

Not long after the Dietrichs moved to Weimar, the capital of the Grand Duchy of Saxe-Weimar-Eisenach, Herr Dietrich died. Although they were very young, the girls missed their father. Their mother, having a penchant for military men, soon met and later married Edouard von Losch, of the highly-respected Regiment of Grenadiers. In the role of stepfather to the girls, von Losch won their immediate love and respect.

Frau von Losch noticed a musical talent in her younger daughter at an early age, and soon Maria Magdalene was taking both piano and violin lessons. In her late teens she made remarkable strides in her violin studies, and by 1921 her mother, now a

At five

widow a second time (Herr von Losch had died at the Russian front during the final months of World War I), managed to enroll Maria Magdalene in Berlin's highly-acclaimed Hochschule für Musik, the State musical academy.

Her future looked bright as a concert artist. Maria Magdalene approached her studies with fantastic vigor and spent many hours daily practicing her lessons over and over until perfection was reached. But a concert career was not to be hers. It was soon discovered that over-practice had produced a large ganglion on the primary nerve of her left wrist, which left but one alternative: stop the study of the violin at once, or suffer serious consequences!

After this tremendous disappointment, Maria

Magdalene, already a movie fan like other girls her age, began to entertain the thought of becoming an actress. This newly-discovered desire soon manifested itself in the idolization of Henny Porten, the popular actress. Maria Magdalene began to wait near the film studios each day for a glimpse of her favorite. One day, after noticing the girl standing near the gate for weeks, Henny Porten stopped to speak to her. Upon learning from Maria Magdalene that she wanted to become an actress, Miss Porten complimented her upon her loveliness and encouraged her desire to act.

Soon she became obsessed with the idea of studying at Max Reinhardt's illustrious Deutsche Theaterschule, which the great producer-director ran in conjunction with his Deutsches Theater, then the mecca for Germany's avant-garde playwrights. But besides presenting current works, Reinhardt also gave the German public lush Shakespearean productions and other classics, as well as popular musical entertainments.

Frau von Losch, still struggling to keep her proper place in society and bring up two girls, refused to give permission to Maria Magdalene for such a wild idea unless the von Losch name was withheld completely. After all, a concert career was one thing, an acting career quite another!

The neatly dressed young blond who faced the great Reinhardt a few days later gave her name as "Marlene Dietrich." It hadn't taken her long to combine her first two names (*Mar*ia and Magda*lene*) and assume her father's surname. Jean Cocteau, in Monte Carlo years later, rhapsodized, "Your name, at first the sound of a caress, becomes the crack of a whip . . ."

Her interview with Reinhardt was brief and painfully to the point. She was not, he felt, ready to study at the Deutsche Theaterschule.

Disappointed but not discouraged, Marlene (as she was to be known from then on) auditioned for a job in a chorus and because of her shapely legs was hired by Guido Thielscher as one of the Thielscher-Girls in a spicy revue that would tour some of the larger cities outside Berlin. Also in this chorus line were Alice Hechy, Trude Hesterberg, Charlotte Ander, and Ellen Müller, all later to appear in films with Dietrich. The experience gained from this engagement proved useful in her career. But outside Berlin wasn't "in."

In the euphoria of this bit of theatrical exposure, Marlene returned to Berlin in the spring of 1922

An eager young student at Max Reinhardt's Deutsche Theaterschule

and auditioned once again for the Deutsche Theaterschule. This time she was accepted. She studied hard and found this *new* world of acting quite unlike anything she had hitherto experienced.

Along with their studies, Reinhardt's young tyros got many opportunities to appear in his various productions (or work behind the scenes in a technical capacity, thus discovering the importance of lighting, costuming, sets, props, etc.) and soon Dietrich got a small role in Shakespeare's *The Taming of the Shrew* which was followed by an appearance as Hippolyta in *A Midsummer Night's Dream*.

Then one day Dietrich was informed at five o'clock in the afternoon that she was to play a small role that very evening in *Der Grosse Bariton* (*The Great Baritone*), starring the renowned actor Albert Bassermann. Another young actress had been forced to drop out of the play because of illness. The première was a success, and Marlene benefited immensely from this sudden experience!

This lucky break led to her being cast in Georg Jacoby's film *So Sind die Männer*, a Union-Film being made at the enormous Ufa (Universum-Film Aktiengesellschaft) Studios just outside of Berlin. Set in Napoleonic times, Dietrich played a housemaid named Kathrin. The cast included Harry

Liedtke, Paul Heidemann, Loni Nest, Antonia Dietrich (no relation), and Kurt Vespermann. When the film was released early in 1923, the title had been changed to *Der Kleine Napoleon.*

It wasn't long after this first film appearance that Marlene was selected by one of director Joe May's production assistants—a young Sudeten Czech named Rudolf Sieber—at the Theaterschule for an important little part in *Tragödie der Liebe,* a drama starring the great Emil Jannings. She was told to report to the Ufa-Studios the next morning. The girl that arrived there that morning made quite an impression in a borrowed red silk dress and sophisticated hair style — but it was the *wrong* impression! The part May was casting was that of Lucie, a judge's mistress bent on attending Jannings' murder trial! Once May had gotten over his initial shock

In Eric Charells' musical revue Von Mund zu Mund

at this vision in red, he asked Rudolf Sieber to take Marlene to the wardrobe department for an over-hauling. The transformation was well worth waiting for. Parading before May was a fuzzy-haired blond floozy clad in a feathered housecoat, sporting a monocle Sieber had given her from the prop room. Everyone on the set was reduced to uncontrollable laughter as Marlene gave her all! But May was not laughing. He was carefully observing this provoca-tive creature and her unique handling of her mono-cle, which would occasionally catch the glare from the kleig lights, creating a halation.

Needless to say, Dietrich was hired, and the char-acter of Lucie suddenly acquired a monocle and, in the courtroom scene, mother-of-pearl opera glasses! Her two scenes in this picture did much to further her career.

With *Der Grosse Bariton* now closed, Dietrich appeared in Wilhelm Dieterle's first directorial ef-fort, *Der Mensch am Wege.* Having won a fine repu-tation as a leading actor in films, Dieterle turned to writing and directing with this film. He adapted his scenario from a short story by Tolstoy. Marlene had the ingenue lead as a peasant girl with golden braids, opposite Dieterle (playing the juvenile lead) and Heinrich George.

Der Mensch am Wege may not have been a great film, but it did set Dieterle on his way to becoming a fine director. In Hollywood he became *William* Dieterle, directing such films as Reinhardt's *A Mid-summer Night's Dream, The Story of Louis Pasteur, The Life of Emile Zola, All That Money Can Buy* and the superb *Portrait of Jennie.* He directed Mar-lene again in M-G-M's lavish spectacle *Kismet* (1944).

Dietrich's next film venture came in the fall of 1923 when she was assigned another ingenue role in *Der Sprung ins Leben,* directed by Dr. Johannes Guter for Oskar Messter-Productions at Ufa. Franz Schulz wrote the script, and the cast included Xenia Desni, Frida Richard, Paul Heidemann and Walter Rilla. It was released early in 1924.

Ever since they had met during the filming of *Tragödie der Liebe,* Marlene and Rudolf Sieber had seen much of each other, and by the spring of 1924 they were inseparable. This handsome young man not only offered security and family life, but per-haps Marlene at this point was also just a bit weary of struggling to get ahead in the acting profession, al-though she had done very well for herself in her first four movies.

With Margo Lion in the musical hit Es Liegt in der Luft

Marriage seemed the solution to her periods of depression. Marlene and Rudolf were wed on May 17, 1924, and for all practical purposes Dietrich retired from stage and screen. It was what she had been longing for. She enjoyed domestic life and cooking large meals for her husband and a close circle of friends.

In 1925, when her daughter Maria was born, Dietrich was indeed the doting mother personified. The Siebers nicknamed their little girl "Heidede" and enjoyed many happy days together. At this time Sieber began shooting a home-movie of his wife and daughter romping and playing together. Three years later he edited it and called his work *Die Glückliche Mutter (The Happy Mother).* Reportedly, this little film *was* released to theaters in Germany during the late 1920's as a short subject.

Sieber then encouraged Marlene to return to acting (which secretly she was longing to do) but she discovered that her old friends and contacts in the business had forgotten her! It seemed almost as if she had never been around theaters or studios at all . . . .

With typical determination, Dietrich canvassed the studios and accepted the first job offered her: an "extra" bit in G. W. Pabst's *Die Freudlose Gasse.*

In a scene with star Jaro Fürth, Marlene huddled in the crowd that gathered outside of the hoarding butcher's (Werner Krauss) shop on "the joyless street." That scene was shot from three angles: a close-up shot of Fürth; a medium-shot of Fürth with Dietrich directly behind him; and a long-shot of the entire group along the street.

In the original print a combination of these shots were edited into a whole, accenting the misery of people whose extreme hunger would soon drive them to a desperate act. But in many countries where *Die Freudlose Gasse* was released, the closer angles were eliminated and only the long-shot remained. In fact, all of the existing prints of this film are incomplete versions of the original work. Thus, a controversy has arisen as to whether, in fact, Dietrich appeared in it at all. She *did!*

Dietrich next got the part of Micheline in Arthur Robison's impressive historical romance *Manon Lescaut,* which began filming in the fall of 1925. She is in the background in several scenes and has some vivid moments which show her to good advantage: her first meeting with the fiery Manon (Lya de Putti), who eventually throws her out, and a scene in the prison workhouse where Micheline is duped into Manon's cell, thereby aiding the latter in a timely escape. She was billed eleventh.

By the time *Manon Lescaut* was released to the public (February, 1926), Dietrich was appearing at Berlin's Staats-Theater as Lou Carrère in Hans J. Rehfisch's comedy *Duell am Lido,* with Fritz Kortner, Lucie Mannheim, Albert Patry, Anton Pointner, Eugen Berg, and Rolf Müller (all of whom she had either appeared with in films or would soon do so.)

Then the Hungarian director Alexander Korda assigned Dietrich a role in one of his wife Maria Corda's vehicles, *Eine DuBarry von Heute.* As a classy coquette, Marlene again made a lasting impression in three well-played scenes. Soon she was cast in Eric Charells' sparkling revue *Von Mund zu Mund (From Mouth to Mouth),* which starred Clare Waldoff. During this run, Korda utilized her again, but this time as a "dress-extra" in another Maria Corda vehicle, *Madame Wünscht Keine Kinder (Madame Doesn't Want Children)* but, alas, Marlene was little more than a set decoration in the large party scenes!

By mid-1926 Dietrich began getting good parts and good billing in two Ellen Richter-Film Productions made for Ufa: *Kopf Hoch, Charly!* and *Der*

Juxbaron. Then came a comedy-melodrama, *Sein Grösster Bluff,* for Nero-Films, which starred Harry Piel, who also directed.

At this time Victor Shutezsky, then associated with Ufa, offered Dietrich a role in *Männer vor der Ehe (Men Before Marriage)* starring Harry Liedtke and Oskar Homolka, but they couldn't agree on salary. After World War II, Shutezsky again approached Dietrich about a lead in Georges Simenon's *Temptation Harbour,* but she refused!

Next, the plum part of Rubie, a razzle-razzle chorus girl, in the stage version of the American hit *Broadway,* by Philip Dunning and George Abbott, which Victor Barnowsky produced and Eugen Robert directed. The cast included Arthur Peiser, Harald Paulsen, Rosa Valetti, Charlotte Ander, Heinrich George, and Mela Schwarz. Dietrich's cohorts in the chorus line included Ruth Albu (Mazie), Cara Guyl (Pearl), Ilse Strobrawa (Grace), and Ingeborg Carlsson (Ann).

While playing Vienna in *Broadway* (with Willi Forst taking over the lead), Dietrich was introduced to Gustav Ucicky, then about to direct Forst in the film *Cafe Electric* for Sascha-Films (a prominent Austrian company). Forst suggested Ucicky sign Dietrich for a role in the film. Ucicky agreed, but after a few days of shooting, regretted this decision. He thought Marlene was inadequate as Erni and would have replaced her had Forst not interceded. "If Dietrich goes," he stated, "then I go!" She remained in the cast. Igo Sym, a handsome young actor also in *Cafe Electric,* taught Marlene how to play the musical saw, which she later demonstrated with skill before GI's in World War II.

Following her appearance in *Broadway,* Marlene was seen at Reinhardt's Josefstädter Theater in *Die Schule von Uznach (The School of Uznach),* a work by Carl Sternheim, one of Germany's minor dramatists of the period. At the same time she began work in the title role of Robert Land's film *Prinzessin Olala.* The cast included Walter Rilla, Carmen Boni and Hans Albers. When released (1928), it was a success.

Next — on the stage — was Max Reinhardt's *Es Liegt in der Luft (It's in the Air)* by Marcellus Schiffer and composer Mischa Spoliansky. The cast included Hubert von Meyerinck, Margo Lion (Schiffer's wife), and Oskar Karlweis. During rehearsals everyone felt that Dietrich was great, and when the show opened all of Berlin was talking about her! Besides a duet with Margo Lion entitled "My Best Girl Friend," Dietrich was a standout singing the title song, accompanied by a piano, a muted trumpet, and a drum.

Robert Land, excited by this reception (and her raves in *Prinzessin Olala*), starred her in his next film, *Ich Küsse Ihre Hand, Madame (I Kiss Your Hand Madame),* with popular Harry Liedtke, which met with considerable success throughout Europe. When it was released, the *Berliner Illustrierte Zietung,* a picture magazine, split its front cover with a half-Garbo, half-Dietrich face!

Then came her portrayals of the unscrupulous Stasha in Kurt Bernhardt's *Die Frau, Nach der Man Sich Sehnt (The Woman One Longs For),* with Fritz Kortner and Uno Henning, and the aviatrix, Miss Ethel, in Maurice Tourneur's *Das Schiff der Verlorenen Menschen (The Ship of Lost Souls),* a German-French co-production.

Her star definitely rising, Dietrich returned to the stage in *Eltern und Kinder* (Shaw's *Misalliance*), followed by Victor Barnowsky's *Zurück zu Methu-*

Dietrich (left) with Lennartz, Kupfer, Charlotte Ander, Cara Guyl, and Ruth Albu in Broadway

In Duell am Lido

salem (*Back to Methuselah*), another Shavian piece. Some critics were already comparing her magnetism to that of Elisabeth Bergner, who, at that time, was also enjoying tremendous success on stage and screen. Bergner said at this time, "If I were as beautiful as Dietrich, I shouldn't know what to do with my talent."

Then came Fred Sauer's *Gefahren der Brautzeit* (*Dangers of the Engagement Period*), which was her last *released* film before *Der Blaue Engel* (*The Blue Angel*). It had actually been started in late 1928 under the title *Eine Nacht der Liebe* (*A Night of Love*). This film gave Dietrich a fine part, which she played quite well, and she was accorded fine photography, which brought much of her beauty to the foreground. It enjoyed greater success, however, when re-released in December of 1930!

As a wealthy American woman in Georg Kaiser's *Zwei Krawatten* (*Two Neckties*), which Reinhardt produced and for which Spoliansky composed the score, Dietrich had another stage hit. The critics were impressed with this show and especially praised her. One evening during its run a short, stocky man

with a grandiose mustache sat in the audience, to catch the performances of Hans Albers and Rosa Valetti. Halfway through, Josef von Sternberg, the American film director, then in Germany to direct Emil Jannings in *Der Blaue Engel,* had already become entranced by Marlene Dietrich on stage. He kept his eyes on her throughout. He was thinking of the pivotal vamp-role of Lola-Lola in *Der Blaue Engel,* still uncast.

Von Sternberg arranged to have Dietrich audition for him with a song in German and another in English. Reports of this first encounter always state that he insisted on a "vulgar" song, but von Sternberg in his autobiography, *Fun in a Chinese Laundry,* says, "... it is impossible that I ever asked anyone to be vulgar. As for my asking her to sing a 'naughty' song for the test, this too is not to be reconciled with what actually happened. As she could only sing what she knew, and that was very little. I sent her to the wardrobe to discard her street clothes and to change into something with spangles and she returned with a costume roomy enough to contain a hippopotamus. I pinned the dress to fit her somehow and asked her to sing something she knew in German and to follow it with an English song if possible.

"I then put her into the crucible of my conception, blended her image to correspond with mine, and, pouring lights on her until the alchemy was complete, proceeded with the test. She came to life and responded to my instructions with an ease that I had never before encountered. She seemed pleased at the trouble I took with her, but she never saw the test, nor ever asked to see it. Her remarkable vitality had been channeled."

Von Sternberg worked hard on *Der Blaue Engel* and even harder on creating a certain effect with Dietrich. His idea differed from that of Heinrich Mann, on whose novel, *Der Blaue Engel* was based. The director wanted the woman, not society and/or the changing times, to be responsible for the professor's decline, thus intensifying the action. The end result was a superb motion picture, the first great German talkie, utilizing the best of the silent screen's techniques with a minimum of dialogue. Jannings gave a portrayal of fantastic power and depth, and the supporting players were excellent. The atmosphere and mood created by von Sternberg's marvelous sense of the visual were stunningly realized. Even when Dietrich was not on camera, the image he had achieved lingered in the minds of the viewer.

16

B. P. Schulberg, Paramount's West Coast chief, then visiting Berlin, saw the "rushes" of *Der Blaue Engel* and, with encouragement from von Sternberg, cabled Paramount to make Dietrich a handsome offer. They complied, but Dietrich was hesitant. After all, her roots were in Germany, with her husband, her daughter, her friends. . . .

Once filming had been completed, von Sternberg sailed alone to the United States, since Marlene had still not decided what to do. Delivered to his stateroom before sailing was a large bon voyage basket from Dietrich. Buried beneath the usual fruit and liquor was a copy of Benno Vigny's novel of the French Foreign Legion, *Amy Jolly*. Her intentions can only be guessed! However, on the way back to the States, von Sternberg read the book and decided that if there was a Foreign Legion for men, there must be a "foreign legion of women" — following their men from one desert encampment to another.

Meanwhile, Dietrich attended the première of *Der Blaue Engel* on April 1, 1930, and since there could be little doubt of the greatness of this film, she left immediately for the United States. Rudolf and young Maria remained in Germany.

Dietrich arrived when the vogue for foreign actresses was at its height. Hollywood in 1930 was eagerly awaiting Garbo's first words in *Anna Christie,* but little did they know that another "mysterious lady" had arrived on the *Bremen*.

The script of her first American film had been prepared by Jules Furthmann from von Sternberg's notes on *Amy Jolly*. The title was changed to *Morocco* and Paramount's top male attraction, Gary Cooper, was assigned the role of Legionnaire Tom Brown, while Adolphe Menjou was engaged to play the artist Kennington.

During the filming of *Morocco*, Dietrich began shedding her somewhat heavy accent and figure. "Svengali Joe," as publicists were now calling von Sternberg, put "Legs" Dietrich on a rigid diet and delivered her into the hands of a masseuse each day as well as a makeup expert. Her gowns and hair styles were checked daily by the director. Dietrich

went along with his every wish and during the transformation she complained not! The effect, and the effort that went into creating that effect, was remarkable. Her old cronies in Berlin wouldn't have recognized her—the plump young *Fräulein* no longer existed. This *new* Dietrich might have come from anywhere . . . anytime. . . .

Her native beauty was enhanced by pencilled eyebrows ("resembling a butterfly taking flight" as one observer put it!); hollow cheekbones; lips purposely left ajar—probably for that hint of humor; and those eyes! The eye makeup was subtle most of the time; von Sternberg wanted nothing to distract one's attention from that sensual stare!

She was photographed through shutters, branches of trees, and in dimly-lit archways. The *illusion of sex* was constant, even if only her legs were exhibited. *Life* magazine later termed this creation "the magic myth."

After seeing a Dietrich picture, John Barrymore reportedly said, "She handles her body like Stradivarius used to handle his violins. And no matter what kind of finish it happens to be wearing at the time, it's still a masterpiece!"

Later on, when Metro-Goldwyn-Mayer's publicity boys superimposed Garbo's face on the famous Sphinx at Gizeh, Paramount's crew, not to be outdone, superimposed Dietrich's face on da Vinci's "Mona Lisa." Nothing was sacred to studio publicity departments! Paramount may have been second, but they at least were original. Theda Bara's face had been superimposed on the Sphinx to pub-

At the Deutsches Theater, 1928, in Shaw's Misalliance (Eltern und Kinder), *directed by Max Reinhardt. With Fritz Odemar, Paul Otto, Otto Walburg, and Else Heims (Reinhardt's first wife). Wallburg, who signed this picture, died at Auschwitz in 1944.*

licize her *Cleopatra* at Fox in 1917! Dietrich more-over, was once likened to Gainsborough's famous "Blue Boy" as Ufa publicity in the late twenties.

The only thing which got in the way of the von Sternberg-Dietrich pictures was the story. What a pity stories had to be used at all! Dietrich was more than enough. Von Sternberg began with a simple idea and then began weaving his images around that idea. He is, without doubt, the greatest abstractionist in motion picture history. Critics seldom understood his aims—perhaps he himself didn't—at that time, but shown today his films take on new meaning and are fully appreciated by audiences and critics alike.

With the opening of *Morocco* and the importation, by Paramount, of *The Blue Angel*, the von Sternberg-Dietrich duo was firmly established. She decided to stay in America and work with her mentor.

The "game" had begun and now Dietrich did all that was expected of her to further the myth that publicists were surrounding her with. This did, however, afford her privacy that other stars didn't get. The "mysterious," "aloof," and "strange" Miss Dietrich was not bothered like her contemporaries.

She settled in a comfortable home with servants and even had a Rolls Royce (courtesy of Paramount). Her social set was limited but luminous. And she was seen only on special occasions: premières, sporting events, night clubs, etc.

The pair now renewed their Paramount contracts (at higher salaries), but Marlene returned to Germany before beginning her next picture. Herr Sieber, Maria, and friend Gerda Huber met her at the train station in Berlin, and they had to push through crowds of admirers to get on their way. *The Blue Angel* had made her a star throughout Europe. Von Sternberg joined them later in Berlin and showed Marlene the script of her new film, *Dishonored*, based on a story he had himself written.

Gerda went along to Hollywood with them as Marlene's secretary-companion, but when *Dishonored* was completed, she and Marlene again left for Germany. Von Sternberg was disappointed that Dietrich had not stayed with him during the editing of the picture (which had become their usual practice). He told an interviewer at this time, "The moment I saw her playing on the stage in Berlin, I knew at once I wanted her for my picture. There was apparent in her a strange mixture of worldly sophistication and cultured refinement. She carried the illusion of perfect indifference. . . ."

With daughter Maria, circa 1928

On this second visit back to Germany, Marlene noticed more than ever before that her country was in the midst of political upheaval. It was late 1931 and the beginnings of the "New Order" were to be seen everywhere. Already, anti-Jewish slogans were chalked on walls all over Berlin. This time husband and daughter returned to Hollywood with her.

Now Sieber and young Maria joined Dietrich and von Sternberg at public events, as she was proud to have her daughter by her side. And every time she was interviewed she would end up by giving the reporter a sample of her cooking or some recipes for her dishes. This domestic aspect of Dietrich might have destroyed a lesser personage, but the public accepted anything she did. Dietrich was the only big female star who was constantly seen publicly with her daughter.

Her passion for male attire was copied at once,

and women everywhere began sporting trousers, men's shirts, ties and hats. Marlene added a strange beauty to these clothes, which cannot always be said of others who wear them. The more masculinely she dressed, the more exciting her feminine appeal became. On her preference for trousers she had this to say: "They are so comfortable. It takes too much time to be a well-dressed woman. I have watched others. Bags, shoes, hats—they must think of them all the time, I cannot waste that time."

booked their pictures all over the country, forcing the Dietrich-von Sternberg team to make two pictures a year so that exhibitors would handle the studio's lesser items. Good stories couldn't be hacked up that fast, and Paramount continually submitted bad scripts, which caused von Sternberg to write his own, as in the case of *Blonde Venus.*

Dietrich played a mother for the first time in *Blonde Venus.* She starts out helping her ailing husband (Herbert Marshall), but soon reaches the

At a press ball in Berlin, 1929: Left to right, Dietrich, Maria Paudler, Luigi Pirandello, Liane Haid, Max Hansen, Anita Davis, Anni Ahlers, and Theodore Däubler

No other von Sternberg-Dietrich film has been imitated more than *Shanghai Express,* their next film together. Here Dietrich was transplanted to China during a revolution, along with eight other first-class passengers aboard the Shanghai Express in Peking. Von Sternberg reached his apex with this film. In ensuing adventures, technical tricks, heretofore hailed as innovations, were reduced to the obvious. His mad devotion to pictorialism and glorifying Dietrich was clouding his otherwise bright talent. Following *Shanghai Express,* Dietrich's contract was rewritten, giving her $125,000 per picture.

Incidentally, the best "copy" of *Shanghai* was Frank Capra's *The Bitter Tea of General Yen,* with Barbara Stanwyck.

The fault of the last three pictures von Sternberg and Dietrich were to make together does not, however, lie entirely with the director. Paramount block-

depths of degradation, dragging her young child all over the South with her. But, in true fashion, she rises up again and becomes the toast of the entertainment world. The musical numbers of *Blonde Venus* are among the wildest ever filmed — at least "Hot Voodoo" is! To the beating of drums, Dietrich enters in a massive gorilla suit, flanked by native girls. Soon she slips out of this outfit and dons a fuzzy blonde wig, a spear, and a shield, and is ready for action. Quite divine!

A young reporter, meeting Dietrich at about this time, made this observation: "She does not smile often, but those infrequent smiles light her whole face."

Von Sternberg wanted time off to work on the story of their next picture. Paramount, meanwhile, offered Marlene *Song of Songs,* which Rouben Mamoulian was preparing. Von Sternberg encour-

With husband Rudolf Sieber, von Sternberg (with cigarette), daughter Maria, and Gerda Huber

aged her to accept this part, which she finally did.

Song of Songs, from the Hermann Sudermann novel, was lushly produced and gave Marlene a fine acting challenge—the first such challange since Lola-Lola! Mamoulian, faced with handling an *image* the public had already accepted, wisely kept her in that frame but gave her more freedom of movement and expression and more depth of character. She sang Frederick Hollander's 1920 song "Jonny" in English in a scene reminiscent of the best von Sternberg ever created for her! Brian Aherne, in his first American picture, was miscast, but struggled along, while character actor Lionel Atwill (being familiar with the attention shown a female star in movies) made the evil baron an outstanding characterization.

During the filming, the famous flyer Amelia Earhart (whose husband, G. P. Putnam, was on Paramount's editorial board) visited with Marlene on the set, probably comparing notes on women wearing male attire, which both of them were noted for!

More than likely, von Sternberg liked *Song of Songs,* since he later cast Lionel Atwill and Alison Skipworth in roles not unlike those they played in the Mamoulian film.

After a short holiday, work was begun on *Her Regiment of Lovers,* based on one of the "secret diaries of Catherine the Great." Shortly after shooting started the title was changed officially to *Cath-*

erine the Great but was again altered when it was learned that Alexander Korda, then making film history in England, had just completed his *Catherine the Great,* with Elisabeth Bergner. Paramount's version became *The Scarlet Empress.*

The strange creation that is *The Scarlet Empress* has to be seen to be believed! For sheer photographic splendor it is doubtful that it has ever seen its match. But everyone and everything was but a thread in a giant tapestry—a most fantastic conglomeration of decorative settings, magnificent costumes (by Travis Banton), and weird symbolism! One critic noted, upon its release, "If the Russia of Catherine the Great wasn't like Mr. Sternberg's, it certainly should have been."

The British production used a subtle approach to the same story and characters weren't lost in the shuffle. *The Scarlet Empress* was a dismal failure at the box office, for the public was growing weary of the von Sternberg-Dietrich formula. Critics, on the other hand, realizing that both these talents were being prostituted for overall "effect," became downright hostile.

Returning home from a European vacation on the *Ile de France* in 1934, Dietrich refused to sit down to dinner one night, for she would be the thirteenth at table. At that moment a ruggedly handsome man offered to join her party and make the total fourteen. This was her first encounter with Ernest Hemingway. They became close friends over the years. Said Hemingway, "If she had nothing more than her voice, she could break your heart with it. But she also has that beautiful body and the timeless loveliness of her face." In her "ABC's" she returned the compliment: "Ernest Hemingway is the most positive life force I have ever encountered. I hate anything negative, and I hate waste. In Hemingway, nothing is wasted!"

By the time Dietrich returned to work in 1935, B. P. Shulberg had gone to Columbia and Ernst Lubitsch had become head of Paramount's production on the West Coast. Even though *Blonde Venus* and *The Scarlet Empress* hadn't made the money expected of them, Lubitsch gave von Sternberg the go-ahead on his next Dietrich picture. This was *Caprice Espagñol,* based on Pierre Louys' novel, *La Femme et le Pantin (The Woman and the Puppet),*

Garbo was portrayed as the Sphinx; Marlene was depicted as Gainsborough's "Blue Boy" and the "Mona Lisa."

which had been previously filmed by Geraldine Farrar in 1920. John Dos Passos wrote the scenario and Dietrich played a Spanish siren named Concha, who ruins a middle-aged grandee in the Seville of 1890.

Lubitsch, exercising his full power, forced von Sternberg to change the title to *The Devil Is a Woman.* Reason? He thought *his* title would appeal to the general movie-going public instead of the intellectuals von Sternberg attracted! He was wrong. The title was not to save this last von Sternberg-Dietrich film from financial disaster. Von Sternberg himself handled the photography (assisted by Lucien Ballard). It is a journey into extravagant style, with a plot that unfolded at an incredibly slow pace. It remains their most personal film together (but far from their best!) and their favorite. Marlene has said many times, "I was more beautiful in it than in anything else." A curious statement indeed.

During the last days of shooting von Sternberg told the press, "Fräulein Dietrich and I have progressed as far as possible together. My being with Dietrich any further will not help her or me. If we continued we would get into a pattern which would be harmful to both of us."

Dietrich was not prepared for his decision. The suddenness of it saddened her completely. Everyone thought that with Svengali's power turned off, Trilby's voice would be forever stilled. Not so with Marlene!

Ernst Lubitsch, giving Dietrich every consideration, personally supervised her next picture, which the talented Frank Borzage directed. *Desire* teamed her for the second time with Gary Cooper. She played an international jewel thief with considerable comic know-how and much charm. Cooper's quiet-talking but effective American engineer proved one of his best characterizations. *Desire* was a definite switch in style for Dietrich, and in a way she was indeed "the new Dietrich" everyone was shouting about, but her personality had only really begun to be tapped. There was, wisely enough, much of the old Dietrich around to help the new one jump those hurdles.

Marlene's publicity, at this juncture, manufactured a running feud with Mae West, the other reigning queen of the Paramount lot. Both ladies found this not only annoying but ludicrous, since they had never even met. So Dietrich visited West on the set of the latter's *Klondike Annie* one day. "She was very kind to me," Dietrich said. "And she's such a witty woman."

Marlene worked hard at picture-making and likewise played hard when away from the studios. At one of the mad costume balls given by the ace hostess Countess di Frasso, Dietrich created a stir when she arrived as "Leda and the Swan"—a dash of beauty right out of mythology! The invitation to this glittering affair asked the guests "to come in a costume depicting other persons they admired."

Another top hostess to film notables was the gifted Carole Lombard. The zany comedienne's party for William Rhinelander Stewart and A. C. Blumenthal at the Venice Amusement Park *begged* everyone to come in "old clothes" to run the concessions—to the management's delight—and also enjoy the various rides and games! Here a bevy of screen stars romped and had a gay ol' time: Dietrich, Lily Damita, Cary Grant, Dolores Del Rio, Cesar Romero, Claudette Colbert, William Haines, and scores of others.

Before *Desire* was released, Paramount assigned

Setting the fashion for mannish attire

Dietrich the old Pola Negri script, *Hotel Imperial* which was now to be filmed as *I Loved a Soldier*. Henry Hathaway, fresh from his highly successful *Lives of a Bengal Lancer,* seemed the right choice, as was Charles Boyer for co-star! By the time shooting began (January 3, 1936) script difficulties had already arisen. After only a few scenes of her had been shot, director Hathaway "shot around" Dietrich while script conferences were taking place. Producer Benjamin Glazier quit and Lubitsch left for a three-month European trip as William Le Baron became Paramount's new head of production. Le Baron and Dietrich didn't get along (she had script approval!). And, after twenty-eight "on-and-off" days of shooting, Dietrich walked out, leaving Paramount holding a $900,000 bag!

After a European trip, she and Clark Gable appeared together on radio in *The Legionnaire and the Lady* for Cecil B. De Mille's Lux Radio Theatre—in fact, their broadcast (June 2, 1936) opened that famous radio series.

Before Dietrich had taken her vacation in Europe, she had had three top offers for her services once her availability became known. Irving G. Thalberg (Metro-Goldwyn-Mayer), David O. Selznick (Selznick International Pictures), and Darryl F. Zanuck (20th Century-Fox) each put in their bids. The offer Dietrich finally accepted was Selznick's to appear in *The Garden of Allah,* to be filmed in the new three-color Technicolor process. Her salary

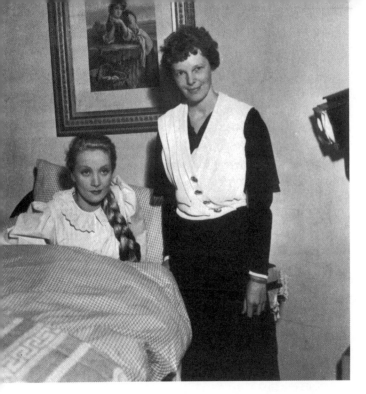

Amelia Earhart, the famous flyer later lost in the Pacific, visits Dietrich on the set of Song of Songs.

was $200,000. Her co-star was Charles Boyer. Location work began at Yuma, Arizona in July 1936.

Actress Merle Oberon was under contract for the part of Domini Enfilden, but once Selznick learned that Dietrich was free, he signed her regardless of the consequences. The "consequences" came in the form of a suit from Miss Oberon. Mr. Selznick, in gentlemanly fashion, awarded her a handsome sum out of court.

Miss Oberon was then to become involved with Josef von Sternberg! She signed with Alexander Korda's London Films to appear in *Claudius* (based on Robert Graves' novel *I, Claudius*) with von Sternberg directing. The cast was notable: Charles Laughton, Emlyn Williams and Flora Robson. This production, like *I Loved a Soldier,* was doomed from the start, but more of it was actually filmed. Laughton and von Sternberg never hit it off, and about halfway through, Oberon was injured in a car accident. The project was abandoned after a great deal of money was spent.

Dietrich, now that *Garden of Allah* was completed, crossed the ocean to work with Korda in his filming of James Hilton's *Knight Without Armour,* to the tune of $450,000. Her co-star was the splendid English actor Robert Donat, and from France, Korda imported director Jacques Feyder, fresh from his triumphant *La Kermesse Herioque (Carnival in Flanders),* which was the talk of Europe. The production had everything to recommend

it, but *Knight Without Armour,* nevertheless, did poorly at the box office. Its setting during the Russian revolution was accurately depicted and no expense was spared. In some ways, the old Dietrich was back again, but some thought in a watered-down version.

Marlene enjoyed working in England, and made many new friends there. Noël Coward, Cecil Beaton, and her constant escort, Douglas Fairbanks, Jr., were but a few of the men in her life. On occasion she would go to Paris and be seen with Erich Maria Remarque, the famous author of *All Quiet on the Western Front,* who had left Nazi Germany and was then living in France.

While she was filming *Knight Without Armour,* Dietrich was approached twice by top-ranking Nazi officials with an offer to return to Germany to make films. She refused, and upon her return to the United States, Marlene applied for American citizenship papers. She told Los Angeles reporters (May 6, 1937), "I am working and living in America and my interests are here. I feel I should be a citizen of this great country."

At Paramount again on a one-picture deal, Dietrich made a sophisticated romance entitled *Angel.* Ernst Lubitsch directed, but his deft hand was hampered by a dull script. The production had lavish values, but it was *too* perfectly done—too stilted.

Seeing the handwriting on the wall, Dietrich commented, "I prefer being a free agent. When I was working with Mr. von Sternberg my admiration of his work and my loyalty to him made me stick close to the movie capital, to be available when he should have plans for me, but I am to indulge myself a little more." She soon departed for England, and in early 1938 she rented a house in London and became a familiar figure at some of London's gayest affairs.

It was then that she was visited by Germany's former Ambassador to England, Joachim von Ribbentrop. He carried an offer directly from Adolf Hitler (whose favorite picture reportedly was *The Blue Angel*). The Nazis desperately wanted Dietrich's services—which would have been quite an international *coup.* They would have made her "Queen of the Reich Cinema." The offer presented was stupendous! Her salary would be in *cash* in any currency she named, and the figure was astronomical. Unlike any other actress of her time, Dietrich would have complete control over script, direction, editing, and cast approval down to the last extra, if she wished. And to top it off, von Ribbentrop promised her a triumphal re-entry into Berlin that would have equalled, if not surpassed, Cleopatra's entry into Rome! Dietrich listened patiently, but was unimpressed. Von Ribbentrop was shown the door.

It is ironic that the actress eventually elevated to the lofty position of "Queen of the Reich Cinema" was Zarah Leander—a Swede!

Meanwhile in Hollywood, Universal producer Joe Pasternak was trying to convince studio executives that Marlene Dietrich would be ideal as Frenchy, the saloon singer with a heart of gold, in his forthcoming production of *Destry Rides Again*. The executives were more than leery, since exhibitors around the country had labelled Dietrich—along with Joan Crawford and Katharine Hepburn—"box-office poison."

With husband Sieber and mentor von Sternberg

Having eventually won their confidence, he placed a transatlantic call to Dietrich and outlined his proposition. Universal could only pay her $75,000, but he felt this role would be the salvation of her sagging career. A vacationing von Sternberg encouraged her to take Pasternak's offer, knowing well that such an outlandish reversal could turn the tide. Indeed it did!

Destry Rides Again is one of the best western films ever made, and under George Marshall's astute direction it moved at a merry clip from beginning to end. James Stewart's Tom Destry was perfect casting and his shy, reticent deputy had an underlying strength and a keen sense of humor. In contrast, Dietrich was hard-boiled, brittle-tongued and festive, singing three top songs especially com-

posed for her by Frederick Hollander. Pasternak was most adroit in getting Dietrich's favorite composer and the songs he wrote for her were all show-stoppers: "Little Joe the Wrangler," "You've Got That Look (That Leaves Me Weak)" (which has since become a Dietrich standard), and "The Boys in the Back Room"—the big hit of the film!

The script also provided a rip-snorting, hair-pulling, knock-down, drag-out fight between Dietrich and Una Merkel, which is finally climaxed when Stewart pours a bucket of water on both "ladies." Doubles were not used—Dietrich and Merkel delivered their own punches!

Pasternak, in his autobiography, *Easy the Hard Way*, said of Dietrich, "Whatever she does, she does very well. Her cakes and cookies—as I can vouch myself—are magnificent. As a hostess at a dinner party, or your guest, or the lady you are lucky enough to sit next to, she is without a peer: she is witty, attentive, charming and lovely. When she gives, she gives utterly."

Dietrich became a United States citizen on June 9, 1939. In Germany, the anti-Jewish newspaper *Der Stürmer* printed a picture of Dietrich taking her oath of allegiance and captioned it: "The German-born Marlene Dietrich has spent so many years among the film Jews of Hollywood that she now becomes an American citizen. Frequent contact with Jews renders her entirely un-German."

This slander had no effect on Dietrich whatsoever. In fact, she had already spent a great deal of her own money getting friends out of Nazi-controlled Germany to the safety of England and the United States—done without benefit of publicity.

With Cecil B. De Mille and Clark Gable during a radio production of Legionnaire and the Lady *on the "Lux Theatre of the Air"*

Universal followed *Destry* with another film full of action, wisecracks, and songs. In *Seven Sinners* she satirized every Sadie Thompson-type as Bijou Blanche, an entertainer roaming from one South Seas island to another. John Wayne was her man in this one. The usual Universal production values were evident, and this film contains some of the best stunt work ever done in Hollywood. Stuntman David Sharpe was chiefly responsible for the superb six-minute fight in the closing moments of the film. The supporting cast was excellent, and Hollander provided Dietrich again with some fine songs: "The Man's in the Navy" and "I've Been in Love Before" were outstanding. He originally wrote another called "I Fall Overboard," but it was cut before release. The song is still listed, however, on the titles.

The public liked *this* new Dietrich and she was once again "box-office."

Herr Sieber was, by this time, employed in the foreign department of Universal, but he and his wife seldom saw each other. He soon left the entertainment world to raise chickens in southern California, at which he became prosperous.

Next, Dietrich appeared in René Clair's *The Flame of New Orleans*. When Pasternak learned that Clair had left the Vichy government of France and had arrived in the United States, he secured his services as director immediately. Dietrich was delighted and played well in this bit of frou-frou about a nineteenth-century opportunist who poses as a countess to snare a wealthy banker, only to fall in love with a rugged sea captain who could offer her nothing but love! Hollywood censorship problems, from the first, took much of the flavor out of what might have been a spicy film, but the Clair touches were everywhere and are still a delight to see.

Marlene now went over to Warner Bros., where she was cast between Edward G. Robinson and George Raft. The picture was *Manpower,* and it gave Dietrich a modern-day *Destry* role—a hostess in a Los Angeles clip joint. Warners, too, got Frederick Hollander to compose for her. Her best number was "He Lied and I Listened." Again action took the place of a good script, with Marlene fighting one man off (her husband, Robinson) while fighting to get another (his pal, Raft).

She next went to Columbia for Mitchell Leisen's *The Lady Is Willing.* As musical-comedy star Elizabeth Madden, Dietrich gave a fine dramatic performance, with comic overtones, in a film that most people tend to forget. It isn't all that bad. The script was weak but the direction sound. Fred MacMurray was her co-star.

Back on the Universal lot, Dietrich made two pictures with John Wayne and Randolph Scott. First was the fourth remake of the ever-popular *The Spoilers* by Rex Beach, with Scott as the bad guy and Wayne the good guy and Dietrich in the middle. In *Pittsburgh,* however, the tables were turned, but not for Marlene! She had the same type of role between two men, with both of them loving her and she getting one of them. This time Wayne was the bad guy and Scott the good guy. Both productions offered plenty of action and superb stunt work in first-class film-making, but Dietrich was

tiring of this "new image" and so was her public. Before leaving Universal, she agreed to appear in the all-star revue *Follow the Boys* as Orson Welles' "victim" in his Mercury Wonder Show. Welles placed Dietrich on the block and sawed her in half, to the consternation of two GI's and the delight of audiences.

Growing weary of her film roles, Dietrich let it be known that she was open to other offers. Broadway responded. It was rumored almost immediately that she was scheduled to appear in Bruno Frank's version of Oscar Wilde's *An Ideal Husband* for Broadway producer Alfred Fisher, who had presented the play in several European capitals. She was also offered the musical version of Somerset Maugham's *Rain!.* (It was done in late 1944 by June Havoc. Called *Sadie Thompson,* even talents like Rouben Mamoulian, Vernon Duke, and Howard Dietz couldn't save it!)

In 1943 she decided to devote her energies to entertaining U. S. troops at bases and hospitals in this country and overseas. She also toured the country on War Bond selling tours. Marlene waited on the GI's in New York's Stage Door Canteen and at the Hollywood Canteen, which Bette Davis and John Garfield had started.

Under the auspices of the Office of War Information, she made many broadcasts in German and French which were transmitted to the peoples under Axis rule in Europe.

During this period, she returned to Hollywood to make a film directed by her old friend William Dieterle. *Kismet* starred Ronald Colman, and M-G-M gave it a lavish budget. The legendary Dietrich legs were painted gold (four coats) for a fabulous dance. It was pure escapism and the public loved it!

In late 1943, after finishing *Kismet,* she joined the U.S.O. (United Services Organization) and toured camps in Italy, Africa, the Mediterranean war theater, Labrador, Greenland, Iceland, England, France, Germany, Czechoslovakia, and the Aleutians. Her show included Milton Frome, Lin Mayberry, Jack Snyder, and an unknown comedian named Danny Thomas. Dietrich sang songs from

With Douglas Fairbanks, Jr., and Alexander Korda at the premiere of the latter's Rembrandt *in London (1936)*

Romping with Claudette Colbert at Carole Lombard's Venice party

her films, did a mind-reading act (which she had "borrowed" from Orson Welles), and created a sensation playing her musical saw. Those GI audiences numbered anywhere from fifty to 22,000 at a single performance.

Dietrich was in Anzio entertaining troops when word came that the Allied Armies had landed in France, and she was given the privilege of announcing this tremendous news during a performance. By this time Marlene had added the song "Lili Marlene" to her repertoire. The German soldiers' song had been picked up by the Allied soldiers in Tunisia, but when Dietrich sang it, it was "for all soldiers." The boys never tired of hearing it. She also sang for German prisoners-of-war, and on one occasion a young German boy, overcome by her song, said, "Why, you *are* Lili Marlene!" General Patton, a bit worried for her safety while entertaining in these areas, lest she get captured, assigned her two bodyguards!

Bill Mauldin in his book *Back Home* happily noted, "Marlene Dietrich was a sweetheart, and the soldiers loved her especially because she spent nearly all her time with them and very little with brass hats." Dietrich paid her own expenses on these tours and thought nothing of "standing patiently in chow lines with her mess kit, sleeping in rat-infested

ruins and dugouts." And through it all she gave a performance that was "a triumph of sheer stamina."

As if those three years of touring weren't enough, Marlene was planning another tour of hospitals and camps when a jaw infection put an end to her activities. Of this wartime period, she has said simply, "It is the only important thing I've ever done."

After the war, Dietrich was scheduled to make *Les Portes de la Nuit* for Marcel Carné, but again script troubles entered into things. However, she and Jean Gabin did make a film for director Georges Lacombe, called *Martin Roumagnac*, which was undistinguished. It took two years of censoring to arrive in the United States under the title of *The Room Upstairs*. She was also slated to appear in another French film with the great character actor Raimu, but his death cancelled those plans.

Returning to the United States, Dietrich was presented with our nation's highest civilian award, The Medal of Freedom, in 1947 by General Maxwell D. Taylor, then commandant of West Point. The citation states as follows:

Miss Marlene Dietrich, civilian volunteer with the United States Service Organization Camp shows, performed meritorious service in support of military operations in North Africa, Sicily and Italy from April 14 to June 16, 1944, and in the North Atlantic Bases in Europe from August 30, 1944 to July 13, 1945, meeting a gruelling schedule of performances under battle conditions, during adverse weather and despite risk to her life. Although her health was failing, Miss Dietrich continued to bring pleasure and cheer to more than five hundred thousand American soldiers. With commendable energy and sincerity she contributed immeasurably to the welfare of the troops in these theaters.

This honor was not the first presented to Marlene Dietrich (she was awarded a special citation by the Treasury Department for her successful War Bond selling tours in 1942), nor was it to be her last.

Marlene's daughter, in the interim, had grown up and by 1946 had married and divorced drama critic Dean Goodman (whom she married at eighteen) and had decided to pursue a career as an actress under the name of Maria Palmer. As such, she played a small part in Tallulah Bankhead's *Foolish Notion* on Broadway and then, following in her mother's footsteps, toured many hospitals for the U.S.O.

In October of 1946, Maria applied at Fordham University for a teaching position. She got that job

With George Jean Nathan and Ernest Hemingway at the Stork Club

and met her present husband there. William Riva, then teaching scenic design, fell in love with Maria and they were married in July of 1947.

At about this time, Paramount offered Dietrich the role of the dark-haired gypsy, Lydia, in Mitchell Leisen's *Golden Earrings,* a part she played with great relish. Ray Milland was the star. Billy Wilder then asked her to portray an ex-Nazi's girl friend living in post-war Berlin in *A Foreign Affair.* Dietrich hesitated, until Wilder screened for her June Havoc's test for the role, which convinced her that the part was tailor-made for her talents. Frederick Hollander again provided some sensuous songs, which she delivered in her own individual style. The film was a success and Dietrich "stole the picture" according to *Life.*

In 1948, Maria Riva gave birth to her first son, John Michael, making the legendary Marlene a very glamorous grandmother. The press had a field day, and to this day the title "glamorous grandmother" sticks. Two years later she was again presented with a grandson, John Peter. Dietrich in an interview at that time, said, "I'm getting a little weary of it. Naturally, I love my grandchildren. But why attach so much importance to my being a grandmother? Countless women have grandchildren—many of them, I am sure, much younger than I."

During this period Maria Riva made a reputation for herself on television through numerous appear-

ances on top dramatic shows, but she has since retired from the limelight to devote herself to raising her children. She now has four boys.

Other than a guest appearance in a film entitled *Jigsaw* in 1949, Marlene didn't make another picture until Alfred Hitchcock's *Stage Fright,* filmed at the Elstree Studios in England. Marlene played a musical comedy star whose husband dies mysteriously, making her a chief suspect throughout. Christian Dior designed her wardrobe, and the cast included Jane Wyman, Michael Wilding, and Richard Todd.

When asked when she would appear on television, Dietrich replied, "If I do television it will have to be something special. People expect something special of me."

Marlene soon made a calculated appearance on an Academy Awards show, shocking everyone by coming out in a high-necked black dress with sleeves to her wrists. The skin-tight gown had one large slit, exposing her beautiful legs as she crossed the stage. She wore no jewelry. Dior had created a masterpiece of understatement, and Marlene carried off the effect beautifully!

In 1951 she was named a Chevalier of the French Legion of Honor for her entertainment of troops during the war in Africa and France. Ambassador Henri Bonnet pinned the decoration on her dress. (She received a similar award from Israel in 1965—the first time their highest award went to a woman—not only for her troop tours, but also for her refusal to return to Nazi Germany to make films!)

Then she returned to England to appear with James Stewart in *No Highway,* from Nevil Shute's story of the unsung men behind the scenes in aircraft research. Dietrich was again an actress.

At this time, she also appeared on the ABC Radio series *Café Istanbul,* which she co-created and for which she wrote some of the scripts.

Next came *Rancho Notorious* for Fritz Lang. As Altar Keane, an ex-saloon singer who runs a hideaway for a band of outlaws, Dietrich was grand fun, but the Ken Darby songs lacked imagination. The color photography, however, was fine. Arthur Kennedy was co-star.

In the early fifties, Columbia Pictures hailed her for the lead in the musical comedy *Pal Joey.* The studio had purchased the film rights to this property back in the forties, but had never done anything with it. With the 1952 revival with Harold Lang sweeping the country, Columbia czar Harry

Cohn revived interest in the picture rights. Dietrich was keen about doing this role and asked Cohen to get Frank Sinatra for Joey. Personal differences with Sinatra prevented a deal with Cohen being made. Dietrich walked out soon afterwards. Frank Sinatra eventually played Joey, with Columbia star Rita Hayworth essaying the role Dietrich would have made immortal!

Good film roles were becoming few and far between, so Dietrich continued with her recording career. Over the years, since the late twenties in Germany, she has appeared on the Decca, Vox, Columbia, RCA Victor, and Capitol labels in this country and many others abroad. CBS Radio hired her for a daytime show called *Time for Love,* and in 1953, as ringmaster, she opened the Ringling Bros.-Barnum and Bailey Circus at Madison Square Garden, the proceeds of which went to the Cerebral Palsy Fund.

In late 1953, Marlene arrived at a third turning point in her illustrious career by hitting the nightclub circuit. The Sahara Hotel in Las Vegas paid her $30,000 a week, for three weeks—to standing-room crowds! "They've been after me for two years to appear at this hotel in a club act. For this money I couldn't refuse."

As the country's highest paid nightclub entertainer she gave the customers just what they wanted, and more. In a Jean Louis creation which cost $6,000, she made history. The skirt was lined with flesh-colored chiffon and the bosom from the waist up was made of a transparent material with rhinestones and sequins *sprinkled* on it. One customer quipped, "That's an expensive striptease."

Throughout the fifties Dietrich returned each year for a few weeks either at the Sahara or the Sands Hotel. Said Marlene of these engagements, "They spoil you. When they love you, it's forever. Of course, I do a different kind of show in Las Vegas. They want more emphasis on sex. In London, and the rest of Europe, I can sing French and German songs as well as English. There's more scope for me. But I enjoy nightclub work wherever it is."

Her club dates have taken her to England, Scotland, France, Canada, South America, Australia, Holland, and Russia. She also played Israel and sang in German there, despite attempts to stop her. The audiences loved her.

In 1956, Dietrich returned to films. In Michael Todd's Academy Award-winning *Around the World in 80 Days* she was cameo-ed as a dance hall queen

With Jean Cocteau at the Theatre de l'Etoile in Paris

in San Francisco. "It's been fun working for Todd," she said at the time. "He still has the enthusiasm that has gone out of Hollywood."

Next she went to Italy to film *The Monte Carlo Story* with Vittorio De Sica, which should have been a better picture than it was. It did, however, offer her a glamorous part with a lovely wardrobe and some songs as well.

She then got the best part of her career in Billy Wilder's *Witness for the Prosecution.* As Christine Vole, the wife of an accused man, her part was many-faceted. She looked extremely beautiful in tailored suits created especially for her by Edith Head. Wilder wisely cast Charles Laughton as Sir Wilfrid Robarts and Tyrone Power as Leonard Vole. Laughton's wife, Elsa Lanchester, was written into the screenplay as an overbearing nurse and their scenes together were hilarious.

Orson Welles, who had wanted Dietrich for his oft-postponed *Mr. Arkadin,* finally got her for his *Touch of Evil.* Charlton Heston and Janet Leigh starred with Welles. Dietrich, Mercedes McCambridge, Zsa-Zsa Gabor, and Joseph Cotten played an assortment of "guest star" parts ranging from bits to several scenes. Dietrich's black-wigged madame in a Mexican bordello fell into the latter category. Of Welles, Dietrich says, "When I talk with him, I feel like a plant that has been watered."

In 1960 she returned to Germany to tour in her

With Adlai E. Stevenson at the premiere of Judgment at Nuremberg

Visiting old friend Billy Wilder on the set of The Fortune Cookie *(1965)*

With Elizabeth Taylor on the set of Who's Afraid of Virginia Woolf? *(1966)*

one-woman show. She faced her first German audiences in over thirty years. In most cities she played without incident, but there were some "Marlene Go Home" signs and some tomatoes thrown. But, on the whole, the Dietrich magic conquered. At the Titania Palast in Berlin she was warmly received. In Munich she received sixty-two curtain calls. This tour, as were her other recent engagements, was recorded by Capitol Records.

The following year Dietrich's book, *Marlene Dietrich's ABC,* was published and was well-received around the country. It was serialized in *Look* and later a paperback edition followed. *The New York Times Book Review* said, in part:

> Marlene Dietrich can write, too. Her first book is a diverting dictionary of observations, enthusiasms, asperities, anecdotes, advice, recipes and autobiographical fragments. With wit and charm she touches on everything from age to zippers, from bordels to Dr. Salk, from kisses to Koaxophilia. In style (and without benefit of ghosts) she achieves an aperitif prose of tang and sparkle; it

spins with a leggy grace all its own. Viewed over Miss Dietrich's shoulder, the alphabet will never seem the same again.

Next she became a member of the all-star cast of Stanley Kramer's *Judgment at Nuremberg,* and as the wife of a German general who had been executed for his involvement at Malmedy, she gave meaning and dignity to a part conceived merely to ease the tension of the trials.

Marlene then narrated the documentary-feature on Hitler called *Black Fox.* In Paris, she did a "walk-on" bit in the Audrey Hepburn–William Holden disaster, *Paris When It Sizzles,* for director Richard Quine.

In October 1967, the lady made her belated Broadway bow in an intermissionless one-woman program of songs. Entitled simply *Marlene Dietrich,* the show was presented by Alexander H. Cohen in a limited engagement that rang up a total of forty-eight performances. Dietrich's favorite conductor, Burt Bacharach, led the orchestra and personally arranged for her such audience favorites as "You're the Cream in

My Coffee," " I Wish You Love," "La Vie en Rose," and "Where Have All the Flowers Gone?" (her German recording of which was among the all-time best-selling ones in Europe). And there were also songs from her films, like "See What the Boys in the Back Room Will Have," "The Laziest Girl in Town," and, of course, "Falling in Love Again." Her show not only was among the most popular of the 1967–68 Broadway season, but it also won Marlene a special Tony Award.

A year later, Cohen brought her back for a successful return engagement that ran an even longer sixty-seven performances. That production was the basis of her only American TV special, a sixty-minute show that aired on CBS in January 1973 under the title *Marlene Dietrich: I Wish You Love.* Curiously, it was lacking in nearly all of the factors that made her stage performances so compelling. The glamour was there, but none of the Dietrich pizzazz; in fact, the lady seemed almost as bored and indifferent in performance as she had been in her barely-civil CBS press conference, designed to promote it.

Also in 1973, Marlene was to have appeared for director Orson Welles in his ill-fated *The Other Side of the Wind*—a never-quite-competed (and unreleased) feature about a troubled movie director (played by John Huston)—but was unavailable for the Arizona filming. Otherwise, she resisted all film offers to tour much of the world with her songs. Asked by Hollywood columnist Hedda Hopper which part of the world impressed her the most, the star unhesitatingly replied, "Israel—that was the greatest!" And she added, "I went there on my own—I didn't go there to make money." She went on to praise the discipline of the Israeli people, who reminded her of the settlers of frontier America.

Finally, in the seventies, Dietrich's personal appearances came to a halt, following leg injuries sustained in performance (it was reported at one engagement that she lost her balance and fell from the stage into the orchestra pit). In 1976, her long-separated husband, Rudi Sieber, died.

Then, two years later, Dietrich was persuaded to perform a cameo in a West German film set in the Weimar Republic, *Schöner Gigolo—Armer Gigolo,* directed by the British actor David Hemmings, who also appeared in a supporting role. The picture wasn't released in the U.S. until 1981, when it attracted little attention under the title *Just a Gigolo.* In the second of her two brief scenes, reportedly shot in Paris especially to accommodate her (the bulk of the movie

Arriving at London's Heathrow Airport (1971)

was filmed in Berlin), Marlene crooned the title song, but in a voice that only faintly echoed her familiar, Teutonic-accented baritone of old. Cast as a aging Prussian baroness, the heavily-veiled star still exuded beauty and glamour enough to make one wonder why director Hemmings made such indifferent use of her: indeed, before the close of her song, the camera deserts Dietrich altogether to follow the movie's leading character, dully portrayed by David Bowie, into the streets.

When asked in a Rex Reed interview whether the thought of death frightened her, Marlene cryptically replied, "No, because all of my friends are dead already." By the end of the seventies, she had found seclusion in her Paris apartment, where she was laid low by a fractured leg bone, the third such in five years. There, in the company of a secretary-companion, she read voraciously, maintained contact with old friends by telephone, and successfully avoided Western Europe's notorious paparazzi. But she denied that she had become a recluse, insisting that she traveled "frequently"—without detection. In a 1981 fall, she also broke a hip.

Always refusing to be photographed, Dietrich nevertheless gave in to actor/director Maximilian Schell's pleas that she cooperate on a documentary film, to be entitled simply *Marlene,* for which the pair endured ten hectic audio-taping sessions. During these meetings, the octogenarian star proved less than charming as she summarily dismissed her film career, praised her friend and colleague Orson Welles ("You should cross yourself when you mention his name"), and frequently raged at Schell, who later reported: "Marlene was very professional." Asked in a press interview how the lady now looked, her director proved to be the perfect gentleman-diplomat: "Well, that should remain a secret. I personally found her more beautiful than ever. She is very sensual, very personal. And I think I understand her refusal to be photographed."

Performing in her CBS-TV special Marlene Dietrich—I Wish You Love *(1973)*

Onstage at London's Wimbledon Theatre (1975)

In October 1991, the German newspaper *Bild* reported Marlene Dietrich dying in her Paris apartment, and that her relatives had gathered for the end. But the star made it publicly known that such was not the case, quipping, "Someone is tempting fate a little."

On the occasion of her ninetieth birthday on December 27, 1991—amid press salutes marking that momentous milestone—Dietrich raised Cain against the Academy of Motion Pictures Arts and Sciences for daring to use her image on its annual report—especially, since the Academy had never seen fit to award her an Oscar, either for a specific performance or for Lifetime Achievement.

Interviewed by phone at that time, Marlene's long-time friend and spokesman, writer Alain Bosquet, told the Paris press: "She will participate in nothing. She wants to keep her distance. Besides, at her age, things aren't so easy." Other insiders revealed that the star was now practically bedridden and a prisoner of her own reclusion. Those few allowed in her presence included Dietrich's maid, her doctor, and her daughter, Maria. Bosquet added: "She is highly vivacious and more lucid than most. She knows exactly what she wants, and what she doesn't want. Dignity is important to her."

On May 6, 1992, Dietrich's lawyer announced her death of "old age" in Paris, informing the press that the actress had been carried from her home covered with the French flag. Survived by her daughter and four grandsons, Marlene was to be buried, as was her wish, next to her mother in Berlin. After the public demonstrations that greeted her performances there in 1960, she had never returned to Germany.

Elderly and infirm though she may have been, Marlene Dietrich remained as intrinsically Teutonic as her word: "My mother tongue is German. I am German and will remain German, German in my soul, German in my upbringing. German philosophy, German poetry—these are my roots."

A Portrait Gallery

Filmography

Early autographed portrait

Introduction to the Filmography

There are two ways a filmography can be arranged and be correct. First, in the order in which the films were made. Second, in the order in which the films were *released*. Europeans prefer the former, Americans the latter.

Thus, the films of Marlene Dietrich are arranged chronologically according to "release" date (in the country of origin). For example: *Cafe Electric,* an Austrian film, opened in Vienna in November, 1927, and wasn't released in Germany and other countries until the following year, or thereafter. But most European reference tools still list this film as a 1928 German production *(Wenn ein Weib den Weg Veliert)* when it was shot and first shown in Austria the previous year!

This, unfortunately, is typical of *all* reference works dealing with the motion picture. Seldom do they agree on the actual release date (day, month, year) or the film's running time. Because of this situation, I have included only the *year* of "release" (except in a few random notes).

Since many films are re-edited—or cut—after their initial screening (whether it be for censorship reasons, or because the film is too long, or because certain sections must be deleted in certain countries where special groups and/or individuals might be offended, etc.), running times have been deleted from this index. However, meter length when a film was first submitted to the censor (before any cutting occurred) *is* supplied for the silent films, since this information has never before been made available. The reason the uncompleted *I Loved a Soldier* (1936) is included in the filmography is that scenes with Dietrich were actually shot—besides the usual

Arriving in America on the Bremen, *1930*

publicity material! But the same is *not* true of Marcel Carné's *Les Portes de la Nuit* (1946) which is discussed in detail below.

The following films are *not* listed in the filmography, even though Miss Dietrich appeared in one; didn't appear in two; and appeared by default in three:

Die Glückliche Mutter (*The Happy Mother*) was a home-movie which Rudolf Sieber directed, photographed, and edited. The stars were his wife and daughter Maria. Shooting began probably in 1925 and ended in 1928. Made only for themselves and friends, I have been told that it *was* released to theaters in Germany in the late 20's as a short-subject.

Stage Door Canteen (1943) was an all-star salute to that New York City organization operated for the benefit of U. S. servicemen during World War II. Dietrich did *not* appear in this film (nor was she scheduled to!), but did make an appearance at the Canteen in April of 1943 and was

sketched by an artist serving refreshments to a young sailor. This sketch was used as advance publicity for the film!

Les Portes de la Nuit (*The Gates of the Night*) (1946). In the autumn of 1945, Dietrich was approached about making this film in Paris. Marcel Carné was directing from a script by Jacques Prévert. Her friend Jean Gabin was signed as the male lead. Filming was to begin December 12, 1945, but Dietrich still had not decided to do the film. Publicity had already begun on the film by January, 1946, and scenes with Gabin as Diego had been shot. Now it was time for the script's Malou (Marlene!), but since she had script approval in her contract with Pathé-Cinéma, everyone waited for her decision. Carné was becoming impatient because he feared without Dietrich, Gabin would leave. After trying to get Prévert to change his script to meet her specifications, (which he refused to do!) Dietrich advised Carné that she would not make this film. In a letter to the Pathé organization she wrote, "I note that several scenes

With Josef von Sternberg during the filming of Dishonored

in the movie *Les Portes de la Nuit* depict negative aspects of life under the Occupation and create in certain parts of this film an atmosphere which seems to me to be bad propaganda for the rest of the world, all of which made it impossible for me to take the part in the picture." No footage had been shot with Dietrich, but she had posed for publicity pictures with Gabin and Carné. Since she had not signed the contract, there was no trouble with the French unions. Gabin did leave and Carné's picture, released with Yves Montand and Nathalie Nattier as stars, was not particularly good. But even less so was *Martin Roumagnac,* which Dietrich and Gabin made for director Georges Lacombe.

Das Gab's Nur Einmal (*It Only Happened Once*) (1958) was a compilation film made in Germany which included film clips of Dietrich. There were many scenes used from pre-war German films, both silents and talkies, and it had a thin storyline: Hans Albers showing a film-struck teenager that the world of films was not all glamour, but hard work as well! There were, among others, scenes from *Tragödie der Liebe* (with Jannings and Glässner) and, of course, *Der Blaue Engel.*

Obiknovennii Fashizm (*Ordinary Fascism*) (1965) a full-length Russian documentary made by Mikhail Romm was, according to the "Monthly Film Bulletin" (August 1966) ". . . not merely another

With René Clair, Joe Pasternak, and Josef von Sternberg, 1941

newsreel account of the rise and fall of the Third Reich but an attempt to pinpoint the nature of fascism, to probe its source as a phenomenon of the 20th century." It used archive clippings of "Marlene Dietrich modelling the black dresses of the time."

The Love Goddesses (1965) was a compilation film concerning the various cinema queens, high priestesses of sex and glamour, which have pervaded the American screen. There were notable omissions but at least Dietrich opened the proceedings with her "Hot Voodoo" number from *Blonde Venus*—which certainly set the pace for the other "love goddesses"!

And, the countless cartoons in which Marlene Dietrich was delightfully caricatured.

Looking over the collected films of Marlene Dietrich would certainly produce some outstanding moments; and, indeed, some best forgotten. But the reason for her prolonged popularity is the continuous "mystique" which surrounds her to this day. It's what people don't know about her that fascinates them. Audiences the world over each have their own reasons for seeing a Dietrich movie.

An early portrait for Ufa Studio (1929)

Dietrich (arrow) on the set with other members of the cast

Der Kleine Napoleon

(The Little Napoleon)

Also known as: So Sind die Männer (Men Are Like This) Napoleons Kleiner Bruder (Napoleon's Little Brother)

A Union-Film Production – 1923

CAST: EGON VON HAGEN (*Napoleon Bonaparte*); PAUL HEIDEMANN (*Jerome Bonaparte*); HARRY LIEDTKE (*Georg von Melsungen*); JACOB TIEDTKE (*Jeremias von Katzenellenbogen*); His Nieces, ANTONIA DIETRICH (*Charlotte*) LONI NEST (*Liselotte*); ALICE HECHY (*Annemarie*); KURT VESPERMANN (*Florian Wunderlich*); PAUL BIENSFELD (*court marshall of the King*); KURT FUSS (*director of the Royal Ballet*); MARQUISETTE BOSKY (*the prima ballerina*); MARLENE DIETRICH (*Kathrin, Charlotte's maid*) WILHELM BENDOW (*Jerome's valet*).

CREDITS: GEORG JACOBY (*Director*); ROBERT LIEBMANN, GEORG JACOBY (*Scenarists*); Released by UFA-FILM, A. G.; LENGTH, 2713 meters.

SYNOPSIS: Following the unfortunate treaty of Tilsit, August 18, 1807, Jerome Bonaparte (Paul Heidemann), the youngest brother of Napoleon I, is made the ruler of the newly created Kingdom of Westphalia. His brilliant court resides in the magnificent Castle Wilhelmshöhe near Kassel. In the castle's beautiful gardens he passes his time with gay garden parties.

The household of Jerome's Police Minister, the Baron von Katzenellenbogen (Jacob Tiedke), is managed by the Baron's niece Charlotte (Antonia Dietrich) whose equally beautiful "foster-sister" is Annemarie (Alice Hechy), the gay daughter of an innkeeper.

During a hunting trip, Charlotte, accompanied by her sister Liselotte (Loni Nest), meets, quite by chance, the young Georg von Melsungen (Harry Liedtke), who has been sent by Napoleon as Official Courier to the Court of King Jerome. Georg is billeted in the house of the Police Minister, and soon he and Charlotte find themselves in love. After a brief romance, Georg succeeds in obtaining Char-

Wolfshagen. Meanwhile, Georg learns of the king's interest in his wife, and hastens to the city dressed in the uniform of the postillion, Florian Wunderlich (Kurt Vespermann), who is Annemarie's sweetheart.

Once in the city, Georg finds their lodgings empty and rushes to the theatre, where he suspects he'll find Charlotte in the company of the king. Georg imagines that he will be too late and that the king will have already given his wife the "golden key," which not only opens the door to the royal box at the theatre but all of the doors in the palace!

But Georg doesn't find Charlotte in the theatre. He is told, however, of her flight to the country by Annemarie, who to the dismay of the prima ballerina (Marquisette Bosky), has been demoted into the corps de ballet of the jovial king by the director of the Royal Ballet (Kurt Fuss).

Jerome is informed of Charlotte's whereabouts and tries to surprise her in Wolfshagen, but Charlotte, with the aid of her maid Kathrin (Marlene Dietrich), escapes dressed in the peasant costume peculiar to that region. In a forest she meets her husband, who has rushed by horseback to find her.

With great courage, Georg has it out with the king and is afterwards jailed in the Löwenburg (Lion's Castle) along with his accomplice Florian. The two men spend quite a time in jail until Annemarie, with the help of the ·"golden key," liberates them!

While Jerome is trying to imprison the two again, Napoleon (Egon von Hagen) appears and straightens out the whole mess. The two young couples begin a life of bliss, while Napoleon's little brother Jerome sadly begins his "forced arrest."

NOTES: This "non-historical comedy," typically cashing-in on the vogue for historical spectacles the German cinema was then enjoying, was Marlene Dietrich's first film. She was not an extra, but a supporting member of the cast, receiving twelfth billing. *Der Kleine Napoleon* was begun in the late fall of 1922. The film's working-title was *So Sind die Männer,* and when released in Austria the title there became *Napoleons Kleiner Bruder.*

But as *So Sind die Männer* it was submitted to the Berlin Censor on December 22, 1922, and was released to the public in January of 1923.

lotte's acceptance to become his wife. And so they are married.

The king, always on the lookout for beautiful women to grace his court—and his private chambers, finally discovers Charlotte. He summons her to appear before him. Charlotte, in order to escape the king's advances, and directly disobeying his command, goes to the country estate of her uncle in

Tragödie der Liebe

(Tragedy of Love)

A Joe May-Film Production—1923

CAST: EMIL JANNINGS (*Ombrade, a wrestler*); ERIKA GLASSNER (*Musette, his mistress*); MIA MAY (*Countess Manon de Moreau*); KURT VESPERMANN (*The Judge*); MARLENE DIETRICH (*Lucie, his mistress*); with Ida Wust, Arnold Korff, Charlotte Ander, Curt Gotz, Rudolf Forster, Ferry Sikla, Loni Nest, Vladimir Gaidarow, Hermann Vallentin, Hedwig Pauli-Winterstein, Paul Grätz, Eugen Rex, Hans Wassmann, Albert Patry.

CREDITS: JOE MAY (*Director*); LEO BIRINSKI, ADOLF LANTZ (*Scenarists*); SOPHUS WANGOE, KARL PUTH (*Photographers*); PAUL LENI (*Decors*); ALI HUBERT (*Costumes*); RUDOLF SIEBER (*Production Assistant*); WILHELM LÖWITT (*Synchronized Music*); Released by UFA-FILM, A.G.; LENGTH (PART I) 1939 meters, (PART II) 1790 meters, (PART III) 1719 *meters,* (PART IV) 1984 meters.

SYNOPSIS: A brutal Parisian wrestler, Ombrade (Emil Jannings), takes his mistress Musette (Erika Glässner) to a local dive. While there, a butler friend of hers (Musette is a chambermaid) slips her a note when Ombrade isn't looking and she puts it into her shoe. Later, the wrestler arrives at her apartment with a present, but Musette isn't there. Seeing a slip of paper on the table (from the butler), Ombrade flys into a rage and discovers the two making love. He chases the butler with murder in his eyes and finally corners him atop the building. The massive wrestler, blind with rage, throws the man from the roof to his death.

Returning to her flat, Ombrade forgets his anger when he sees Musette dressed in the fur-lined neg-

Dietrich (right)

Dietrich is third from right in first row of spectators on left side of courtroom. Emil Jannings is in light suit, left foreground.

ligee he bought for her. He embraces her, but he cannot erase the crime he has just committed from his mind. Trying to forget the incident, Ombrade dresses up and takes the saucy chambermaid to a swank apartment being used as a gambling casino. Luck makes him the big winner, but suddenly the police raid the place. Not wanting to lose his fabulous winnings, he escapes, leaving Musette there to be arrested.

Musette gives the police her boy friend's address, and they go to arrest him. But the charge is not merely gambling or resisting arrest, but murder! At the jail the fighter and the chambermaid are placed in cells next to each other, so a police stenographer can take down every word that is spoken.

Meanwhile, the trial date is set. One of the judges (Kurt Vespermann) to try the case gets a call from Lucie, his mistress (Marlene Dietrich). She wants to attend the trial that all of Paris is talking about. The judge refuses her request, but she is not discouraged.

At the opening of the wrestler's trial the judge's mistress and her girl friend appear in the spectator's gallery—in the front row, so as not to miss a thing. They have come equipped with opera glasses and watch the expressions on the wrestler's face all during the trial. Musette, on the stand, tells all, and soon Ombrade is found guilty.

NOTES: Prior to her triumph in *Der Blaue Engel*, Lucie was Marlene Dietrich's favorite role. It brought her much attention in her early career. After all, it was an Emil Jannings vehicle, and everyone would see a Jannings picture. Her first scene on the phone, clad in feathers and a monocle, was almost entirely in close-up. And she received some close-up shots at the trial too, playfully peeking at everyone through her opera glasses.

Dietrich's second film was one of the few *major* German films she was to appear in and brought her instant recognition, for her scenes (although short) were distinctive.

Tragödie der Liebe was filmed in four parts (a total of 20 reels). Parts I and II were submitted to the Berlin Censor on March 6, 1923, and released a few weeks later, while Parts III and IV weren't submitted to the Censor until May 8, 1923, and released shortly thereafter.

A considerably abbreviated edition of this four-part epic tragedy is now a part of the George Eastman House of Photography's collection.

Der Mensch am Wege

(Man by the Roadside)

An Osmania-Film Production—1923

CAST: ALEXANDER GRANACH (*Schuster*); WILHELM DIETERLE (*The Human-Angel*); with Heinrich George, Wilhelm Völker, Wilhelm Diegelmann, Dr. Max Pohl, Ernst Gronau, Ludwig Rex, Gerhard Bienert, Brockmann, Georg Hilbert, Fritz Kampers, Max Nemetz, Werner Pledath, Fritz Rasp, Rausch, Emilie Unda, Marlene Dietrich, Sophie Pagay, Liselotte Rolle, Bäck, Gerlach-Jacobi, Hegewald, Härling, Herbst, Hermine Körner, Dolly Lorenz, Seeberg, Lotte Stein.

CREDITS: WILHELM DIETERLE (*Director and Scenarist*); WILLY HAMEISTER (*Photographer*); WILLI HABENTZ (*Assistant Photographer*); HERBERT RICHTER-LUCKIAN (*Decors*); From a short story by LEO TOLSTOY; LENGTH, 1657 meters.

SYNOPSIS: Old and half-starved Schuster, the village nonentity (Alexander Granach), finds a young man by the roadside one day and offers aid to this stranger although he himself has very little! It seems this stranger (Wilhelm Dieterle) is really an angel and soon will bring Schuster's family good luck.

With Wilhelm (later William) Dieterle

This fable is expanded further with the mysterious death of a cruel landlord, a man of great means and property, as suspicion falls on Schuster! His family refuses to believe the slim evidence brought forward but can do little but endure the suspicions with humility. The human-angel, working in the house of Schuster, then prepares to rescue him from these injustices!

NOTES: This sketchy synopsis was pieced together from a review which appeared in *Der Kinematograph* (June 17, 1923). This review further stated that Dieterle was heavily influenced by the Russian film *Polikuschka* and by many Swedish film makers of the time, but when sentimentalized in the traditional German fashion, the fable lost its impact. The photography was praised, as was the acting of Alexander Granach. The acting was generally considered "naturalistic," but only Granach was singled out for comment. At first glance, the film contained good pictorial composition, but in the final analysis remained "artificial" and "staged."

Dieterle patterned his scenario after a short story by Leo Tolstoy, who had patterned his short story after Russian folk tales. Dieterle, best known at that time as a popular young actor in German films and on the stage, turned to directing and script-writing with this film, and also played one of its leading roles.

Dietrich appeared as a peasant girl, obviously the ingénue, complete with long golden braids—a characterization which would again appear in her career: the disguise in *Dishonored;* the early Lily of *Song of Songs;* and certain scenes of the uncompleted *I Loved a Soldier*.

On June 4, 1923, *Der Mensch am Wege* was submitted to the Berlin Censor and it was agreed, upon release, that it was not a film for a juvenile audience. It was released to the public two weeks later at the Alhambra Theatre in Berlin.

Der Sprung ins Leben

(The Leap into Life)

An Oskar Messter-Film Production—1924

CAST: XENIA DESNI (*a circus acrobat*); WALTER RILLA (*her partner*); PAUL HEIDEMANN (*a young scholar*); FRIDA RICHARD (*his aunt*); KATHE HAACK (*the scholar's associate*); LEONHARD HASKEL (*the ringmaster*); with Olga Engl, Marlene Dietrich, Hans Brausewetter.

CREDITS: DR. JOHANNES GUTER (*Director*); OSKAR MESSTER (*Producer*); FRANZ SCHULZ (*Scenarist*); FRITZ ARNO WAGNER (*Photographer*); RUDI FELDT (*Decors*); Released by UFA-FILM, A.G.; European Distribution by PAN-FILM, A.G.; LENGTH, 2075 meters.

SYNOPSIS: A young scholar (Paul Heidemann), attending the circus one day, falls for a young acrobat (Xenia Desni) and proposes that she leave the show and allow him to transform her into a social belle. Almost against her will, the girl is brought into the home of the young man's aunt (Frida Richard), who will instruct her in the ways of society. The fellow plans to marry the girl once she has proved herself fit for his social position.

Instead of feeling happy in these new surroundings, however, the former acrobat longs for her former partner (Walter Rilla), whom she didn't realize she loved so deeply until she was parted from him. The young scholar's ardent pursuit of her affections heightens her longing to be with the handsome young acrobat again.

The following week the young man takes her to a mountain spa and again forces his attentions on her, but she breaks loose and flees down the mountainside. Running after her, the young man runs directly in front of a passing train and is badly hurt. The girl, having seen this unfortunate accident, runs back to help him and, finding him still alive, rushes him to a nearby hospital. She remains with him, tortured by guilt, until he has fully recovered.

Meanwhile, the big circus comes to town and the young girl goes to see it. She furtively looks for her former partner, but he spots her first and begs her to return to the life she was meant for. Realizing the truth, she agrees.

Soon they have prepared a marvelous trapeze act (over a lion's cage) and while they are on the high wire, the young scholar, in a last desperate move to get her to reconsider his way of life, runs into the arena and shouts at her to come down to him. But she prefers the arms of her partner. The scholar, upon returning home, finds his young assistant (Käthe Haack) waiting with open arms.

NOTES: Dr. Johannes Guter avoided a tragic story here and appealed to the public's taste for a happy ending for all concerned. His production displayed great taste and beauty. The circus performers and animals were from the Leipzig Zoo. Dietrich probably played one of the young ladies yearning for the young scholar's attention, which, unfortunately, is never realized.

Der Sprung ins Leben was filmed in the fall of 1923 and was submitted to the Berlin Censor on January 21, 1924. It premiered in Berlin on January 31, 1924.

Die Freudlose Gasse

(The Joyless Street)

Released in England in 1926 as The Joyless Street; Released in The United States in 1927 as The Street of Sorrow

A Hirschal-Sofar-Film Production

CAST: JARO FURTH (*Councillor Josef Rumfort*); GRETA GARBO (*Grete Rumfort*); LONI NEST (*Mariandl*); ASTA NIELSEN (*Maria Lechner*); MAX KOHLHASE and SILVA TORF (*her parents*); KARL ETTLINGER (*Director General Rosenow*); ILKA GRUNING (*his wife*); COUNTESS AGNES ESTERHAZY (*Regina Rosenow*); ALEXANDER MURSKY (*Dr. Leid, the lawyer*); TAMARA (*Lia Leid*); HENRY STUART (*Egon Stirner*); ROBERT GARRISON (*Ganez*); EINAR HANSON (*Lieutenant Davy, U.S.A.*); MARIO CUSMICH (*Colonel Irving, U.S.A.*); VALESKA GERT (*Mrs. Greifer*); COUNTESS TOLSTOI (*Miss Henriette*); MRS. MARKSTEIN (*Mrs. Merkl*); WERNER KRAUSS (*Josef Geiringer, the butcher*); HERTA VON WALTHER (*Else*); OTTO REINWALD (*her husband*); GRIGORY CHMARA (*a waiter*); RASKATOFF (*Trebitsch*); KRAFT RASCHIG (*An American Soldier*); and (*unbilled*) MARLENE DIETRICH.

CREDITS: GEORG WILHELM PABST (*Director*); WILLI HAAS (*Scenarist*); GUIDO SEEBER, CURT OERTEL and WALTER ROBERT LACH (*Photographers*); HANS SOHNLE, OTTO ERDMANN (*Decors*); MARC SORKIN (*Assistant Director*); ANATOL LITVAK (*Editor*); DR. NIKOL. KAUF-MANN (*Medical Advisor*); Based on the novel by HUGO BETTAUER; LENGTH, 3738 meters.

SYNOPSIS: In post-World War I Vienna's inflation period some of its citizens become powerful through the suffering and poverty of others. Such a man is the notorious banker Rosenow (Karl Ettlinger), who must see that his wife (Ilka Grüning) and daughter (Countless Agnes Esterhazy) enjoy all the comforts of their class-conscious society.

There is much speculation on the stock market at this time (for those who can afford such luxuries), and Councillor Josef Rumfort (Jaro Fürth), a declining high official, gets carried away, sells property, and speculates on industrial stocks with the cash. When it becomes apparent that these stocks will soon fail, Rosenow cleans up, while small investors like Rumfort lose everything!

This is a time when the local butcher, baker, and even the dressmaker, have a certain power, for everything depends upon their issuing credit. The butcher, Josef Geiringer (Werner Krauss), is notori-

Dietrich is just left of two officers, with hands clasped.

ous for his ways of getting female customers to pay their debts! And Mrs. Greifer (Valeska Gert), the local dressmaker, provides a little extra service for her customers when her girls, struggling for support of their families, are forced to "entertain" in the back rooms at night.

One night in these rooms a terrible murder is committed. Lia Leid (Tamara), the faithless wife of the lawyer Dr. Leid (Alexander Mursky), is found strangled. Suspicion falls immediately on Egon Stirner (Henry Stuart), an official of the bank, who has been having an affair with this wealthy woman. The young man is sentenced to a long prison term despite his continual denials.

Meanwhile, to help out her father, Grete Rumfort (Greta Garbo) decides to take in lodgers. A young American lieutenant (Einar Hanson) comes to inspect the rooms and falls in love with Grete, but her father refuses to allow the American to rent from them.

Now Grete must go to Mrs. Greifer for credit and also gets a daytime job in her dressmaking shop. When the Rumforts' problems increase, Grete is resigned to meeting a customer in the "back room," but is rescued from such a fate by young Lieutenant Davy!

The murder case, meanwhile, takes another turn. Maria Lechner (Asta Nielsen) has confessed to the crime of murdering Lia Leid, and Egon Stirner is set free. But these terrible times finally manifest themselves when one of the women seduced by the butcher kills him and the populace of the neighborhood raid his vast storage bins of food.

NOTES: Pabst's *Die Freudlose Gasse* accented the general atmosphere of misery that prevailed in the early post-war years of Vienna and remains one of the great sociological dramas made during that period. Filmed in both Vienna and Berlin, it starkly presented sex and mores with unusual candor (note a medical doctor hired as "Technical Advisor!").

In *The Film Till Now*, Paul Rotha stated that "No film or novel has so truthfully recorded the despair of defeat, and the false values of social life that arise after war, as *The Joyless Street*. With unerring psychology by which he caused the smallest actions of his characters to convey meaning, Pabst brought to his picture moments of searing mental anguish, of sheer unblemished beauty. His extreme powers of truthfulness, of the understanding of reality, of the vital meaning of hunger, love, lust, selfishness and greed, rendered this extraordinary film convincing."

Garbo, giving a telling performance here, firmly established herself as an actress of power and soon left for America. Others in the international cast included Asta Nielsen (Danish); Countess Agnes Esterhazy (Hungarian); Henry Stuart (Egyptian); Grigory Chmara–Nielsen's husband–(Russian); and Werner Krauss (German)!

There are many who don't believe that Marlene Dietrich played one of the women in the butcher's line in this film. First, let's remember that no *complete* version of this film (originally 3738 meters) exists today. The English-titled versions are greatly cut, and naturally it is difficult, perhaps impossible, to find Dietrich in the scene which she made. Also, the medium-shot of Dietrich standing behind Jaro Fürth may never have been used in the finished print but only for advertising purposes. The long shot is definitely in the picture but the lighting is such that she cannot be spotted anyway.

Die Freudlose Gasse was submitted to the Censor on May 15, 1925, and released two weeks later.

With Jaro Fürth

51

A beguiling Dietrich flirts at the sidewalk cafe

Manon Lescaut

Released in the U. S. in December, 1926 as Manon Lescaut

An Ufa-Film Production—1926

CAST: LYA DE PUTTI (*Manon Lescaut*); VLADIMIR GAIDAROV (*des Grieux*); EDUARD ROTHAUSER (*Marshall des Grieux*); FRITZ GREINER (*Marquis de Bli*); HUBERT VON MEYERINCK (*son of de Bli*); FRIDA RICHARD AND EMILIE KURTZ (*Manon's aunts*); LYDIA POTECHINA (*Susanne*); THEODOR LOOS (*Tiberge*); SIEGFRIED ARNO (*Lescaut*); TRUDE HESTERBERG (*Claire*); MARLENE DIETRICH (*Micheline*); with Karl Harbacher, Albert Paulig, Hans Junkermann.

CREDITS: ARTHUR ROBISON (*Director*); HANS KYSER and ARTHUR ROBISON (*Scenarists*); THEODOR SPARKUHL (*Photographer*); PAUL LENI (*Decors and Costumes*); Based on *L'Histoire de Manon Lescaut* by ABBE PREVOST; Released by UNIVERSUM-FILM-VERLEIH, G.m.b.H.; LENGTH, 2645 meters.

SYNOPSIS: Manon Lescaut (Lya de Putti), a beautiful young girl from the provinces, is being sent by her severe aunts (Frida Richard and Emilie Kurtz) into a convent. It is hoped that the good sisters will be able to tame Manon's dangerous temper. En route to the convent in a coach, Manon's thoughts are not on the convent and prayers, but already on planning her escape. In Amiens, while spending the night at an inn, she meets the wealthy Marquis de Bli (Fritz Greiner), a man of the world, whom she tells of her planned escape.

De Bli promises her that his coach will be ready for her at midnight and that he will follow her later to Paris. Manon escapes from her aunts and the elderly suitor by taking a trip with a handsome young man about to enter the priesthood, whom she has met at the inn. He is the Chevalier des Grieux (Vladimir Gaidarov), the son of the Marshall of France. They plan to stay at Susanne's (Lydia Potechina) home in Paris, but their luck is of short duration. Soon they are without money.

While young des Grieux is out trying to sell a ring, the old Marquis, having observed these two turtle doves, arranges a nasty intrigue. Manon's step-brother (Siegfried Arno), dependent upon the old Marquis, keeps des Griex occupied for quite a while, during which time the creditors get the police to put Manon into debtors' prison. While Manon is about to be taken away, de Bli appears to save her, but forces the helpless girl to write a letter to her be-

Dietrich (left) taunts Lya de Putti, with assistance from Fritz Greiner

loved's father (Eduard Rothauser), asking him to have his son arrested. The girl commits this drastic act with a sad heart and hides when the Marshall's men come for des Grieux. The young man sees Manon's letter and escapes, but returns to her later because he cannot believe she would have written such a note.

The old Marquis offers Manon beautiful clothes and jewels which makes the vain girl stop crying about her young lover. Soon Susanne enters the room dressed like a peacock, which causes gales of laughter from Manon and de Bli. At this moment des Grieux enters and is now convinced of Manon's faithlessness.

The Marquis takes Manon into his home and presents her to the world. But Manon, who is basically not a bad girl, feels that she is living in a gilded cage, and eventually escapes! She seeks out des Grieux, about to become a priest the next day, and persuades him to follow her again. In Paris she leaves him at a sidewalk café, and goes to tell the Marquis of her true love. De Bli's anger enrages Manon. He then has her locked up.

Now he hatches another sinister plot, sending the enticing Micheline (Marlene Dietrich) to des Grieux with the following letter:

Manon won her bet. She succeeded with her looks to win you back to the sinning world, and in order to console you is sending you the good-natured Micheline. The amused round table of the Marquis de Bli.

Des Grieux reads the letter and faints! Micheline has him brought inside the café where she attempts to console him. Meanwhile, Manon (who has outwitted de Bli's son [Hubert von Meyerinck] and has again escaped) arrives on the scene. Micheline, seeing Manon, makes a swift departure.

Manon and des Grieux, together again, must again face poverty, which Manon soon finds she is unable to bear!

Manon's stepbrother, meanwhile, persuades des Grieux to try his luck *cheating* at cards in a gambling establishment. He joins the Marquis and Micheline in a game of cards and is enjoying quite a "winning streak" when the Marquis catches him cheating!

At this time, the young de Bli buys Manon a shopfull of clothes, and when des Grieux returns home with the money he has won, he notices her new acquisitions. In a rage, he throws all the money on the floor, saying, "Money won by cheating and the wages of a loose woman belong together!" She replies, "What do you want from me? Do you want me to starve? I am not even married to you!" Des Grieux, realizing the truth, decides to marry Manon immediately and goes for a priest.

During his absence, the old Marquis appears with the police to throw Manon into jail. The young man returns to find his beloved gone!

Manon is brought into a prison workhouse, where she weaves at a loom. The Marquis arrives shortly thereafter with his new mistress (Micheline!) and offers Manon freedom if she will become his. She

At the casino, with Vladimir Gaidarov and Fritz Greiner

refuses. Manon manages, however, with the help of her stepbrother, to lock Micheline into her cell. She takes the mistress's hat and coat and escapes, leaving her in the cell.

Manon rushes to the palace of the old des Grieux in order to find his son. But the old man is furious because of her many deceptions and hastens to his friend, the president of the police, with the intention of having Manon deported to the American colonies, since she is undesirable. And, it seems, young des Grieux doesn't trust Manon either. Without hope, Manon staggers from the palace, into the arms of the police!

The day of the deportation has arrived. The Marquis is present with his gay friends to enjoy Manon's unhappiness, but his pleasure is spoiled when Manon, who has escaped from her keeper, attacks him, and he flees with a scratched face. Des Grieux finally learns the truth from his friend and priestly adviser Tiberge (Theodor Loos) and hastens to free Manon. But he is too late. The convoy of women, packed like cattle in wooden carts, has already left.

On the way to Le Havre, Manon becomes violently ill and is left, like a dying animal, by the roadside, where des Grieux comes upon her. He rushes her to the palace of his father. Moved by his great love for his son, the Marshall of France forgives his son. In the arms of her beloved, dreaming of marriage and the bridal wreath, Manon closes her eyes forever. . . .

NOTES: This beautifully tragic story was given a sumptuous production by Ufa-Films and it was immediately popular with critics and the public alike. It was released in Berlin in February of 1926 and arrived in America in December of that year, the first Marlene Dietrich picture to play the United States. (It was submitted to the Berlin Censor on January 22, 1926.)

Manon's star, Lya de Putti, was hardly a stranger to American audiences, for in 1925 she had appeared for D. W. Griffith in *The Sorrows of Satan,* and her famous German film, *Variety* (with Emil Jannings), was still playing around the country.

Dietrich's role was not a small one. It provided her with seven scenes with the film's stars and was the second most important female role.

Paul Rotha, in *The Film Till Now,* says of this film, ". . . The acting material was well chosen, no easy task with a costume picture of this type, the Manon of Lya de Putti and the Chevalier des Grieux of Vladimir Gaidarov being admirable, whilst the supporting cast, particularly Siegfried Arno, Frida Richard, and Lydia Potechina, were exceptionally competent. Robison succeeded in establishing an air of intimacy, of dramatic relationship between one character and another, of the deep passion that linked the two lovers, by a continual use of close-ups. The decorations of Leni gave to the film a reality that is lacking in the vast majority of costume pictures . . . The costumes, designed with a wealth of accurate detail that was fully revealed by the close penetration of the camera, were more faithful to their period, both in cut and wear, than any others that have been seen in historical film reconstruction."

Eine Du Barry von Heute

(A Modern Du Barry)

Released in the U.S. in 1928 as A Modern Du Barry

A Felsom-Film Production

CAST: MARIA CORDA (*Toinette, a modern Du Barry*); ALFRED ABEL (*Sillon*); FRIEDRICH KAYSSLER (*Cornelius Corbett*); JULIUS VON SZÖREGHY (*General Padilla*); JEAN BRADIN (*Sandro, King of Asturia*); HANS ALBERS (*Darius Kerbelian*); ALFRED GERASCH (*Count Rabbatz*); ALFRED PAULIG (*Clairet*); HANS WASSMANN (*the theater director*); KARL PLATEN (*a servant*); EUGEN BURG (*Levasseur*); MARLAINE (*sic*) DIETRICH (*a coquette*); HILDA RADNAY (*Juliette*); JULIA SERDA (*Aunt Julie*); HEDWIG WANGEL (*Rosalie*); LOTTE LORRING (*a mannequin*).

CREDITS: ALEXANDER KORDA (*Director*); ROBERT LIEBMANN, ALEXANDER KORDA, PAUL REBOUX (*Scenarists*); FRITZ ARNO WAGNER (*Photographer*) OTTO FRIEDRICH WERNDORFF (*Decors*); From the Story "Eine Du Barry von Heute" by LUDWIG (LAJOS) BIRO; Released by UFA-FILM, A. G.; LENGTH, 3004 meters.

SYNOPSIS: Toinette (Maria Corda), a young shop girl, lives in a hotel owned by her Aunt Julie (Julia Serda). One evening she is seduced by Darius Kerbelian (Hans Albers), a silk underwear salesman. Half out of her mind, the young girl decides to end it all by drowning herself, but is rescued by a painter named Sillon (Alfred Abel), who gives her a new lease on life. Soon she becomes a mannequin in a stylish shop. Now Toinette's climb begins! One day when an attractive coquette (Marlene Dietrich) and her friend Juliette (Hilda Radnay) come into the shop, Toinette takes a fancy to a frock the young woman buys and leaves for alterations. That night, Toinette "borrows" the gown, to go out on the town! Escorted by Sillon, Toinette is having a riotous time, in a fashionable club, when the young coquette ap-

pears with Juliette and their dates: Count Rabbatz (Alfred Gerasch) and a noted theater director (Hans Wassmann). When the coquette notices her gown being worn by a shop model, she becomes furious and storms out of the club. Meanwhile, Toinette meets the Count and the theater director, and soon becomes the toast of Paris. The next morning, not knowing this meeting has taken place, the coquette calls the shop to insist on the girl's being fired, but, alas, she has already quit!

Toinette soon meets a young man named Sandro (Jean Bradin), quite by accident, in the street one afternoon, and they enjoy a friendly chat.

The young man is actually Sandro, King of Asturia, whose throne is shaky, for he is too young and pleasure-loving, and because the Commander of

the Army, General Padilla (Julius von Szöreghy) hopes to get rid of him and seize the throne. The king, meanwhile, is trying to negotiate a loan with Cornelius Corbett (Friedrich Kayssler), a wealthy American banker. Corbett is in Paris and has seen Toinette at many gay affairs and desires her.

Toinette, knowing that the wish to possess a woman becomes stronger the more difficult it is made, finds no trouble in turning Corbett down. Toinette's thoughts are still focused on Sandro, the young man to whom she refused a kiss that afternoon weeks before. Once Corbett and Sandro have agreed to terms concerning the loan, Corbett throws a swank party and asks Toinette if she will preside over the affair and welcome the guests as they arrive.

This is when Toinette discovers Sandro is a monarch and he discovers that she is not an innocent girl but a popular actress and hostess at such parties. Despite their mutual disappointment in one another's pretense, Sandro offers marriage if she'll accompany him back to his country. Corbett, hearing of this plan, tells the young King that if *he* doesn't get Toinette, the King will not get his loan. After a time, Sandro decides that love is stronger than money and takes Toinette to his kingdom.

This move is grist to General Padilla's mill and he soon launches a revolution which had been building up for many months! The people turn against Toinette and blame her for their high taxes. Corbett's money, meanwhile, finances the revolution. Sandro is dethroned and Toinette is imprisoned. Soon their lives are in great danger.

Corbett, aboard his yacht in the harbor, hearing of this danger to the young lovers' lives, realizes he's gone too far, and rescues the young pair in the nick of time. He helps them escape aboard his yacht and takes them to a foreign country so that they may establish a new kingdom—a kingdom of love!

NOTES: This was Dietrich's first film for director Alexander Korda, and although she had only three scenes, she played the role of the coquette with great candor and humor—and just a hint of bitchiness. *Du Barry* was filmed at Ufa's Babelsberg studios in the spring of 1926. It was intended primarily as a vehicle for Korda's wife, Maria (Corda). The film was released in the United States in 1928 as *A Modern Du Barry,* but had a limited distribution. A print is now in the collection of the National Film Archive of the British Film Institute.

Dietrich was billed for the first and only time as *Marlaine* Dietrich, which may have been a typographical error—or perhaps an experiment on her part.

Du Barry was submitted to the Berlin Censor on November 9, 1926, and released soon thereafter.

Madame Wünscht Keine Kinder

(Madame Doesn't Want Children)

Released in the U.S. in 1927 as Madame Wants No Children

A Fox Europa-Film Production

CAST: MARIA CORDA (*Elyane Parizot*); HARRY LIEDTKE (*Paul Le Barroy*); MARIA PAUDLER (*Louise Bonvin*); TRUDE HESTERBERG (*Elyane's mother*); DINA GRALLA (*Lulu, Elyane's sister*); HERMANN VALLENTIN (*Paul's uncle*); CAMILLA VON HOLLAY (*Louise's maid*); OLGA MANNEL (*Louise's cook*); ELLEN MULLER (*Elyane's maid*); with Marlene Dietrich, John Loder.

CREDITS: ALEXANDER KORDA (*Director*); ADOLF LANTZ, BELA BALAZS (*Scenarists*); THEODOR SPARKUHL, ROBERT BABERSKE (*Photographers*); OTTO FRIEDRICH WERNDORFF (*Decors*); KARL FREUND (*Producer*); KARL HARTL (*Associate Producer*); RUDOLF SIEBER (*Production Assistant*); Based on the novel, *Madame ne veut pas d'enfants,* by CLEMENT VAUTEL; Re-

leased by DEUTSCHE VEREINSFILM, A. G.; LENGTH, 2166 meters.

SYNOPSIS: Paul Le Barroy (Harry Liedtke), has found in his friendship with lovely Louise Bonvin (Maria Paudler) an idyllic, peaceful relationship, but, it seems, Louise doesn't like belonging to just one man. So Paul, aching to have a home of his own and be surrounded by children, marries Elyane Parizot (Maria Corda), the attractive daughter of wealthy parents. As soon as the wedding ceremony is over, however, Paul learns from Elyane's own lips that her only motive for entering the ranks of the *grande confrèrie* was a desire for greater freedom than a young bourgeois girl was allowed at that time.

To show she means what she says, Elyane makes Paul promise not to have any children—the principal luxury of the poor! After the honeymoon the couple settle in a *moderne* apartment and Elyane continues giving parties, showing little interest in anything but the Charleston and beautiful clothes. This carefree attitude is influenced by the behavior of Elyane's mother (Trude Hesterberg) and her sister (Dina Gralla), who are, in Paul's opinion, nothing more than "loose ladies," albeit fashionable ones.

Now Paul thinks more and more of his contented life with Louise, and finally walks out on Elyane. When Elyane finds Louise's address in her husband's things, she suspects the worst and now wants Paul back more than ever!

Elyane goes to Louise's flat, gun in hand, but is calmed down by Louise, who comforts her and advises her how to regain and retain Paul's affection and secure happiness for both—by granting him the pleasure of fathering her children. Soon their marriage becomes stabilized and all is bliss for the Le Barroys. And Madame has a baby!

NOTES: In the mid-20's Fox Film Corporation set up a European branch, known as Fox Europa, under the guidance of Julius Aussenberg. Korda made *Madame* under this banner and employed Dietrich and young Britisher John Loder as *Edel-comparses* ("dress-extras") for the party scenes. It was filmed in two weeks' time, for the Kordas were Hollywood-bound! Fox released an English-titled version in the United States in 1927. This "modern marriage" tale was given deft direction and was full of Korda's touches and production gloss! The acting as well as the sets and photography were well regarded at the time. The script, based on a young Belgian writer's popular novel, was later turned into a hit play on the French stage (1927) by Paul Veber.

In the early 1930's, *Madame Wünscht Keine Kinder* was re-made as a "talkie," with slight modifications. It was produced by Lothar Stark and directed by Hans Steinhoff and opened in New York's Tobis Theatre (a German-language house) on June 1, 1933. The cast included Liane Haid, Georg Alexander, Lucie Mannheim, Otto Wallburg, Erika Glässner, Willi Stettner and Hans Moser.

Not only did Maria Corda, Marlene Dietrich, and John Loder later invade American films, but so did young Camilla von Hollay, who played Maria Paudler's maid. Soon after this Korda production, Camilla won a juicy part in Emil Jannings' celebrated *Faust*, which soon brought her an American offer—to co-star with John Barrymore in *Eternal Love*, using the name Camilla Horn!

In 1928, Alexander Korda directed his wife Maria Corda in *The Private Life of Helen of Troy* for First National. After a few more years in America, Korda crossed the Atlantic to set the British film industry on its feet and win international recognition.

The reason Dietrich accepted a "dress-extra" part was probably that her husband was engaged by Korda as a production assistant and, it must also be remembered, Dietrich had just completed *Eine Du Barry von heute* for Korda.

Madame was submitted to the censor on December 9, 1926, and was released two weeks later.

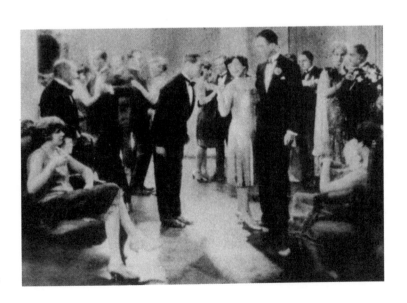

With Harry Liedtke and Maria Paudler

Kopf Hoch, Charly!

(Heads Up, Charly!)

An Ellen Richter-Film Production—1926

CAST: ANTON POINTNER (*Frank Ditmar*); ELLEN RICHTER (*Charlotte "Charly" Ditmar*); MICHAEL BOHNEN (*John Jacob Bunjes*); MAX GULSDORFF (*Harry Moshenheim*); MARGERIE QUIMBY (*Margie Quinn*); GEORGE DE CARLTON (*Rufus Quinn*); ANGELO FERRARI (*Marquis d'Ormesson*); ROBERT SCHOLZ (*Duke of Sanzedilla*); NIKOLAI MALIKOFF (*Prince Platonoff*); TONI TETZLAFF (*Frau Zangenberg*); MARLENE DIETRICH (*Edmée Marchand*); BLANDINE EBINGER (*the seamstress*); and Albert Paulig.

CREDITS: DR. WILLI WOLFF (*Director*); ROBERT LIEBMANN, DR. WILLI WOLFF (*Scenarists*); AXEL GRAATKJAR (*Photographer*) ERNST STERN (*Decors*); Based on a novel by LUDWIG WOLFF; Released by UFA-FILM, A. G.; LENGTH, 2512 meters.

SYNOPSIS: Frank Ditmar (Anton Pointner) leaves his wife Charlotte (Ellen Richter) to begin a new life in America. In her depression, Charlotte falls for the first man who comes along, ship-owner John Jacob Bunjes (Michael Bohnen). At first, Bunjes thinks Charlotte is an adventuress, but discovers his mistake too late. Charlotte, meanwhile, has found out that she too has made a mistake and leaves Bunjes. She writes her husband in America about her infidelity and tells him that she can never again be his wife.

Ditmar does not understand the letter he receives (because he doesn't know his wife has been seeing Bunjes—a fact she neglected to mention!). Life in America has not turned out as Frank had hoped and he is depressed until he meets an attractive American girl named Margie Quinn (Margerie Quimby). Charlotte somehow learns of this "affair" and realizes that all hopes are lost for her and her husband ever to get back together again.

Now Charlotte moves about with different men quite openly. The old fear of being disloyal to her husband has left her. Soon she becomes involved with a gigolo, the Marquis d'Ormesson (Angelo Ferrari), who has an eye on her money, but she is saved in the nick of time by Bunjes, who has been following her.

With Bunjes, Charlotte decides upon a new life and a new name, Charly—casting everything old aside. She and the handsome ship-owner go together.

NOTES: This was Dietrich's first film for the Ellen Richter-Film Company, which released its films through Ufa. Dr. Willi Wolff, Miss Richter's husband, devoted most of his time directing his wife or making films for her company. Filming began on *Kopf Hoch, Charly!* in the fall of 1926 and on November 10 it was submitted to the censor. It was released in December of that year.

The film was distinguished by unusually beautiful photography of the countryside. The handling of the melodramatic plot was well done, with its moods shifting from sadness to bright comic moments with equal ease. Dietrich played a French charmer named Edmée Marchand.

"Charly" of the title has also been spelled "Charlie" and "Charley."

With Reinhold Schünzel

Der Juxbaron

(The Imaginary Baron)

An Ellen Richter-Film Production—1927

CAST: REINHOLD SCHUNZEL (*The "Imaginary Baron"*); HENRY BENDER (*Hugo Windisch*); JULIA SERDA (*Zerline Windisch*); MARLENE DIETRICH (*Sophie, her daughter*); TEDDY BILL (*Hans von Grabow*); COLETTE BRETTL (*Hilda von Grabow*); ALBERT PAULIG (*Baron von Kimmel*); TRUDE HESTERBERG (*Fränze*); KARL

With Trude Hesterberg, Henry Bender, Reinhold Schünzel, Teddy Bill, Colette Brettle, and Julia Serda

With Reinhold Schünzel

HARBACHER (*Stotterwilhelm*); HERMANN PICHA (*a tramp*); FRITZ KAMPERS (*a policeman*); KARL BECKMANN (*the landlord*).

CREDITS: DR. WILLI WOLFF (*Director*); ROBERT LIEBMANN, DR. WILLI WOLFF (*Scenarists*); AXEL GRAATKJAR (*Photographer*); ERNST STERN (*Decors*); Based on the operetta by PORDES-MILO, HERMANN HALLER (*Book*) and WALTER KOLLO (*Music*); Released by UFA-FILM, A. G.; LENGTH, 2179 meters.

SYNOPSIS: A young couple, Hans von Grabow (Teddy Bill) and his wife Hilda (Colette Brettl), having just returned from their honeymoon, are presently entertaining, for a day or two, a childhood friend of Hans, the very rich Baron von Kimmel (Albert Paulig), who is known not only for his millions but for his bad manners.

When writing to his mother-in-law, Zerline Windisch (Julia Serda), Hans boasts of his house guest to the point that he and his wife receive a telegram stating that soon the whole family will descend upon them. And, the telegram further demands, keep the rich Baron there, for Zerline is thinking of her still-unmarried second daughter Sophie (Marlene Dietrich).

To ward off this "attack" from his in-laws, Hans writes them that the Baron, although very rich, has spent years in the tropics, where he reverted to primitivism, and he is now like a wild man.

Mama, despite all this, wants to get Sophie a husband, and soon the two ladies, accompanied by Hugo Windisch (Henry Bender), the easy-going father, prepare for the journey to the eldest daughter's estate.

Unfortunately, Baron von Kimmel had prior commitments and has left. Now the von Grabows are without a "baron." But, at this moment, a pair of vagabonds appear at the estate: a likeable itinerant tramp-musician (Reinhold Schünzel) and his girl friend Fränze (Trude Hesterberg). After chatting with this couple, Hans von Grabow is convinced that this otherwise intelligent and suave tramp-musician could be passed off as a baron.

Thus, this "imaginary baron" saves the day! He is cleaned up and dressed in new clothes and is presented as an elegant gentleman to the Windischs upon their arrival.

Actually this "baron" was hired only for one night, but Zerline and Sophie intercede and beg him to remain as a guest. It seems that the tramp-musician

With Reinhold Schünzel

was once an elegant gentleman, but his wanderlust drove him to a life without cares.

In record time the "baron" has proposed to Sophie and he invites all the guests of the von Grabows to the annual Tramp Ball for an unusually "wild" time! Everyone is game, and fun is had by one and all until the affair is raided by the police. All are arrested except the "baron," who is allowed to go free since he is a baron.

Soon Sophie discovers the "baron's" true identity and turns away from him with disgust. He returns to the willing arms of Fränze, and off the pair go, entertaining with dances, songs, and sketches, with the tramp-musician having a merry time beating a drum (strapped on his back), playing an accordion strapped on in front, a lyre attached to his hat, and bells jingling from his pants' legs.

NOTES: Dietrich's second film for Dr. Willi Wolff gave her a fine opportunity at playing farce. It was an important leading role indeed. *Der Juxbaron* had fine production values and was popular in Europe.

The star, Reinhold Schünzel, was a noted actor and director in the German cinema until he fled Nazism in the mid-1930's. In Hollywood he became known as a fine character actor in such productions as *New Wine* and *Notorious*. In 1946 he appeared in Dietrich's *Golden Earrings*—nineteen years after she had "co-starred" with him in *Der Juxbaron*.

Der Juxbaron was first submitted to the Censor on December 20, 1926, and released to the public in March of 1927.

With Reinhold Schünzel

With Colette Brettl, Julia Serda, Henry Bender, Teddy Bill, and Reinhold Schünzel

Sein Grösster Bluff

(His Greatest Bluff)

A Nero-Film Production—1927

CAST: HARRY PIEL (*Henry Devall, Harry Devall*); TONY TETZLAFF (*Madame Andersson*); LOTTE LORRING (*Tilly, her daughter*); ALBERT PAULING (*Mimikry*); FRITZ GREINER (*Hennessy*); CHARLY BERGER (*"Count" Koks*); BORIS MICHAILOW (*Sherry*); MARLENE DIETRICH (*Yvette*); PAUL WALKER (*"Goliath," a dwarf*); KURT GERRON (*the Rajah of Johore*); EUGEN BURG (*Police Superintendent*); OSSIP DARMATOW (*"Count" Apollinaris*); VICKY WERCKMEISTER (*Suzanne*); PAUL MOLESKA, OSWALD SCHEFFEL, CURT BULLERJAHN, CHARLES FRANCOIS, WOLFGANG VON SCHWINDT (*gangsters*); with Hans Breitensträter.

CREDITS: HARRY PIEL (*Director*); HENRIK GALEEN (*Scenarist*); GEORG MUSCHNER, GOTTHARDT WOLF (*Photographers*); ZEISKE-LEONARD (*Assistant Photographer*); W. A. HERRMANN (*Decors*); EDMUND HEUBERGER (*Assistant Director*); DR. HERBERT NOSSEN (*Titles*); Released by SUDFILM, A. G. (EMELKA); LENGTH, 2984 meters.

SYNOPSIS: Henry Devall (Harry Piel) and his twin

With Harry Piel

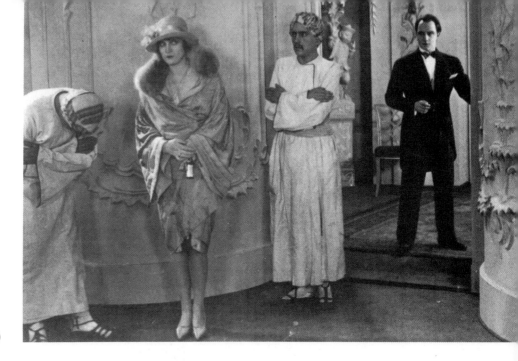

With Harry Piel (in doorway)

brother Harry (Harry Piel) look so much alike that Harry leaves for America while Henry becomes employed at Madame Andersson's jewelry shop in Paris. Henry proves himself quickly and soon holds a highly trusted position.

One day the Andersson firm gets an order from the Rajah of Johore (Kurt Gerron) for a spectacular piece of jewelry. Soon the word is all over Paris, and the shop is filled with ladies and gentlemen (crooks in disguise) to see the fabulous creation.

At the same time, Harry returns to Paris from America and goes into a guest house near the railway station to look up his brother's address. Mim-

ikry (Albert Paulig), head of one of the gangs, spots him and thinking he's Henry, tries to interest him in a "deal." Harry realizes the mistaken identity and refuses Mimikry's proposition.

Yvette (Marlene Dietrich), a call girl, also has an interest in the jewelry and together with Goliath (Paul Walker), a dwarf dressed as a child, they enter the store. The dwarf overhears a conversation between Madame Andersson (Tony Tetzlaff) and Henry and sees Henry put the gems into his pocket. When walking out, the dwarf lifts the piece out of his pocket.

At home, Henry prepares for the trip to Nice to

With Harry Piel

65

deliver the jewel to the Rajah, but he discovers it has been stolen. He immediately considers suicide, but at that moment Harry arrives. Before long, Madame Andersson and her daughter Tilly (Lotte Lorring) arrive to take Henry to the station. Henry and Harry decide to switch places, and Henry gets into a large trunk and Harry becomes Henry. The ladies, of course, are not aware that the jewelled piece has been stolen.

Another gang follows them to the station, where they grab Harry's briefcase. Now Madame Andersson *knows* the piece has been stolen. Harry decides to leave for Nice anyway, tricks all the crooks at the station into a deserted car, and departs with his trunk and the Anderssons.

Meanwhile, Mimikry calls "Count" Apollinaris (Ossip Darmatow), his accomplice, to set a trap for Henry when he arrives in Nice. At the hotel, Harry checks a bag in the hotel safe, then goes to his room and lets Henry out of the trunk. Just then Tilly comes in and the brothers have a little fun with her. First one comes in from the bedroom and then he leaves and the other comes in—she doesn't know whom she's talking to. Tilly finally kisses Harry, thinking it's Henry.

Now Yvette arrives in Nice, hoping to sell the piece of jewelry to the Rajah, but through some sensational tricks Count Apollinaris gets it away from her. And the Rajah, a crook too, goes to the hotel and flees with the empty bag that Harry had placed

With Harry Piel

in the safe. Now crooks are everywhere, and Madame Andersson discovers that her personal jewelry is missing. The Rajah realizes that he's got the wrong bag, but at least his expenses will be paid.

Henry and Harry now devise a plan to catch all of the crooks and recover the missing jewelry. Henry calls the police to a deserted farm house and explains the whole thing, and soon Harry, being chased by the crooks, arrives. They are all being arrested when the Rajah drives by and is greeted by the police. He is being told about the crooks when Harry recognizes him and has *him* arrested. Soon all is solved, and Harry and Tilly fall in love.

NOTES: This film, also known as *Der Grosse Bluff* (The Great Bluff), starred the popular Harry Piel in a dual role. He also directed. His forte was adventure yarns displaying dare-devil exploits, making him extremely popular with men and women alike. Piel looked at length for a suitable partner to play one of the twin brothers in the film but could find no one. Finally he decided to essay both roles besides his directorial chores—a challenge he met with verve!

Dietrich again played farce well and looked quite lovely in the gowns and hats of the period. The production was slick, and action never flagged.

Sein Grösster Bluff was submitted to the Censor on May 5, 1927, and released shortly thereafter.

With Harry Piel

Cafe Electric

Released in Germany in 1928 as *Wenn ein Weib den Weg Verliert.*
(When a Woman Loses Her Way)

A Sascha-Film Production (Austrian—1927)

CAST: FRITZ ALBERTI (*Göttlinger*); MARLENE DIET-RICH (*Erni, his daughter*); ANNY COTY (*one of her friends*); WILLI FORST (*Ferdl*); NINA VANNA (*Hansi*); IGO SYM (*Max Stöger, an architect*); FELIX FISCHER (*the editor*); VERA SALVOTTI (*Paula*); WILHELM VÖLKER (*Dr. Lehner*); ALBERT E. KERSTEN (*Mr. Zerner*); with Dolly Davis.

CREDITS: GUSTAV UCICKY (*Director*); JACQUES BACHRACH (*Scenarist*); HANS ANDROSCHIN (*Photographer*); ARTUR BERGER (*Decors*); KARL HARTL (*Executive Producer*); Based on the play, *Die Liebesbörse*, by FELIX FISCHER; Released by SASCHA FILMINDUSTRIE, A. G.; German release by SUDFILM, A. G.; LENGTH, 2400 meters.

SYNOPSIS: Erni (Marlene Dietrich), a flighty young woman, the daughter of a building contractor, Göttlinger (Fritz Alberti), has met and been seduced by a young gigolo named Ferdl (Willi Forst), habitué of the notorious Café Electric, where only prostitutes and pimps gather.

Also to be found there is Hansi (Nina Vanna), whom a cruel twist of fate has forced into that "profession."

Max Stöger (Igo Sym) is an architect working for Göttlinger—a busy young man with his own problems, who cannot be concerned with worrying about the boss's daughter. One day in the contractor's

With Willi Forst

office, the architect surprises Erni as she is stealing—for Ferdl—a ring belonging to her father. Ferdl gives the ring to Hansi, who starts wearing it constantly. She has, meanwhile, gotten to know the architect, who is charmed by her. He visits her at the Café Electric, where he also runs into his boss, Göttlinger, making love to her. When he sees the ring on Hansi, Göttlinger accuses Max of being the thief.

During this interlude, Ferdl is arrested, after a jilted former mistress, who is jealous of Erni, informs on him. He believes, however, that he has been betrayed by Hansi and swears vengeance. Max and

With Willi Forst

Hansi live together, but as he is now unemployed and cannot find a job, they are soon reduced to poverty. An unfortunate coincidence causes Max to believe that Hansi has returned to her old way of life, and he rejects her.

Hansi goes back to the Café Electric and is stabbed by Ferdl, who has just been released from prison. Max, now a reporter, learns the truth and decides to begin a new life together with Hansi.

NOTES: *Cafe Electric* was filmed entirely in Vienna while Dietrich and Willi Forst were appearing in the popular stage hit *Broadway*. The famous Dietrich legs were given their due here, and her carefree attitude and classy clothes added the proper accent. The Sascha-Film Production was released on November 25, 1927, in Vienna and in Germany as *Wenn ein Weib den Weg Verliert*, in 1928!

The strong script was tastefully and effectively handled; Igo Sym was excellent, according to the critics, as was Nina Vanna. Dietrich was thought "quite gifted" and "most provocative." Willi Forst likewise turned in a fine job, "vital and full of life."

With Willi Forst

With Carmen Boni

Prinzessin Olala

(Princess Olala)

Released in England in 1929 as Art of Love.

A Super-Film Production—1928

CAST: HERMANN BÖTTCHER (*the Prince*); WALTER RILLA (*Prince Boris, his son*); GEORG ALEXANDER (*the Chamberlain*); CARMEN BONI (*Princess Xenia*); ILA MEERY (*Hedy, her friend*); MARLENE DIETRICH (*Chichotte de Gastoné*); HANS ALBERS (*René, Chichotte's friend*); KARL GÖTZ (*an old cavalier*); JULIUS VON SZÖREGHY (*a strong man*); LYA CHRISTY (*Lady Jackson*); ARIBERT WASCHER (*police superintendent*); and ALFRED ABEL.

CREDITS: ROBERT LAND (*Director*); FRANZ SCHULZ, ROBERT LAND (*Scenarists*); WILLI GOLDBERGER (*Photographer*); FRITZ BRUNN (*Assistant Photographer*);

With Hans Albers

With Hans Albers

ROBERT NEPPACH (*Decors*); Based on the operetta by JEAN GILBERT (*Music*); RUDOLF BERNAUER, RUDOLF SCHANZER (*Libretto*); Released by DEUTSCHES LICHT-SPIEL-SYNDIKAT, A. G.; LENGTH, 2122 meters.

SYNOPSIS: Prince Boris (Walter Rilla) has had a perfect upbringing, and at the age of 25 he knows just about everything—except love! His father (Hermann Böttcher) has chosen the beautiful Princess Xenia (Carmen Boni) for him to marry. However, the Prince feels that his son should first learn about the "art of love" and therefore sends him to Paris, where he will take *love lessons* from the infamous Chichotte de Gastoné (Marlene Dietrich). Chichotte's fame is known throughout the country, where she enjoys a reputation for showing many European princes "how"—and is thus nicknamed Princess Olala!

Princess Xenia, who has never seen her husband-to-be (except in a photograph), also lives in Paris. By accident she learns the reason for Boris' journey

With Carmen Boni

With Hans Albers

to Paris. She cannot get used to the idea that he should be taught by Chichotte, so she contacts the woman and offers her a handsome sum of money to let her pose as Princess Olala. Chichotte gladly accepts the offer and leaves for Deauville with her lover, René (Hans Albers).

Boris arrives at Olala's apartment and faces his wife-to-be, thinking she is Chichotte de Gastoné. However, the Princess Xenia is as inexperienced in the "art of love" as Boris, and their first "lesson" merely produces a kiss! At that very moment three of Olala's jealous lovers knock on the door. Afraid that the wicked plot will be uncovered, Xenia leads Boris out by a back exit, and they head for Deauville. They stay at a cheaper hotel than Olala and René—and their lessons never seem to get anywhere. Boris finally claims that she is making a fool of him. He feels that she has been cold during their relationship, while with other men she has apparently been quite the opposite. (He is thinking of the three lovers left banging on her door!)

Meanwhile, René (not only Chichotte's lover but a thief as well) has stolen a valuable piece of jewelry from a rich Englishwoman, Lady Jackson (Lya Christy), whom he has met under the assumed name of "Prince Boris." Therefore the police are now hunting the Prince, while Olala and René return to Paris.

The real Boris is found and arrested, and it takes three days for this misunderstanding to be cleared up. When he is released, he calls Chichotte, but gets the real one on the phone. When he mentions his name, she, thinking that it's René, hangs up. Quite upset, Prince Boris leaves for home. Trying to push bad memories of his French trip out of his mind, he wants to get married as soon as possible.

Everything is arranged, and at the wedding ceremony, as the bride appears, her face veiled, Boris begins to think of his Princess Olala. He almost walks out, until Princess Xenia raises the veil. The Prince is overjoyed, the wedding takes place, and happiness is theirs!

NOTES: This delightful romantic comedy enjoyed a successful run in the German-speaking countries and the following year went abroad (to England) where it played as *Art of Love*. Robert Land's direction provided Dietrich with a self-assurance she had hitherto lacked. Not only was she glamorous, but she looked most attractive in a short hair style. Again much attention was paid to those famous legs. She had definitely reached the "featured-billing" plateau!

Prinzessin Olala was submitted to the Censor on July 13, 1928, and first viewed by the public approximately two weeks later.

Ich Küsse Ihre Hand, Madame

(I Kiss Your Hand, Madame)

Released in the U.S. in 1932 as I Kiss Your Hand, Madame

With Harry Liedtke

A Super-Film Production—1929

CAST: HARRY LIEDTKE (*Jacques*); MARLENE DIETRICH (*Laurence Gerard*); PIERRE DE GUINGAND (*Adolf Gerard, her ex-husband*); KARL HUSZAR-PUFFY (*Tallandier, her lawyer*).

CREDITS: ROBERT LAND (*Director*); FRIEDEL BUCKOW (*Assistant Director*); ROBERT LAND (*Scenarist*); KARL DREWS, GOTTHARDT WOLF (*Photographers*); FRITZ BRUNN, FRED ZINNEMANN (*Assistant Photographers*); ROBERT NEPPACH (*Decors*); From an original story by ROLF E. VANLOO, ROBERT LAND; Title Song by RALPH ERWIN (*Music*); FRITZ ROTTER (*Lyrics*); English titles, HELENE TURNER; U. S. Release by STANLEY DISTRIBUTING CO.; German Release by DEUTSCHES LICHTSPIEL-SYNDIKAT, A. G.; LENGTH, 2020 meters.

SYNOPSIS: Laurence Gerard (Marlene Dietrich), a handsome young Parisian divorcée, having just been given her final decree by her lawyer Tallandier (Karl Huszar-Puffy), stops her car in a darkened street thinking that the man she sees there is her current lover. Asking him to get in the car, Laurence at once realizes her mistake, but is drawn to the handsome man nevertheless. She lets him out at the

*With Karl Huszar-Puffy
and Harry Liedtke*

corner, and he mistakenly picks up her divorce papers and takes them with him.

A few nights later Laurence has prepared an elaborate dinner for her lover, but he calls to say he cannot come. Laurence is convinced he's two-timing her and, in a rage, decides to go out on the town. This thought is interrupted by the door bell. Her maid lets a man in and asks him to wait in the living room. He notices the splendidly set table as Laurence appears. He introduces himself as Count Leisky, formerly of the Russian Imperial Guard, and hands the divorce papers back to her. Soon the couple are in close harmony.

At this moment Tallandier drops in. He was hoping that her current lover hadn't appeared so he might take Laurence out. He is introduced to the Count, but recognizes him to be Jacques, the headwaiter at the Café Grillon, but does not let on. Laurence, now with two men on her hands, sends Tallandier out to walk her dogs.

She then suggests to the Count that they dine out, but he insists on serving the already-prepared meal to her, which she thinks is charming. After they eat, the Count takes Laurence to the Café Grillon for an after-dinner drink. His colleagues realize that the young woman doesn't know he is the headwaiter, and give him supreme service. Meanwhile, Tallandier picks up Laurence's ex-husband, Adolf (Pierre de Guingand), and they take a table near the couple at the café.

*With Harry Liedtke and Karl
Huszar-Puffy*

With Harry Liedtke

After Laurence and Jacques dance, they leave the café, closely followed by Tallandier and Adolf. The latter are delighted when Laurence says good night to Jacques on the street and doesn't ask him in.

Laurence is eventually told that Jacques is a bogus count. That evening she dines at the Café Grillon with Tallandier and she accomplishes the feat of getting Jacques fired, saying that he has insulted her.

Tallandier, now distressed by the happenings, offers money to the manager of the café to give to

With Harry Liedtke

Jacques, but is informed that the headwaiter is *actually* Count Leisky and would be insulted by such an act.

Jacques finally becomes employed as a service man on the third floor of a first-class hotel and becomes immensely popular with the ladies. Laurence, now aware that he *is* a count and sorry for getting him fired, takes a room on his floor and rings for his services. Discovering that Laurence has placed the call, Jacques gets himself transferred to another floor. Again she pursues him! Finally convinced of her love, Jacques and Laurence discover each other anew in the hotel's elevator, riding it up and down.

NOTES: This was a popular comedy when initially released, due mainly to Liedtke's fans. When it arrived in the United States in 1932, however, to capitalize on Dietrich's new image, critics and public alike turned thumbs down. Obviously, everyone was spoiled by the von Sternberg-ized Dietrich! One critic noted that "Marlene is too firmly established to be affected by her early errors."

Ich Küsse Ihre Hand, Madame isn't that bad, and Dietrich performed with a freshness and vitality then lacking in her Paramount releases.

The English titles for the United States version (a copy of which is in the collection of the George Eastman House) changed Dietrich's name to "Lucille" and Liedtke's to "Pierre." In the synchronized sound print, Richard Tauber dubbed the singing of the title song for Liedtke.

The assistant photographer, Fred Zinnemann, is now one of the finest directors in films, with notable achievements like *High Noon, From Here to Eternity, The Nun's Story,* and *A Man for All Seasons* to his credit.

This film was submitted to the Berlin Censor on January 14, 1929, and released soon after.

With Fritz Kortner

Die Frau, Nach der Man Sich Sehnt

(The Woman One Longs For)

Released in the U.S. as Three Loves (silent) by Moviegraphs, Inc. in 1929 and with a synchronized score by Associated Cinemas in 1931.

A Terra-Film Production—1929

CAST: MARLENE DIETRICH (*Stascha*); FRITZ KORTNER (*Dr. Karoff*); FRIDA RICHARD (*Mrs. Leblanc*); Her sons, OSKAR SIMA (*Charles Leblanc*) and UNO HENNING (*Henry Leblanc*); BRUNO ZIENER (*Philipp, the Leblanc's valet*); KARL ETTLINGER (*the old Poitrier*); EDITH EDWARDS (*Angela Poitrier,* his daughter).

CREDITS: KURT BERNHARDT (*Director*); LADISLAS VAJDA (*Scenarist*); KURT COURANT (*Photographer*); ROBERT NEPPACH (*Decors*); Based on the novel by MAX BROD; Synchronized Score by EDWARD KILENYI, WALTHER BRANSEN; LENGTH, 2360 meters.

SYNOPSIS: The young Leblanc brothers, Henry (Uno Henning) and Charles (Oskar Sima), are in charge of a large smelting company. Henry is the managing engineer, working between the running wheels and hissing valves, while Charles handles the business end. The company, however, needs finan-

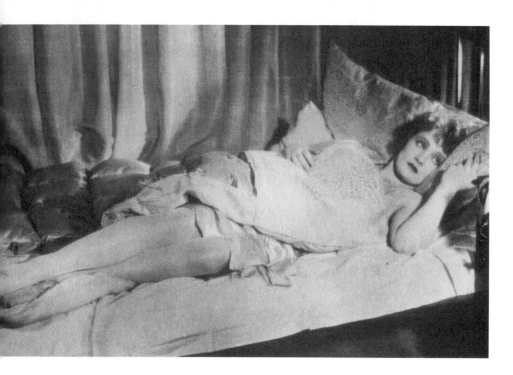

cial assistance, or else its giant works will be forced to shut down.

Fortunately, Henry is loved by Angela (Edith Edwards), the daughter of rich industrialist Poitrier (Karl Ettlinger), who loves his daughter immensely and would do anything for her. Henry *likes* Angela, but doesn't love this homespun type of girl. But he gives in and marries Angela, while old Poitrier helps the Leblancs financially.

Henry and Angela take a wedding trip to the Riviera by train. When the couple retire to their sleeping compartment, Angela (being alone with her beloved for the first time) gives into the happiness of the situation and lets Henry make love. As he begins to help her undress, Angela gets frightened and opens the compartment door and pushes him out into the passageway. Inside, she prepares herself for the night without interference. This was a fateful gesture, since it is here that Henry meets the woman Fate has placed there for him to meet!

In the moment he is waiting for Angela to get undressed, the door of another compartment opens and Stasha (Marlene Dietrich) appears! She is a woman of glorious beauty and sophistication. Stasha

With Uno Henning

is travelling with Dr. Karoff (Fritz Kortner), who is completely captivated by her charms, but she has fled Karoff's revolting love-making. Although Karoff loves her totally, she has tired of him. Karoff leaves to tend the luggage, since he and Stasha are getting off at the next stop. Stasha lures Henry by feigning a fainting spell, and Henry quickly takes her into his arms and pulls her into her compartment. Angela, now ready to receive her husband, opens her door just in time to see him disappear into the next compartment.

In her compartment, Stasha begs Henry not to leave her and to protect her from Karoff. Fascinated by the beauty of this woman, Henry has become completely her slave, and promises anything. Dr. Karoff, returning to the compartment, sees Stasha holding Henry's hand. She quickly introduces Henry as her cousin whom she has just met by accident. The train stops. Before leaving, Stasha implores Henry to follow her and protect her from Karoff. Henry, now in a condition bordering on insanity, rushes back to his compartment and finds his wife crying bitterly. Completely beside himself, Henry escapes to the compartment of his old valet, Philipp (Bruno Ziener), who has accompanied the young couple. He tells him of his decision to leave the train at the next stop and return to Cannes and orders him to calm his wife down by telling her some story. The old valet cannot dissuade Henry from executing this insane plan. Because of the violent discussion between Henry and Philipp, the other passenger sharing the valet's compartment wakes up from a deep sleep and in his fright pulls the emergency cord. During the confusion that ensues, Henry jumps off the train!

Soon Henry arrives at the elegant hotel where Stasha and Karoff are staying. She is happy to see her "cousin," of whom Dr. Karoff is most suspicious! In a villa on the Riviera, meanwhile, Angela is alone on her wedding night. Philipp cannot rouse her from her lethargy. Angela, however, makes a heroic decision and writes a telegram to send to Henry's mother: "Arrived two days ago, weather is beautiful. We are very happy. Angela & Henry." But the valet does not send this telegram, and instead wires: "Am very unhappy, come immediately. Angela."

In the meantime, Stasha, Karoff, and Henry enjoy the New Year's celebration in the hotel. Stasha and

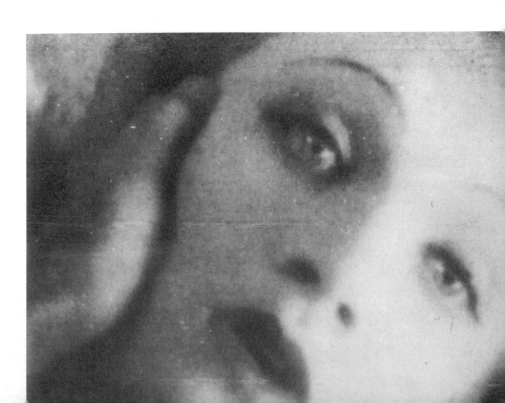

A frame from Dietrich's first death scene

With Uno Henning

Henry intend to escape at midnight, Karoff sees through this plan and threatens Stasha—he'll inform the police if she ever tries to sever their relationship. It seems that Karoff killed Stasha's husband with her knowledge. Henry, weary of waiting for Stasha to appear, returns to the hotel to find Stasha and Karoff dancing together.

In the morning, in Stasha's suite, Henry attacks Karoff, who fights back and knocks him out. A waiter and Stasha revive Henry.

Soon two policemen arrive at the hotel in order to take the murderer and his accomplice into custody. Stasha has informed Henry about their dastardly deed while Karoff prepares to flee. The police appear and take him into custody. They ask for Stasha. Karoff shows them the door behind which she is hiding. When the police enter the room, Karoff follows and shoots her. As she dies in Henry's arms, he feels that he is just awakening from a terrible dream. He returns later to Angela and begs forgiveness.

NOTES: Interesting direction and a taut script pro-vided an above-average melodrama. Dietrich in her first *femme fatale* part was not totally convincing but looked sinister enough throughout. Uno Henning and Fritz Kortner gave good support. The sets and photography were quite effective. It was submitted to the Berlin Censor on April 26, 1929.

The English-language title, *Three Loves*, derives from one of the frame titles which explains that Stasha has had *three loves* (her husband, her husband's killer, and the young Frenchman Leblanc), and as she dies, she says that she's lost them all.

This was the first time Dietrich was shot on the screen but certainly not the last! She was later executed in *Dishonored*, shot by Brian Donlevy in *Destry Rides Again*, murdered by Gabin in *Martin Roumagnac*, and again shot while protecting her man in *Rancho Notorious*.

Kurt Bernhardt, the director, later became Curtis Bernhardt at Warner Bros., directing Humphrey Bogart (*Conflict*), Barbara Stanwyck (*My Reputation*), and Bette Davis (*A Stolen Life*), among others.

With Robin Irvine

Das Schiff der Verlorenen Menschen

(The Ship of Lost Souls)

A German-French Co-Production. French Title: Le Navire des Hommes Perdus.
Released in England in 1930 as The Ship of Lost Men.

A Max Glass-Wengeroff-Film Production—1929

CAST: FRITZ KORTNER (*Captain Fernando Vela*); MARLENE DIETRICH (*Miss Ethel, an aviatrix*); GASTON MODOT (*Morian, the escaped convict*); ROBIN IRVINE (*T. W. Cheyne, a young American doctor*); BORIS DE FAST (*sailor*); VLADIMIR SOKOLOFF (*Grischa, the cook*); ROBERT GARRISON, ALFRED LORETTO, FEDOR CHALIAPIN, JR. and HARRY GRUNWALD (*the crew*); MAX MAXIMILIAN (*the second mate*).

CREDITS: MAURICE TOURNEUR (*Director* and *Scenarist*); MAX GLASS (*Producer*); NIKOLAUS (NICK) FARKAS (*Photographer*); FRANZ SCHROEDTER (*Decors*); JACQUES TOURNEUR (*Assistant Director*); Based on the novel by FRENZOS KERZEMEN; Released by ORPLID-METRO, A. G.; LENGTH, 2638 meters.

SYNOPSIS: Miss Ethel (Marlene Dietrich), a young American millionairess, is attending a swank party when she is called to the phone. She is told that her airplane is ready for her trans-ocean flight. Miss Ethel hopes to break the European record across the Atlantic Ocean.

After leaving the party, Miss Ethel arrives at the airfield in true aviatrix garb: leather flight suit,

goggles, and gloves! Soon she is flying out over the ocean, and it looks as though she might just break the previous record set—until the plane develops engine problems.

Far below in the murky sea is the *Galathée,* a mystery ship carrying as its crew quite a group of "lost souls"—smugglers, pirates, escaped prisoners, and criminals of all types on the run! Among this strange group is T. W. Cheyne (Robin Irvine), a young American doctor who was forced to make the journey with them. Apart from Cheyne, only Grischa, the cook (Vladimir Sokoloff), is a decent human being.

On this particular night Cheyne and Grischa see a plane crash and secretly haul the half-dead pilot aboard. When they remove her cap, they realize it is a woman, and a woman aboard this ship could only spell disaster! So they take Miss Ethel down to a room near the galley.

Soon the big secret is out that a woman is aboard! The severe Captain Fernando Vela (Fritz Kortner) has his hands full with a woman-hungry crew getting out of hand. Morian (Gaston Modot), an escaped convict, is the one who discovered Miss Ethel and the one who causes the other men to panic. With the crew set off like a pack of animals, it's difficult indeed for Cheyne and Grischa to protect her, but they do the best they can. As the situation gets most critical (the crew have begun to close in on Miss Ethel on deck), bright searchlights pierce through the dense fog to reveal a giant ocean liner alongside them.

With Robin Irvine (left)

It's not there by accident, we soon find out, but because Grischa had sent S.O.S.'s via Morse code and light signals. The motley crew is taken prisoner, and the young couple and Grischa are joyfully welcomed aboard the ocean liner.

NOTES: This German-French production was directed by the great director Maurice Tourneur (with his son Jacques assisting him on direction and editing), but the film did poorly outside of Europe. It was released in England in 1930, but never made it to the United States.

Tourneur's characters were well conceived and the storyline was skillfully developed. His use of photography and lighting—the dismal ship, the water spraying the deck, the light and dark shadows of the cabins, the dramatic sea—all added atmospheric effects to his general conception. Although much of the plot seemed contrived at times. Dietrich's sequences were quite exciting. In male attire most of the time (except for the early party sequence), Dietrich generated great feminine charm.

The interiors were shot in Berlin and the exteriors at Hamburg and Travemunde in 1929. It was her last silent film, although *Gefahren der Brautzeit* would be released later. It was submitted to the Berlin Censor on August 26, September 2, and again on September 5, 1929 and was premiered on September 16, 1929, in Berlin.

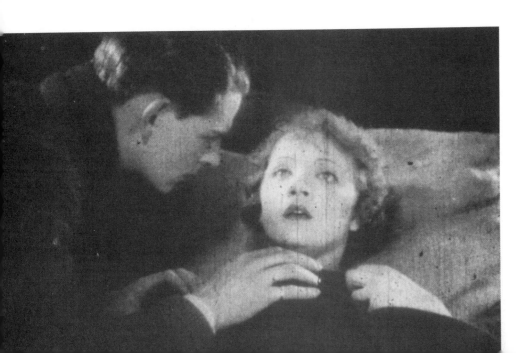

With Robin Irvine

Gefahren der Brautzeit

(Dangers of the Engagement Period)

A Strauss-Film Production—1929

Also known as:

> Aus dem Tagebuch eines Verführers (From the Diary of a Seducer)
> Eine Nacht der Liebe (One Night of Love)
> Liebesnächte (Nights of Love)
> Liebesbriefe (Love Letters)

CAST: WILLI FORST (*Baron van Geldern*); MARLENE DIETRICH (*Evelyne*); LOTTE LORRING (*Yvette*); ELZA TEMARY (*Florence*); ERNST STAHL-NACHBAUR (*McClure*); BRUNO ZIENER (*Miller*); with Oskar Sima.

CREDITS: FRED SAUER (*Director*); WALTER WASSERMANN, WALTER SCHLEE (*Scenarists*); LASZLO SCHAFFER (*Photographer*); MAX HEILBRONNER (*Decors*); Released by HEGEWALD-FILM, A. G.; LENGTH, 2183 meters.

SYNOPSIS: Young Baron van Geldern (Willi Forst) is a Casanova. He has so many loves that he doesn't even remember their names. One day he notices the husband of one of his "loves" outside and pulls his maid into the bed as the husband bursts into the room, thinking he will find his wife in Geldern's arms. Angered, the husband vows vengeance, because he knows his wife and the Baron are having an affair. When the opportunity is ripe, the husband makes an attempt on Geldern's life, but the young Baron is saved by an American named McClure (Ernst Stahl-Nachbaur) and they become close friends.

But the pattern continues. Baron van Geldern meets Florence (Elza Temary), a dangerous gangster's moll, and again McClure saves the Baron's life when the gangster, Miller (Bruno Ziener), tries to shake him down.

One day the Baron gets a telegram from McClure inviting him to Scheveningen, which he gladly accepts. On the train the Baron meets, and immediately falls in love with, a sweet, lovely girl named Evelyne (Marlene Dietrich). She feels secure with

With Ernst Stahl-Nachbaur

Baron van Geldern and explains the sad circumstances which have brought her to this compartment, on this train. It seems that her father lost all his money and she is being forced into a marriage with a man she does not even know.

The train stops near a station and cannot proceed because of a landslide. The passengers must spend the night in a small Dutch town. That night Evelyne is seduced by Baron van Geldern. In the morning he finds just a note: "It's better this way."

Arriving several hours later at Scheveningen, the Baron tells McClure about the woman on the train, but McClure has a big surprise for his friend and scarcely listens. He is going to marry the daughter of a business partner. Suddenly Geldern sees Evelyne approaching and is about to tell McClure who she is, when the American jumps up and introduces her to the Baron as his future bride.

Realizing that he has "cheated" on his friend McClure, the Baron decides to leave. There is a

With Willi Forst

knock at his door and Evelyne enters. She insists that Geldern tell McClure of their mutual love, but he says he cannot. Suddenly there is another knock at the door and Evelyne hides.

McClure comes in, then notices the diamond brooch he had just given to Evelyne lying on the floor. He seizes the Baron's gun, which is lying atop the trunk, and fires. Evelyne runs into the room screaming! The Baron gives McClure his word that nothing has happened between them and says that he is not badly hurt. McClure and Evelyne leave.

The Baron then takes the gun, wipes it off, and holding it in his own hand, dies, thus making the incident look like suicide. Evelyne, meanwhile, has told McClure everything and the American gives in, but when they return to Baron van Geldern's room, they discover that they're too late!

NOTES: There has been much confusion about this film for a number of years. In all listings of Marlene Dietrich's films it manages to get listed twice—as a 1926 production, *Gefahren der Brautzeit,* and as a 1929 production, *Liebesnächte (Nights of Love).* Actually, as we shall see, this is *one* film with **not** two but five titles connected with it!

Gefahren der Brautzeit was *not* filmed in 1926 (then Dietrich would hardly have had a leading role, much less top billing) but was begun in late 1928 as *Eine Nacht der Liebe (One Night of Love).* During its filming the·title became *Aus dem Tagebuch Eines Verführers (From the Diary of a Seducer)* (a press release in early 1929 stated that the film was "a modern melodrama built on the Don Juan theme.") When it was completed, the title became *Liebesbriefe (Love Letters).* But by the time it was submitted to the Berlin Censor, in November 1929, the title was *Liebesnächte!* It was released later that month, finally, as *Gefahren Der Brautzeit* and was mildly successful. Soon though, it became known that Dietrich had won the coveted role of Lola-Lola in *Der Blaue Engel,* then filming, and business picked up!

She was beautifully photographed in this film and sported a smart wardrobe.

Der Blaue Engel

(The Blue Angel)

Released in the U.S. in 1931 as The Blue Angel

An Erich Pommer-Production
An Ufa-Sound-Film—1930

CAST: EMIL JANNINGS (*Professor Immanuel Rath*); MARLENE DIETRICH (*Lola-Lola, Fröhlich*); KURT GERRON (*Kiepert, a magician*); ROSA VALETTI (*Guste, his wife*); HANS ALBERS (*Mazeppa*); REINHOLD BERNT (*the clown*); EDUARD VON WINTERSTEIN (*director of the school*); HANS ROTH (*the beadle*); *Students:* ROLF MULLER (*Angst*), ROLANT VARNO (*Lohmann*), KARL BALHAUS (*Ertzum*) and ROBERT KLEIN-LORK (*Goldstaub*); KARL HUSZAR-PUFFY (*the publican*); WILHELM DIEGELMANN (*the captain*); GERHARD BIENERT (*the policeman*); ILSE FÜRSTENBERG (*Rath's housekeeper*).

CREDITS: JOSEF VON STERNBERG (*Director*); ERICH POMMER (*Producer*); ROBERT LIEBMANN (*Scenarist*); GUNTHER RITTAU, HANS SCHNEEBERGER (*Photographers*); OTTO HUNTE, EMIL HASLER (*Decors*); SAM WINSTON (*Editor*); FRIEDRICH HOLLANDER (*Musical Score*); FRITZ THIERY (*Sound*); WEINTRAUB'S SYNCOPATORS (*Orchestra*); Based on *Professor Unrath* by HEINRICH MANN; Adapted for the screen by CARL ZUCKMAYER and KARL VOLLMÖLLER; Released by UFA-FILM, A. G.; U. S. Release by PARAMOUNT PICTURES; LENGTH, 2965 meters.

SONGS: *By* FRIEDRICH HOLLANDER and ROBERT LIEBMANN; "Nimm Dich in Acht vor Blonden Frauen";

"Ich Bin Die Fesche Lola" ("I'm Naughty Little Lola"); "Kinder, Heut' Abend Such Ich Mir Was Aus"; "Ich Bin Von Kopf Bis Fuss Auf Liebe Eingestellt" ("Falling in Love Again"); English lyrics by SAM LERNER.

SYNOPSIS: Immanuel Rath (Emil Jannings), a respected middle-aged professor of English literature in a German boys' high school, one day finds his pupils passing around souvenir postcards of saucy Lola-Lola (Marlene Dietrich) of the Blue Angel cabaret. Suspecting that his young students are idling away their after-school hours in this forbidden den, he sets out to catch them there, reprimand them, and show them the right path.

At the Blue Angel the professor becomes confused by the general pandemonium and ends up,

With Emil Jannings

strangely enough, in Lola-Lola's dressing room. She is pretty and quite nonchalant and unlike any woman he has ever met. He soon finds himself fascinated by this provocative creature. Later in the cabaret she sings her songs to him as he drinks and drinks in the box seat, reserved for special guests. Next morning, the professor realizes he has spent the night in her bed.

Arriving at school late, he discovers that his students have misinterpreted his mission at the Blue Angel and have covered the blackboard with obscene caricatures to taunt him. When the director of the school (Eduard von Winterstein) hears the commotion and learns the circumstances, he has no alternative but to fire Professor Rath.

Rath goes to Lola-Lola for consolation. His predicament and his need for understanding bring them close together. But this little charmer is playing him for all she can get. Soon they are married. Unable to find work and not wanting to leave Lola-Lola, the professor is forced to sell pictures of his wife at various cabarets where the traveling troupe plays. Eventually he also becomes a member of the troupe: a stupid buffoon.

The manager of the troupe (Kurt Gerron), hoping to capitalize on the professor-turned-clown, decides to return to the town where the professor once taught. Rath, half-crazed and humiliated beyond endurance, goes on with the usual act. During these antics the curtain man cracks an egg on the professor's head and Rath, on cue, crows like a rooster, which he had done for laughs in his rational days. Now, quite out of his senses, Rath races from the stage, seeking solace, and finds Lola-Lola in the arms of her lover Mazeppa (Hans Albers). He tries to strangle her, but is subdued and thrown out of the theatre.

That evening he wanders aimlessly in the town and finds himself back at the school. He staggers into his old classroom and sits at the desk from which he had once commanded respect. Before rows of empty seats, the professor dies.

NOTES: *Der Blaue Engel* was produced at Ufa's Neubabelsberg Studios outside Berlin from November 4, 1929, to January 22, 1930. The premiere was held at the Gloria Palast Theatre in Berlin on April 1, 1930. An English-speaking version, shot simultaneously, ran 99 minutes and was first viewed at the Rialto Theatre in New York City on December 5, 1930, but Paramount (the United States distributors) held up general release until Dietrich's

With Emil Jannings,

first American film, *Morocco,* had opened. *The Blue Angel* opened to the general public in January of 1931. The accents were thick, which many a critic complained of, but Mordaunt Hall, in his *New York Times* review, said, "Lola is a rather taciturn creature, but occasionally she reveals subdued enthusiasm, coupled with a dry sense of humor." This film enjoyed its greatest success in America when the

With Kurt Gerron

With Emil Jannings and Rosa Valetti

With Kurt Gerron and Emil Jannings

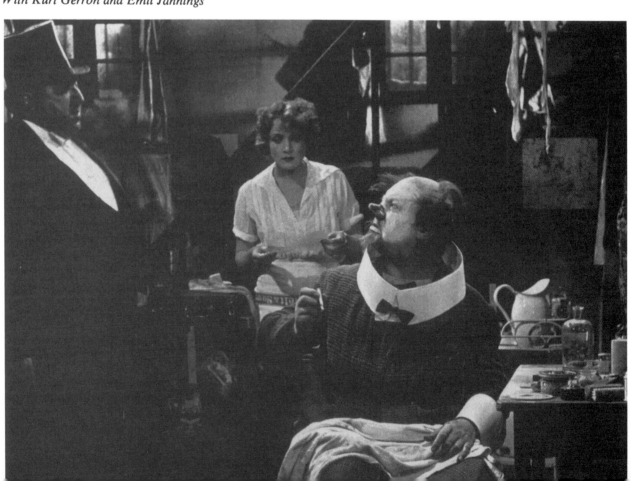

With Hans Albers and Emil Jannings

original German-language version was released with English subtitles.

Emil Jannings' Hollywood career was brief but brilliant and was halted when sound came to the cinema. He returned to Germany and Ufa began searching for a suitable vehicle for him as his talkie debut. Jannings wanted to film the life of Rasputin and convinced Erich Pommer, Ufa's powerful producer, that he should hire the American director Josef von Sternberg, who had directed him in the excellent *The Last Command*. Von Sternberg wanted top money but didn't want Rasputin. Finally, Heinrich Mann's 1904 novel, *Professor Unrath*, was decided upon. Von Sternberg wanted Brigit Helm for the role of Lola-Lola (the double name was used by the scenarists, who felt it would be *twice* as sexy!) but she was unavailable. Mann wanted Trude Hesterberg but it was decided that her box-office appeal was limited only to Berliners. Jannings wanted Lucie Mannheim.

Von Sternberg then "discovered" Marlene Dietrich and his quest for the "eternal woman" was over! But the heads of Ufa didn't want to entrust such an important role to an actress whose popularity was confined chiefly to what we would term "B" films.

Once the director got his way, the basic elements of Mann's novel were scrapped. No longer was society and/or the changing times reason enough for the professor's degradation. It was now up to Lola-Lola to accomplish this with a glance, a shrug, a puff of smoke . . . It was during the filming that Mann told Jannings ". . . the success of this film will be found in the naked thighs of Miss Dietrich!"

Two of the cast members, Kurt Gerron and Karl Huszar-Puffy, later became victims of Nazi tyranny and died in concentration camps.

In 1959, 20th Century-Fox unwisely re-made *The Blue Angel*, which not only didn't approach the original, but helped to convince everyone that copies of originals are just that—*copies!* Its only virtue was fine color photography, which should have been put to better use.

Morocco

A Paramount Picture—1930

CAST: GARY COOPER (*Tom Brown*); MARLENE DIET-RICH (*Amy Jolly*); ADOLPHE MENJOU (*Kennington*); ULLRICH HAUPT (*Adjutant Caesar*); JULIETTE COMPTON (*Anna Dolores*); FRANCIS MCDONALD (*Corporal Tatoche*); ALBERT CONTI (*Colonel Quinnevieres*); EVE SOUTHERN (*Madame Caesar*); MICHAEL VISAROFF (*Barratire*); PAUL PORCASI (*Lo Tinto*) with Emile Chautard.

CREDITS: JOSEF VON STERNBERG (*Director*); JULES FURTHMAN (*Scenarist*); LEE GARMES (*Photographer*); HANS DREIER (*Art Director*); TRAVIS BANTON (*Costumer*); SAM WINSTON (*Editor*); Based on the novel *Amy Jolly* by BENNO VIGNY.

SONGS: *By* LEO ROBIN and KARL HAJOS; "Give Me the Man," "What am I Bid," By CREMIEUX; "Quand L'Amour Meurt."

SYNOPSIS: Amy Jolly, a young cabaret entertainer (Marlene Dietrich), arrives by ship in the North African city of Morocco. She has already stirred the emotions of a wealthy artist named Kennington (Adolphe Menjou) on board but refuses his offer of "assistance" in the strange desert city. Shortly after arriving, she gets a job as the new headliner in a local cabaret, which caters not only to the sophisticates but to the officers and men of the French Foreign Legion.

Her first exposure before the unruly audience quickly sets the mood for what is to come. They quiet down and await her second number with longing. Then Amy Jolly reappears armed with a basket of shiny apples and sings, in a sultry manner, "What Am I Bid for My Apples," selling each apple for a high price to the patrons. Kennington, a leader in Morocco's social set, beckons to her again, and to taunt him—and shock the audience at the same time—Amy plants a kiss on the mouth of a woman in the audience.

92

Legionnaire Tom Brown (Gary Cooper) suddenly confronted by Amy, wants to buy one of her apples, although he is broke. He borrows some francs from his buddies and Amy hands him an apple. The good-looking legionnaire is the ladykiller of the outfit and usually gets what he goes after. To his surprise, Amy gives him change and at the same time slips him a key to her rooms.

Later, in Amy's boudoir, Tom, usually the aggressive one, plays the scene cool. He acts bored with Amy and confesses that "I met you ten years too late." He hands her key back and departs. Amy, probably turned down for the first time, follows him.

On his way back to the barracks, Tom sees Madame Caesar (Eve Southern) standing in the shadows. She has followed him to Amy's rooms and has been waiting for him. Not far behind is her husband, the Adjutant (Ullrich Haupt), who suspects his wife of infidelity with Tom Brown. Amy then comes upon them and Madame Caesar disappears into the night just as the Adjutant approaches. He confronts Tom and Amy and summons them to his office the following day.

Kennington, a friend of Adjutant Caesar's, is with him in the office when Amy Jolly is brought in. Tom is cleared of suspicion when she alibis that they were together. Kennington asks the Adjutant not to be too harsh on Amy and she is released. Brown, on the other hand, is soon sent on a dangerous patrol. Befor leaving, however, he visits Amy's dressing room and speaks of quitting the Foreign Legion, but when Amy finishes her number and returns, he has left a message on the mirror: "I changed my mind, Good Luck." Kennington proposes marriage and Amy, bitter over Tom's departure, accepts. At an elegant dinner party held at Kennington's lush estate, Amy realizes she must find Tom when she hears the returning troops entering the city.

She stops Tom's buddy Corporal Tatoche (Francis McDonald), to ask where he is, but the Corporal thinks Tom is dead. Amy tells Kennington she must go. She must make sure he's dead before marrying Kennington. Together they visit hospitals in the area to which the patrol was sent, but find nothing. Amy then visits a cheap dive and comes upon Tom sitting at a table with a native woman. He tells her he doesn't care for her anymore and she almost believes him—until she notices that he is carving her name into the wooden table.

The next morning as the legionnaires prepare to depart for another encampment, Amy asks Kennington why a small group of women are huddling

With Gary Cooper

With Adolphe Menjou and Paul Porcasi

near the town's gate. He explains that they follow their men wherever they go. As the troops move out, and the women follow them, Amy, standing on three-inch heels, watches in silence. Suddenly she begins to walk out into the sands. Finally, taking her shoes off, she follows her man into the desert with the wind blowing against her face.

NOTES: Marlene Dietrich, as seen through the eyes of Josef von Sternberg, began to take full shape in *Morocco*. She was the cool, calculating woman whose past had brought her nothing but misery. Determined to change all that, she chases her man first with subtle charms then openly defying all standards and customs. They matter not to her. The wealthy artist offers marriage, wealth, and security which indeed tempts her—as before. But she finally listens to herself and goes after the cynical legionnaire who has turned away from her.

Von Sternberg's Dietrich thus became a *femme fatale* to end all femme fatales. Her very presence could drive men to desperate acts, while, in most cases, she would remain indifferent.

Dietrich's indifference was in perfect contrast to Gary Cooper's insolent anti-hero—one of the finest performances of his early career. Adolphe Menjou, on the other hand, was suave, debonair, and slick. He knew what he wanted but seldom got it. His money could buy everything but love.

Von Sternberg's technique of endlessly varied photography and the skillful way he employed sound put *Morocco* years ahead of its time. The dialogue was kept to a minimum, thus intensifying the mood, action, and atmosphere of his theme. Audiences were captivated by the desert splendor, and the "mysterious foreigner" had conquered all. Dietrich,

With Gary Cooper

94

With Adolphe Menjou, Ullrich Haupt, and Gary Cooper

von Sternberg, and photographer Lee Garmes were accorded Academy Award nominations for their superb work.

Outlook noted, "Whether or not Marlene Dietrich really resembles Greta Garbo—as Paramount has hinted—you will have to decide for yourself. It is certain, however, that she is a vividly beautiful young lady and an excellent actress. Moreover, while she comes from the German musical comedy stage, she speaks flawless English." *Films in Review* years later said, "The theme of the soldier and the lady (who ultimately becomes a camp follower), following her man into battle or wherever he goes is a familiar one, but von Sternberg did it first and best. Her decision to follow him is made in utter silence save for the howling desert wind. There is no atmospheric music in *Morocco* at all. *Morocco* is a love story written, directed, and played for intelligent adults. It picks up a love story where other love stories end and takes it from there. The humor of *Morocco* is wry, subtle, perverse. It has irony tinged with grace and reminiscent with regret."

Dietrich's throaty voice, loaded with implications, delivering songs with a pleasing note of humor. Her style was unlike any other chanteuse. Her manner was highly individual and endlessly diverse.

The celebrated climax: Dietrich determines to follow her man into the desert.

Dishonored

A Paramount Picture—1931

CAST: MARLENE DIETRICH (*X-27*); VICTOR McLAGLEN (*Lieutenant Kranau*); LEW CODY (*Colonel Kovrin*); GUSTAV VON SEYFFERTITZ (*Head of Secret Service*); WARNER OLAND (*General von Hindau*); BARRY NORTON (*young lieutenant*); DAVISON CLARK (*court officer*); WILFRED LUCAS (*General Dymov*); BILL POWELL (*manager*); with GEORGE IRVING.

CREDITS: JOSEF VON STERNBERG (*Director*); DANIEL H. RUBIN (*Scenarist*); LEE GARMES (*Photographer*); KARL HAJOS (*Musical Score*); TRAVIS BANTON (*Costumer*); HARRY D. MILLS (*Sound Recorder*); Based on a story by JOSEF VON STERNBERG.

SYNOPSIS: In World War I Vienna, the Head of

With Gustav von Seyffertitz

the Secret Service (Gustav von Seyffertitz) is impressed by a young streetwalker (Marlene Dietrich) when he hears her tell a police officer, "I'm not afraid of life or death!" To get out of the rain, the young woman invites him up to her apartment, where he asks if she is interested in making easy money by spying against Austria. She quickly turns him over to the police. Convinced of her loyalty, he gives the police officer, who has escorted him out, his official card to give to the girl.

At Secret Service Headquarters the chief explains the dangers and thanklessness of the profession and why he has chosen a woman for a dangerous task. She accepts without hesitation and is dubbed "X-27."

X-27's first assignment is to learn if General von Hindau (Warner Oland) is a traitor passing information to the Russians. She meets him at a masked ball, flirts with him, and leaves with him for his home. On the way they drop off a man in a clown suit on crutches they met at the ball. During the ride the clown offers the general a cigarette, which he does not smoke, but puts in his coat pocket.

At the general's home X-27 has time to look around when he gets a well-timed phone call from the Head of the Secret Service. While snooping around, a butler comes in with champagne. To cover up, X-27 asks for a cigarette, but is informed that the general doesn't smoke and none are in the house. Remembering the cigarette the clown had given the general, X-27 finds it in his coat pocket and discovers a note in the mouthpiece section. When the general returns, X-27 is smoking the cigarette. Realizing all is lost,

With Victor McLaglen

With Warner Oland

and that X-27 is a spy, the general goes into the next room and shoots himself.

The objective now is to locate the clown—actually H-14 of the Russian Secret Service disguising himself as Austrian Lieutenant Kranau (Victor McLaglen). Later she meets him at a casino and sets a trap for him, but he escapes. He, in turn, enters her bedroom one evening and discovers her instructions to proceed to the Russian-Polish border and plans to entrap her there. After flying to the border, X-27 assumes the identity of a peasant maid working in the Russian officers' barracks, where Colonel Kovrin (Lew Cody) takes a fancy to her. In his rooms that night she gets the colonel drunk and then transcribes some vital military information into ciphers of music, which she can play at any time. Kranau, meanwhile, recognizes her black cat—which she takes everywhere she goes—and eventually finds her and has her arrested. In his quarters she slips a drug into his wine and forges a pass to get by the guards.

Following her, Kranau is caught at the Austrian

With Victor McLaglen

border and is to be executed at dawn. By this time X-27 realizes her love for the husky Russian spy and requests a few moments alone with him. While toying with her revolver, she "carelessly" drops it, and Kranau escapes into the night. The Austrian government condemns her to death for treason. In the clothes of her choice (the garments of her former profession!) she faces the firing-squad. A young lieutenant (Barry Norton), about to give the command to fire, balks, saying he can't kill a woman. While he is being replaced, X-27 calmly applies her lipstick. The orders are then carried out!

NOTES: Von Sternberg reportedly stated during the filming of *Dishonored* that Marlene Dietrich "has everything" and that he was "planning her pictures to show her various phases." This was, undoubtedly, her "international spy phase," for as a Mata Hari type, pulling off brilliant capers until she falls for a spy from the other side, she was quite divine!

The characterization (a woman unafraid of any-

With Lew Cody

With director Josef von Sternberg on the set

thing, including death, fastening her energies to a *job* and not a man, slowly but surely drawn to his charms, which drives her to a desperate act, thus bringing about her execution!) was perfectly suited to the Dietrich face, manner, voice, and style.

Von Sternberg's taste and his ability to elevate a hackneyed script into a visual work of art are to be admired. His use of the dissolve (one scene beginning while the previous one ends) was most evident and brilliantly effective, but, alas, was used much too often. His symbolism (which he denies exists) is as fascinating now as it was then, no matter how overworked or confused it may be.

Dietrich's disguise as a Russian peasant girl was beautifully executed. The entire Dietrich image was scrapped and a full-cheeked, plump, giggling little wench was placed in its stead. The transition was accomplished not only by the physical reversal but the substitution of another voice and the mannerisms of the peasant.

This offered more acting range than Dietrich had thus far known under von Sternberg. She was not only creating varying moods, but was letting herself be created within those moods. Thus, we see many Dietrichs in this film.

The piano music "played" by Marlene containing the awe-inspiring message of earth-shattering importance is the waltz "Danube Waves" by Ion Ivanovici.

Richard Watts, Jr. in his review of *Dishonored*, wrote, "Of Miss Dietrich, it need only be said that she proves once more that her hasty rise to film celebrity was the result of neither luck, accident, nor publicity. There still may be some doubt whether she possesses that technical expertness on which so many observers place such store, but there can be little question by now that her almost lyrically ironic air of detachment and, to be as frank about it as possible, her physical appeal, make her one of the great personages of the local drama."

Shanghai Express

A Paramount Picture—1932

CAST: MARLENE DIETRICH (*Shanghai Lily*); CLIVE BROOK (*Captain Donald Harvey*); ANNA MAY WONG (*Hui Fei*); WARNER OLAND (*Henry Chang*); EUGENE PALLETTE (*Sam Salt*); LAWRENCE GRANT (*Mr. Carmichael*); LOUISE CLOSSER HALE (*Mrs. Haggerty*); GUSTAV VON SEYFFERTITZ (*Eric Baum*); EMILE CHAUTARD (*Major Lenard*); with Claude King, Willie Fung.

CREDITS: JOSEF VON STERNBERG (*Director*); JULES FURTHMAN (*Scenarist*); LEE GARMES (*Photographer*); HANS DREIER (*Art Director*); W. FRANKE HARLING (*Musical Score*); TRAVIS BANTON (*Costumer*); Based on a story by HARRY HERVEY.

SYNOPSIS: At the Peking Railroad Terminal the great Shanghai Express is being loaded with baggage and passengers for the journey to Shanghai. This is a time of great unrest in China, and rebels have threatened to attack the train. The passengers who board the first-class car include Shanghai Lily (Marlene Dietrich), a notorious adventuress, known everywhere as "the White flower of the Chinese coast"; Henry Chang (Warner Oland), a Eurasian merchant; Hue Fei (Anna May Wong), an American-educated Chinese girl with a questionable reputation; Captain Donald Harvey (Clive Brook), a British officer in the Medical Corps; Sam Salt (Eugene Pallette), an engineer who loves to gamble; Mrs. Haggerty (Louise Closser Hale), a prim boarding house keeper; Eric Baum (Gustav von Seyffertitz), a dope-smuggling invalid; Mr. Carmichael (Lawrence Grant), a fanatical missionary; and Colonel Lenard (Emile Chautard), a disgraced

With Clive Brook

French officer wearing his uniform without authorization.

Before boarding the train, Captain Harvey is told by a friend that the infamous "Shanghai Lily" will be travelling on the same train. He has been so submerged in his work that he doesn't know of her reputation, nor has he heard her name. Once inside, the Captain runs smack into an old flame, Madeline, whom he hasn't seen in five years. When she tells him that she now has a new life and a new name, he asks if she has married. She glances at him and slowly replies, "It took more than one man to change my name to Shanghai Lily!"

Before the train pulls out of the station, a rebel spy is caught and arrested. The train is not out of Peking more than an hour or two when it is overtaken by rebels, and soon everyone is made aware that the unassuming Mr. Chang is actually the notorious rebel leader. It seems that the spy who was arrested in Peking was one of his top aides and is now in the hands of officials in Shanghai. Chang orders all passengers to be held in an old station currently being used as the Rebel Headquarters until he decides which of the group will best suit his needs as hostage.

All passports are checked and backgrounds delved into. Soon there are no secrets among the eight first-class passengers. Before making his decision, however, Mr. Chang asks Shanghai Lily to become his mistress but is flatly refused. Captain Harvey, in

the next room, partially overhears this conversation and misinterprets the meaning.

The passengers are returned to the train the next day. Lily notices that Captain Harvey is missing and

With Clive Brook

returns to the station house, to find Mr. Chang about to have the captain's eyes put out. To save him, Lily agrees to accept Mr. Chang's previous offer only if the captain is released unharmed. The captain is freed, not knowing of Lily's sacrifice.

This deed is short-lived, though, for Hui Fei, loathing the rebel leader and what he stands for, has hidden herself in his quarters and stabs him to death when he enters the room. The area is in utter chaos

as Shanghai Lily and Captain Harvey return to the train. As it departs for Shanghai, the couple make plans for a future together.

NOTES: Probably the best of the von Sternberg-Dietrich films, this "Grand Hotel on Wheels" moved at a crisp pace and was full of excitement. Everything von Sternberg wanted to say with Dietrich he accomplished here. His use of light, shadows, reflec-

With Clive Brook

With Anna May Wong

tions, the bustling crowds, the dissolves, the shutters filtering the sun's rays on Marlene in conjunction with her moods and/or the situations unravelling around her, suggested tremendous sexual excitement, although little more than the Dietrich ankle was exposed.

Travis Banton, Paramount's brilliant costume designer, again created exotic outfits for Dietrich. She was feathered, veiled, gloved; furs changed with her moods; beads became crystals became lace. She was literally smothered in clothes. Someone had to bring something to this image in order for it to work fully. Without that added "something" von Sternberg's illusions might not have worked.

Lee Garmes worked closely with von Sternberg and outdid himself in the photography of *Shanghai Express*. He won an Academy Award, while the picture and director each received nominations.

The London *Times* thought "Her acting finds its strength and impulse in her careful elimination of all emphasis, and the more seemingly careless and inconsequent her gestures the more surely do they reveal the particular shades and movements of her mind." Another critic was impressed with "the Oriental impassiveness of Miss Wong meeting its match in the equal impassiveness of Miss Dietrich's Western sophistication." *The New York Times* felt this was "the best picture von Sternberg has directed . . . many of the scenes are so beautifully lighted that they recall etchings."

*With Anna May Wong
and players*

103

With Herbert Marshall

Blonde Venus

A Paramount Picture—1932

CAST: MARLENE DIETRICH (*Helen Faraday*); HERBERT MARSHALL (*Edward Faraday*); CARY GRANT (*Nick Townsend*); DICKIE MOORE (*Johnny Faraday*); GENE MORGAN (*Ben Smith*); RITA LA ROY ("*Taxi Belle*" *Hooper*); ROBERT EMMETT O'CONNOR (*Dan O'Connor*); SIDNEY TOLER (*Detective Wilson*); FRANCIS SAYLES (*Charlie Blaine*); MORGAN WALLACE (*Dr. Pierce*); EVELYN PREER (*Iola*); ROBERT GRAVES (*La Farge*); LLOYD WHITLOCK (*Baltimore manager*); CECILE CUNNINGHAM (*Norfolk woman manager*); EMILE CHAUTARD (*Chautard*); JAMES KILGANNON (*janitor*); Students: STERLING HOLLOWAY (*Joe*), CHARLES MOR-

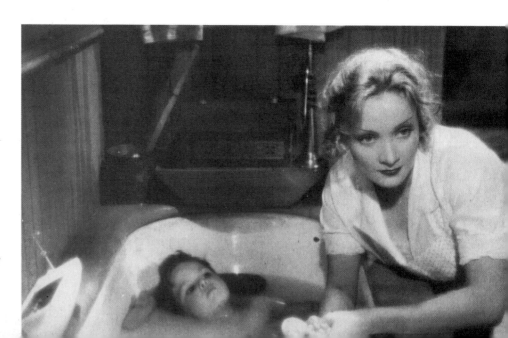

With Dickie Moore

TON (*Bob*) and FERDINAND SCHUMAN-HEINK (*Henry*); JERRY TUCKER (*Otto*); HAROLD BERQUIST (*big fellow*); DEWEY ROBINSON (*Greek restaurant proprietor*); CLIFFORD DEMPSEY (*night court judge*); BESSIE LYLE (*Grace*); MILDRED WASHINGTON (*Negro girl*); GERTRUDE SHORT (*receptionist*); HATTIE MCDANIEL (*Negro girl*); BRADY KLINE (*New Orleans cop*).

CREDITS: JOSEF VON STERNBERG (*Director*); JULES FURTHMAN and S. K. LAUREN (*Scenarists*); BERT GLENNON (*Photographer*); WIARD IHNEN (*Art Director*); OSCAR POTOKER (*Musical Score*); TRAVIS BANTON (*Costumer*); Based on a story by JOSEF VON STERNBERG.

SONGS: *By* SAM COSLOW and RALPH RAINGER; "Hot Voodoo," "You Little So-and-So. *by* LEO ROBIN and DICK WHITING; "I Couldn't Be Annoyed."

SYNOPSIS: American chemist Edward Faraday (Herbert Marshall) falls madly in love with a German café singer named Helen (Marlene Dietrich) after seeing her only once—bathing in a mountain pond. In no time, he has her on a ship bound for the United States as his bride.

Life is happy for them both, and later when their son Johnny (Dickie Moore) is born, Helen becomes a devoted mother, while Edward keeps busy working in the laboratory on various experiments. One day Helen learns that her husband has become contaminated with radium poisoning and may die unless he receives proper treatment. The only clinic equipped for such cases is in Europe, and the cost is beyond anything Edward can afford. Helen decides to return to her former profession to aid her husband.

At a local bistro she opens as the featured singer. She is an overnight success. Among those present on this auspicious occasion is young playboy Nick Townsend (Cary Grant), who is quite taken with her. At first Helen is uninterested in his advances but is soon won over by his innate charm and good looks. When Nick discovers that Helen is working to pay her husband's medical bills and bring up their infant son, he offers to set her up in a swank apartment and help financially. She accepts.

In due course, Faraday returns from Europe cured, but he is heartbroken when he learns of his wife's infidelity. Without waiting for an explanation, he begins proceedings to gain custody of their son, but Helen takes the boy and runs away. Their trip together is a long, hard one, and downhill all the way; Faraday has detectives following her everywhere, but she's always one jump ahead of them.

With Cary Grant

Finally she is found and relents. Faraday takes his son back with him to New York.

Unencumbered now by husband or son, Helen begins the hard road back to the top of the entertainment world. Soon she's a headliner in a Parisian nightclub and the rage of Paris. Nick Townsend is again at her side.

Taking the hit show to New York, Helen is encouraged by Nick to visit her husband and son, which she agrees to do. Edward, finding out the

With Dickie Moore and Herbert Marshall

whole story of his wife's loyalty, forgives her and they are reunited.

NOTES: In this fifth picture for von Sternberg, Dietrich again was cast as a nightclub entertainer. But it was the first time she played a devoted mother. Because Paramount had submitted so many wretched scripts, von Sternberg was forced to sketch out another fast storyline which he turned over to the scenarists. The action was, by this time, getting considerably slower and his exposition much more pronounced. The trip to Skid Row seemed an eternity—puffing trains, miles of tracks, scenes of various cities en route, etc.

Bert Glennon, who photographed some of von Sternberg's earlier silents, worked on *Blonde Venus*. Whether Miss Dietrich was in a housedress and apron or an evening gown, her loveliness was most apparent. Her musical numbers were wild and provided her with great variety both in style and dress. In "Hot Voodoo" she enters in a gorilla suit flanked by native girls and proceeds to remove her suit and slip on a fuzzy blonde wig not to be believed! Then, carrying a spear and shield, Dietrich sings the

In the ape suit for the "Hot Voodoo" number

In the "Hot Voodoo" number

song. Another number, done in white top hat, tie and tails before a sophisticated audience, demonstrated her power to get away with just about anything. Her third number was done in a gown of shimmering beads. She carried a large picture hat.

Herbert Marshall was a staunch Britisher playing an American, while Cary Grant, in his fifth picture, exhibited considerable charm and personality. Young Dickie Moore, one of the better child actors, was thoroughly believable, which is more than can be said of the script.

Mr. von Sternberg in his autobiography stated that *Blonde Venus* was "written swiftly to provide something other than the sob stories that were being submitted."

The New York Times had to admit that this was an "excellent example of von Sternberg's preoccupation with style and method."

Song of Songs

A Paramount Picture—1933

CAST: MARLENE DIETRICH (*Lily Czepanek*); BRIAN AHERNE (*Waldow*); LIONEL ATWILL (*Baron von Merzbach*); ALISON SKIPWORTH (*Frau Rasmussen*); HARDIE ALBRIGHT (*Walter von Prell*); HELEN FREEMAN (*Fräulein von Schwartzfegger*); with James Marcus, Morgan Wallace, Wilson Benge and Hans Schumm.

CREDITS: ROUBEN MAMOULIAN (*Director and Producer*); LEO BIRINSKI, SAMUEL HOFFENSTEIN (*Scenarists*); VICTOR MILNER (*Photographer*); TRAVIS BANTON (*Costumer*); Music by KARL HAJOS and MILAN RODER; NATHANIEL W. FINSTON (*Musical Director*); S. C. SCARPITTA (*Sculptor*); From the novel by HERMANN SUDERMANN and the play by EDWARD SHELDON.

SONG: *By* FREDERICK HOLLANDER with English lyrics by EDWARD HEYMAN; "Jonny."

SYNOPSIS: Lily Czepanek, a guileless country girl (Marlene Dietrich), desolated by her father's death, goes to Berlin to live with her aunt, Mrs. Rasmussen (Alison Skipworth). She works for her keep in her

With Brian Aherne

With Alison Skipworth

aunt's bookshop, where she meets a young sculptor named Waldow (Brian Aherne) who lives across the street. He notices her legs while she is on a ladder dusting the books, and he expresses a desire to have her pose for him. The girl declines but is intrigued.

That night Lily waits for her aunt to fall asleep, then runs across the street. Although innately shy, she finally agrees to pose in the nude for Waldow. His life-size statue of Lily represents the Song of Solomon. The couple soon fall in love and spend Sundays in the country and nights working late in the studio.

After the statue is completed, Baron von Merzbach (Lionel Atwill) the sculptor's wealthy patron, visits and is at once taken by the beauty of the statue. When its model appears from behind a curtain, he is dazzled.

Soon sculptor and model are inseparable, but he is rather frightened of her expressions of never-dying love and a strong desire for marriage and children, which he feels would hamper him in his work. Meanwhile, the Baron is giving Lily's aunt money and rum—buying her support for his plans to marry her niece and make her a lady of quality.

Then the Baron cunningly persuades young Waldow to give her up, since he can do much more for Lily and convinces him that "for his art's sake" the best thing to do is to leave immediately. That night Lily's aunt—on schedule—throws her out when she discovers her trying to sneak out of the bookshop.

109

Lily disappears. Waldow hunts everywhere, but has no luck. One evening he enters a Berlin nightclub and there sees Lily—now a "fancy lady" singing the naughty song "Jonny." Later, he takes her out of the nightclub and convinces her of his love and asks her to marry him. She consents.

NOTES: This handsomely produced but only mildly dramatic film was Dietrich's first American picture directed by someone other than Josef von Sternberg. Rouben Mamoulian, fresh from his triumph, *Dr. Jekyll and Mr. Hyde,* accepted the dual assignment of handling an old-fashioned story and the von Sternberg-ized Dietrich. He directed *Song of Songs* in a sophisticated and finely stylized manner which contained many moments of visual excitement. He removed Dietrich, somewhat, from the pedestal on which von Sternberg had placed her by enabling her to find freedom of characterization and expression. The result was a satisfying performance indeed. This must rank among her best screen work. Dietrich had proved what a fine choice she was for the buffeted heroine; she gave Lily grace, sympathy and ineffable beauty. No role could ask for more!

Lily dashes across the street and up to the garrett, only to find the lustful Baron waiting there. He tells her that the sculptor has left her and offers marriage and all the advantages associated with being a Baroness.

Lily finally accepts and becomes the Baroness von Merzbach. She is tutored in everything a woman of her station must know. The Baron's housekeeper, Fräulein von Schwartzfegger (Helen Freeman), jealous of the new mistress, insists that the Baroness learn to ride and persuades the Baron that young Walter von Prell (Hardie Albright) should give her the necessary lessons. The housekeeper urges the young man to make advances to the Baroness, who just ignores them.

One evening the Baron brings Waldow to dinner to view his cultured creation and insists that the two become friends again. Meanwhile he drinks himself into a stupor and the Baroness tries to convince Waldow she does not love the Baron by arranging for him to see her enter von Prell's cottage on the estate for an assignation. But a lamp is knocked over when von Prell carries Lily into the bedroom and the cottage is set aflame. Von Prell carries the Baroness out to safety and in the confusion Fräulein von Schwartzfegger warns her to leave before the Baron learns of this scandal.

With Lionel Atwill

110

Mamoulian speaks highly of his association with Dietrich (despite the obvious battles that must have taken place). He appreciated her "great sense of discipline" and is justly proud of her acting accomplishment under his guidance. In fact, it was *Song of Songs* that Mamoulian showed privately to Greta Garbo at Paramount before agreeing to direct her in *Queen Christina* at Metro-Goldwyn-Mayer. Miss Garbo was impressed!

Song of Songs had twice been filmed before, with two of the silent screen's great ladies essaying the part of Lily: Elsie Ferguson and Pola Negri.

Sydney W. Carroll in the London *Times* said, "Marlene will appear, probably for the first time in her career, as an innocent country girl. Why should she not? It is true this actress has made the vamp queen of the pictures; it is true that every grade of scarlet womanhood has found in her ideal expression; it is true that no more glamorous, seductive, disintegrating personality ever before represented sex upon the films. Such is her range that even virginity is not beyond it. The way of the world, the sneer of the sophist, the leer of the lewd, these are of the dead past. Our cinemas, always fickle in their taste, now yearn for simplicity and purity. Marriage has become a necessity."

Newsweek noticed that "so vibrant and compelling is Marlene Dietrich . . . that she turns material into an individual triumph." The *London Daily Telegraph* said, "Miss Dietrich's fans ask nothing more than that she should be well photographed in suitable situations and unsuitable clothes." *The New York Times,* on the other hand, stated, "Marlene Dietrich floats through it with the lyric grace of that apparition which was sent by Heaven to be a moment's ornament. Mr. Mamoulian has the eye of a poet and Victor Milner the poet's skill."

Dietrich waits as the set is being lighted.

With Helen Freeman and Lionel Atwill

Other than singing a few notes in French at a piano, Dietrich's only song was "Jonny," the famous Frederick Hollander song of 1920 which she had recorded in Germany as early as 1929. Edward Heyman wrote her some English lyrics, a fact she totally forgot during her nightclub tours and in her Broadway show. She said that since no English lyrics had ever been written for it, she would sing the song in German. Ralph Rainger and Leo Robin also composed a song entitled "You Are My Song of Songs," but it was not in the final release prints.

This was Brian Aherne's first American-made motion picture, although he had appeared earlier in several British films. For some reason he appeared ill-at-ease and unsure of himself. His performance is—today—the only liability in the film. Lionel Atwill, always virile and robust, almost stole the show as the lecherous Baron. Alison Skipworth was properly unpleasant as the rum-guzzling old aunt. Helen Freeman was deliciously wicked as the Baron's full-time housekeeper, part-time mistress.

And all of them owe a great big bow to Tchaikovsky's Symphony No. 6 (the "Pathetique"), which kept booming on the sound track whenever a glimpse of the nude statue occurred.

Here again sex in the form of a nude statue (which bore a striking resemblance to Dietrich) captivated audiences, but the most they saw of Dietrich herself was bare shoulders. The rest of the time she was fully clothed.

Maria Sieber, Dietrich's daughter, playing Sophia Frederica as a child

The Scarlet Empress

A Paramount Picture—1934

CAST: MARLENE DIETRICH (*Sophia Frederica, Catherine II*); JOHN LODGE (*Count Alexei*); SAM JAFFE (*Grand Duke Peter*); LOUISE DRESSER (*Empress Elizabeth*); MARIA SIEBER (*Sophia as a child*); C. AUBREY SMITH (*Prince August*); RUTHELMA STEVENS (*Countess Elizabeth*); OLIVE TELL (*Princess Johanna*); GAVIN GORDON (*Gregory Orloff*); JAMESON THOMAS (*Lieutenant Ovtsyn*); HANS VON TWARDOWSKI (*Ivan Shuvolov*); DAVISON CLARK (*Archimandrite Simeon Tevedovsky, also Arch-Episcope*); ERVILLE ALDERSON (*Chancellor Bestuchef*); MARIE WELLS (*Marie*); JANE DARWELL (*Mlle. Cardell*); HARRY WOODS (*the doctor*); EDWARD VAN SLOAN (*Herr Wagner*); PHILIP G. SLEEMAN (*Count Lestocq*); JOHN B. DAVIDSON (*Marquis de la Chetardie*) GERALD FIELDING (*Officer, Lt. Dmitri*); JAMES BURKE (*guard*); BELLE STODDARD JOHNSTONE (*first aunt*); NADINE BERESFORD (*second aunt*); EUNICE MOORE (*third aunt*); PETRA MCALLISTER (*fourth aunt*); BLANCHE ROSE (*fifth aunt*); JAMES MARCUS (*innkeeper*); THOMAS C. BLYTHE (*1st Narcissus*); CLYDE DAVID (*2nd Narcissus*); RICHARD ALEXANDER (*Count von Breummer*); HAL BOYER (*Paul, 2nd lackey*); BRUCE WARREN (*7th lackey*); GEORGE DAVIS (*jester*); ERIC ALDEN (*5th lackey*); AGNES STEELE, BARBARA SABICHI, MAY FOSTER and MINNIE STEELE (*Elizabeth's ladies-in-waiting*); KATHERINE SABICHI, JULANNE JOHNSTON, ELINOR FAIR, DINA SMIRNOVA, ANNA DUNCAN, PATRICIA PATRICK and ELAINE ST. MAUR (*Catherine's ladies-in-waiting*).

CREDITS: JOSEF VON STERNBERG (*Director*); MANUEL KOMROFF (*Scenarist*); BERT GLENNON (*Photographer*); HANS DREIER, PETER BALLBUSCH and RICHARD KOLLORSZ (*Art Directors*); W. FRANKE HARLING, JOHN M. LEIPOLD and MILAN RODER (*Music Arrangers*); Based on the music of TCHAIKOVSKY, MENDELSSOHN; TRAVIS BANTON (*Costumer*); GORDON JENNINGS (*Special Effects*); Based on a Diary of CATHERINE THE GREAT.

SYNOPSIS: As a child in Germany young Princess Sophia Frederica (Maria Sieber) is told of her great destiny. When a young woman, the princess (now played by Marlene Dietrich) is brought to Russia by the Empress to wed her son, the Grand Duke Peter, heir to the throne. Sophia is a shy, innocent, roman-

until she learns that he is an intimate friend of the Empress. From then on she decides to live a "free life" and romances many men, including the Captain of the Guards. From this affair a son is born, which the Grand Duke disclaims but which the court acknowledges as heir to the throne.

As soon as the Empress dies and the Grand Duke becomes Emperor, he plans to kill Catherine and marry his mistress. But, Catherine is immensely popular with the Army and the ministers—and with the peasants, who are suffering injustices at the hands of their new Emperor. Soon these men rally to her support. The Emperor is murdered and Catherine is proclaimed Empress of all the Russias!

NOTES: Von Sternberg and his art director, Hans Dreier, decided from the first to abandon historical accuracy and give the story of Catherine a stylized Russian background to "build up the drama of the story." This was an understatement!

tic girl, dreaming of happiness with her husband. She and her aunt, the Princess Johanna (Olive Tell), are escorted on the long, tedious journey by handsome Count Alexei (John Lodge), of the Russian Court. Sophia is led to believe that her future husband is far handsomer than Alexei.

One evening, while stopping over at an inn, the young Count makes advances to the little princess but Princess Johanna intervenes and journey continues without further incident. Arriving at the palace, Sophia Frederica is overwhelmed by the immensity of it all. She is presented to the Empress Elizabeth (Louise Dresser), who immediately takes a dislike to the name Sophia Frederica and dubs her "Catherine."

When the Grand Duke Peter (Sam Jaffe) is presented to her, all her girlish dreams vanish. Standing before her is a grinning half-wit in a powdered wig. She is further disillusioned when she discovers that he hates her and prefers to be with his mistress, the Countess Elizabeth (Ruthelma Stevens). Catherine refuses to live with him and thus suffers many humiliations from the Empress.

Slowly driven into the arms of other men, Catherine has many affairs. Her first is Count Alexei,

busch, a young Swiss sculptor, created the fantastic figures which were everywhere: arms of chairs, legs of tables, etc. etc.

Bert Glennon's superb camera zoomed amongst these figures and often made them seem quite alive. Von Sternberg created, and inspired his entire crew to create with him, a gorgeously mad tapestry of Catherine's Russia. Everything, strangely enough, jelled into a whole. Only the characters were lost, but what did that matter? Here was real spectacle.

Dietrich's performance, without proper transitions, was good as could be expected under the circumstances. Her earlier sequences as the shy princess were near perfect, but when she later becomes the power within the palace, there was no believeability! Young John Lodge, grandson of the great Massachusetts senator, Henry Cabot Lodge, in his first important film role, provided a handsome figure with a fine voice.

If *The Scarlet Empress* were a silent, Louise Dresser would have been magnificent (as she was in *The Eagle*) but her "American" voice and frontier manner ruined the Empress characterization. The Grand Duke of Sam Jaffe left nothing for the imagination: he came on like "Gang Busters" and departed in much the same manner. Von Sternberg got Marlene's permission to use her daughter Maria for the role of Sophia Frederica as a child. She was most charming.

What helped kill this picture's box-office potential was the release, a few months earlier, of Alexander Korda's handsome production, *Catherine the Great,* with Elisabeth Bergner (sensitively beautiful); Doug-

Never before had there been such pomp and pageantry: all attention was geared to the visuals. Ferocious icons, ominous serfs, bells, cuckoo clocks, pillars, brought a Byzantine flavor to the surroundings, a kind of German expressionism. Peter Ball-

With Sam Jaffe

114

las Fairbanks, Jr. (as the subtly insane Grand Duke); and Flora Robson (callous, yet understanding, as the Empress). Korda's emphasis was on character not spectacle.

Seen today, *The Scarlet Empress* is a treat in style, mood, and expressionism, and the words of von Sternberg himself can now be understood more clearly: "I did make a serious if overly pedantic effort to use the medium properly and weld sound and sight into an integral unity."

The critics then said it was ". . . a sadistic spectacle" . . . "foolishness" . . . "sheer idiotic affectation."

Richard Watts, Jr., in the New York *Herald Tribune* took Dietrich's side: "Under his tutelage Miss Dietrich has become a hapless sort of automaton, while his passion for brooding ponderously over a scene and going in heavily for pompous affectations in settings, symbolism and costuming have resulted in mannered and ostentatious dullness."

André Sennwald in the *New York Times* said of von Sternberg, ". . . he possesses so many obvious talents, inextricably confused with so many obvious faults, that no one who is vitally interested in the cinema can afford to ignore him."

Time magazine cried out: "A tedious hyperbole in which Director Josef von Sternberg achieved the improbable feat of burying Marlene Dietrich in a

With John Lodge and C. Aubrey Smith

welter of plaster-of-Paris gargoyles and galloping cossacks, it seems all the more inadequate by comparison with Elisabeth Bergner's *Catherine the Great* . . . Worst Shot: Marlene Dietrich clattering up the palace steps on a white horse."

All things considered, *The Scarlet Empress* was great fun . . . and still is when viewed today!

With Louise Dresser and Sam Jaffe

115

With Cesar Romero

The Devil Is a Woman

A Paramount Picture—1935

CAST: MARLENE DIETRICH (*Concha Perez*); LIONEL ATWILL (*Don Pasqual*); CESAR ROMERO (*Antonio Galvan*); EDWARD EVERETT HORTON (*Don Paquito*); ALISON SKIPWORTH (*Senora Perez*); DON ALVARADO (*Morenito*); MORGAN WALLACE (*Dr. Mendez*); TEMPE PIGOTT (*Tuerta*); JILL DENNETT (*Maria*); LAWRENCE GRANT (*conductor*); CHARLES SELLON (*letter writer*); LUISA ESPINAL (*Gypsy dancer*); HANK MANN (*foreman, snowbound train*); EDWIN MAXWELL (*superintendent, tobacco factory*); with Donald Reed, Eddie Borden.

CREDITS: JOSEF VON STERNBERG (*Director and Photographer*); JOHN DOS PASSOS and S. K. WINSTON (*Scenarists*); LUCIEN BALLARD (*Assistant Photographer*); HANS DREIER (*Art Director*); TRAVIS BANTON (*Costumer*); SAM WINSTON (*Editor*); Based on the novel *The Woman and the Puppet* by PIERRE LOUYS. SONGS: *By* LEO ROBIN and RALPH RAINGER; "(If It Isn't Pain) Then It Isn't Love," "Three Sweethearts Have I."

SYNOPSIS: During a wild carnival in Seville in the 1890's, young handsome political refugee Antonio Galvan (Cesar Romero) meets the notorious Concha Perez (Marlene Dietrich) and arranges to see her again that evening. Meanwhile, the young man meets Don Pasqual (Lionel Atwill) an old Army friend, and tells him of the strange compulsion he feels towards this woman.

Don Pasqual, once a proud officer in the Civil Guard but now a civilian derelict, relates to his young friend the story of his own masochistic humiliations at the hands of Concha Perez, in hopes of deterring him from seeing her again.

He tells Antonio how they met on a snowbound train five years earlier. He, too, immediately captivated by her charms, let her go after a fight with another woman. He began showering her with gifts and money—paying all of her debts—to the delight of her scheming mother (Alison Skipworth). The more

With Lionel Atwill

mysterious and aloof she became, the more excited he was. He was rewarded by her disappearance. Later he saw her in a Cadiz bar dancing and singing. Again she permitted his advances and allowed him to spend money. But again she disappeared. Some time later, while performing his official duties, he

With Lionel Atwill (in uniform) and Alison Skipworth

With Cesar Romero

saw her rolling cigarettes in a tobacco factory and the same infatuation stirred in his blood. Again Concha took all and gave nothing in return.

When Don Pasqual concludes his story, his young friend is more intrigued than ever, but for his friend's sake he is sympathetic and says he will not see the woman that evening. Just the opposite occurs, however, and Don Pasqual challenges Antonio to a duel.

The older man lets Antonio win because he believes that Concha really loves the younger man, and so fires into the air.

Once Concha has visited Don Pasqual in the hospital he tells her to go. He says he's through with her. She leaves for the border with Antonio to elope to Paris. At the border she changes her mind after going through customs, leaves him there. She then

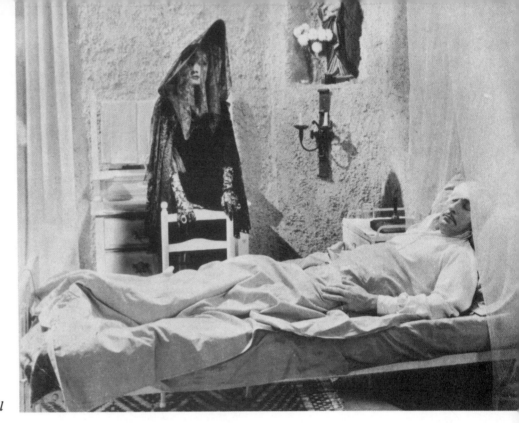

With Lionel Atwill

returns to Seville and . . . Don Pasqual . . . and . . . NOTES: Von Sternberg reached the end of the road with *The Devil Is a Woman*. He had brought Marlene Dietrich as far as he could. Feeling that nothing *new* could come from their association, he announced to the press that they would separate after this film was released. Dietrich was crushed but, as time went on, she became self-propelled. Like Concha Perez, Marlene Dietrich seemed to drain everything that was good out of von Sternberg, the only switch being that he walked out on her, not she on him. He was never to accomplish without her what he had created with her. Dietrich, on the other hand, would go on in pictures (some bad; some good), conquer the nightclub world, continue recording songs in her own seductive style.

With Edward Everett Horton

Von Sternberg's photography in *The Devil Is a Woman,* which he prefers to call *Caprice Espagñol,* is magnificent. Despite its total lack of pace and narrative style, this film remains a favorite with them both. Dietrich thinks she looked better in it than in any other picture—which is certainly open for debate. She did prove, however, that even as a Spanish wench, she could captivate men and ruin them if it pleased her to do so!

When originally released, *The Devil Is a Woman* caused quite a sensation when the Spanish Government asked Paramount to withdraw it from the world market and destroy the negative. There were many reasons for their anger, i.e. the character of Don Pasqual libeled the Spanish Civil Guard, as did the character of Edward Everett Horton who, as the police chief, felt that arresting lawbreakers was a waste of time—why not shoot them instead? However, the drinking sequences of the men of the Civil Guard were singled out. If that were all that was wrong, a scene or two could have been deleted.

The temper of Europe at that time being what it was, the State Department asked Paramount to withdraw all of their existing prints of the picture from circulation. They did so, but whether the negative of *The Devil Is a Woman* was really destroyed has never been established. Very few prints of the film are available for showing today. Miss Dietrich's own print was shown at the Museum of Modern Art's tribute to her in 1959, but since that time various copies have been springing up around the country.

Most critics didn't care for the film, except for *The New York Times,* which said, "the cultivated filmgoer will be delighted by the sly urbanity which is implied and in von Sternberg's direction; as well as excited by the striking beauty of his settings and photography . . . it is the best production of the von Sternberg-Dietrich alliance since *The Blue Angel.*"

The critic of the *New York Journal-American* felt "the action is so absurd, so artificial, so repetitious, that every scene fairly shrieks for Jim Cagney and a grapefruit."

With Gary Cooper

Desire

A Paramount Picture—1936

CAST: MARLENE DIETRICH (*Madeleine de Beaupré*); GARY COOPER (*Tom Bradley*); JOHN HALLIDAY (*Carlos Margoli*); WILLIAM FRAWLEY (*Mr. Gibson*); ERNEST COSSART (*Aristide Duval*); AKIM TAMIROFF (*Police Official*); ALAN MOWBRAY (*Dr. Edouard Pauquet*); ZEFFIE TILBURY (*Aunt Olga*); HARRY DEPP (*clerk*); MARC LAWRENCE (*valet*); HENRY ANTRIM (*Chauffeur*); ARMAND KALIZ (*jewelry clerk*); GASTON GLASS (*jewelry clerk*); ALBERT POLLET (*French policeman*); GEORGE DAVIS (*garage man*); CONSTANT FRANKE (*border official*); ROBERT O'CONNOR (*customs official*); STANLEY ANDREWS (*customs inspector*); RAFAEL BLANCO (*driver of haywagon*); ALDEN CHASE (*clerk in hotel*); TONY MERLO (*waiter*); ANNA DELINSKY (*servant*); ALICE

With Ernest Cossart

With Gary Cooper

FELIZ (*Pepi*); ENRIQUE ACOSTA (*Pedro*); GEORGE MACQUARRIE (*clerk with gun*); ISABEL LA MAL (*nurse*); OLIVER ECKHARDT (*husband*); BLANCHE CRAIG (*wife*); ROLLO LLOYD (*clerk in Mayor's office*); ALFONSO PEDROSA (*oxcart driver*).

With Gary Cooper

CREDITS: FRANK BORZAGE (*Director*); ERNST LUBITSCH (*Producer*); EDWIN JUSTUS MAYER, WALDEMAR YOUNG and SAMUEL HOFFENSTEIN (*Scenarists*); CHARLES LANG (*Photographer*); HANS DREIER, ROBERT USHER (*Art Directors*); FREDERICK HOLLANDER (*Musical Score*); TRAVIS BANTON (*Costumer*); From a comedy by HANS SZEKELY and R. A. STEMMLE.

SONG: *By* FREDERICK HOLLANDER and LEO RUBIN, "Awake in a Dream."

SYNOPSIS: Continental jewel thief Madeleine de Beaupre (Marlene Dietrich) devises a clever scheme of gaining possession of a valuable string of pearls from Parisian jeweler Aristide Duval (Ernest Cossart) while also implicating Dr. Edouard Pauquet (Alan Mowbray), a psychiatrist. Once she has duped both of these refined gentlemen, Madeleine races for the Spanish border.

Driving leisurely on the same road, going in the same direction, is Tom Bradley (Gary Cooper) a good-natured American engineer from Detroit enjoying his first vacation in years. Madeleine soon passes Tom on the road, nearly running him off and leaving him in a cloud of dust.

Tom catches up with her at the border. Standing in line awaiting inspection, Madeleine sees a customs official look into a lady's handbag and quickly slips the "hot" necklace into Tom's coat pocket. Once Tom's baggage is checked, he drives off. Madeleine follows him and passes him several times on the

With John Halliday, Gary Cooper, and Zeffie Tilbury

road flirting outrageously to get his attention. That technique not working the way she wants, Madeleine speeds ahead and stops her car on the road and proceeds to smash its engine with a hammer. Tom pulls up and offers assistance to the lady in distress. One look at that engine and he asks Madeleine if she'd like a lift, which she gratefully accepts.

At one point, Tom gets out of his car to check the tires, and Madeleine, thinking she has the necklace with her in the car, zooms off leaving Tom, and his jacket with the pearls, to walk to the nearest town.

Madeleine and her confederate, Carlos Margoli (John Halliday), then try to retrieve the pearls from an unknowing Tom. They invite him to a mountain inn, and it is there that he discovers what they are after. Up till then, Tom thinks Madeleine is in love with him, but now he knows what she has been after. What he doesn't know is that she really has fallen for him.

Tom then tries to reform Madeleine, and the third member of the mob, Aunt Olga (Zeffie Tilbury), is called in. She tries to reason with Madeleine, but has little success. Tom finally wins, and Madeleine

With Alan Mowbray, Gary Cooper, and Ernest Cossart

With director Frank Borzage

returns the necklace to Duval, marries Tom, and leaves for Detroit and domesticity.

NOTES: Once Dietrich was on her own, producer Ernst Lubitsch got three scenarists at work on this screenplay. It was familiar, to be sure, but, with deft playing the unusual happened. Dietrich was beginning to become more alive and her hitherto subdued humor finally flourished. Being teamed again with Gary Cooper was perfect casting. No one personified the American image better than Cooper, and in the mid-thirties, his adroitness at this was at its peak. Dietrich joined all the great female stars of the period as a jewel thief. Hers was a little more down-to-earth than most, but she gave Madeleine de Beaupre the slickness and appeal she deserved.

Although Frank Borzage, of *Seventh Heaven* fame, directed, the entire production received the personal supervision of Ernst Lubitsch, then head of Paramount's West Coast Productions. Dietrich, on her own for the first time in America, felt secure in Lubitsch's hands, and working with Borzage and Cooper proved a rewarding experience. Originally entitled *The Pearl Necklace,* which made more sense than *Desire,* this comedy was given expert support by John Halliday, Ernest Cossart, Alan Mowbray, and Zeffie Tilbury.

Frank Nugent in *The New York Times* was delighted that "Ernst Lubitsch . . . has freed Marlene Dietrich from Josef von Sternberg's artistic bondage and has brought her vibrantly alive in *Desire*. . . . Permitted to walk, breathe, smile and shrug as a human being instead of a canvas for the Louvre, Miss Dietrich recaptures . . . some of the freshness and gayety of spirit that was hers in *The Blue Angel* and other of her early successes."

This film is continually revived around the country and is shown on television more than any other Dietrich film of the 1930's. The reason is simple: It's fun!

In 1962, Eugenia Sheppard, the women's feature editor of the *New York Herald Tribune* told her readers, after seeing *Desire* on television, ". . . Before the picture was over, Marlene appeared in a sports costume that marked the beginning of today's good taste. It was a fitted, double-breasted sports jacket worn over a white dress. At the end she was married, though, in everything they could pile on her, hats, scarfs, veils, and more fox than you ever saw on a single garment. I could have sat right through the picture a second time. Though it was all terrible taste as today's fashions go, there was something delicious about it. It was a real binge, like switching to chocolate after a diet of whole wheat bread."

Frederick Hollander and Leo Robin wrote two songs for *Desire,* but only one was used. "Awake in a Dream" is sung by Dietrich at a piano. "Whispers in the Dark," not used, was later re-vamped for Paramount's *Artists and Models.*

I Loved a Soldier

A Paramount Picture (Never completed)—1936

CAST: *In the order hired*: MARLENE DIETRICH, CHARLES BOYER, AKIM TAMIROFF, WALTER CATLETT, PAUL LUKAS, VICTOR KILLIAN, SAMUEL S. HINDS, TED OLIVER, NESTER ABER, SIEGFRIED RUMANN, LIONEL STANDER, JOHN MILJAN, HARRY CORDING, BRANDON EVANS, BOB KORTMAN, ROBERT MIDDLEMASS, FRED KOHLER, SAM JAFFE, MICHAEL MARK.

CREDITS: HENRY HATHAWAY (*Director*); BENJAMIN GLAZER (*Producer*); JOHN VAN DRUTEN (*Scenarist*); CHARLES LANG (*Photographer*); HARRY MILLS (*Sound Recorder*); Additional Dialogue and re-writes, GROVER JONES; Based on a play by MELCHIOR LENGYELL; Translated from Hungarian by ALICE DE SOOS.

NOTES: Hollywood has had its disasters (unfin-ished films abandoned for one reason or another; completed films shelved and forgotten), but few have cost as much as this picture. A Dietrich picture at Paramount always commanded a full-scale budget.

The weeks of planning that went into this pro-duction had already put the cost up. Location shoot-ing began on January 3, 1936, at Triunfo, with co-star Charles Boyer. The film at that time was entitled *Invitation to Happiness*. Four days later, with the title now *I Loved a Soldier*, producer Benjamin Glazer withdrew after a row with Dietrich over the script. He later told Lubitsch that he "would not supervise a story over which the star was given so much authority." Dietrich's association with von

With director Henry Hathaway on the set

Sternberg was the main reason for one of the most stringent contracts in Hollywood. She had script approval and was fully exercising her rights.

Lubitsch then began to supervise the picture, which was "shooting around" Miss Dietrich while director Henry Hathaway and scenarist Grover Jones revamped the John Van Druten screenplay. But soon Lubitsch left for Europe on a three-month jaunt, and William Le Baron became head of production at Paramount.

Dietrich and Le Baron never saw eye to eye and on February 11, 1936 (after 28 days of recorded shooting time), she walked out for good! The money spent up to that date was a cool $900,000.

Margaret Sullavan was borrowed from Universal in mid-March to co-star with Boyer. The title was now back to the original *Hotel Imperial,* the title of the story from which the film was adapted. Shooting began, and Stuart Erwin was added to the cast.

After three days shooting Margaret Sullavan tripped over a light cable, fell and broke both bones of her left forearm after being chased around the set by Erwin between "takes." This caused more delays, and the cost was rapidly approaching the $1,000,000 mark.

By this time *Hotel Imperial* was known as "Paramount's jinx picture," and in a desperate move, Paramount executives tried successively to get Bette Davis, Elissa Landi, and Claudette Colbert, but all were tied up.

In 1939 Paramount released a fully re-shot version of *Hotel Imperial* with Ray Milland and the lovely Isa Miranda. Miss Miranda, it was more than casually noted, bore a fantastic resemblance to Dietrich and had been directed in much the same manner. Her Hollywood career, alas, was short-lived.

Hotel Imperial had been previously filmed in 1927, starring Pola Negri.

The Garden of Allah

A Selznick-International Picture in Technicolor:

Released through United Artists—1936

CAST: MARLENE DIETRICH (*Domini Enfilden*); CHARLES BOYER (*Boris Androvsky*); BASIL RATHBONE (*Count Anteoni*); C. AUBREY SMITH (*Father Roubier*); TILLY LOSCH (*Irena*); JOSEPH SCHILDKRAUT (*Batouch*); JOHN CARRADINE (*sand diviner*); ALAN MARSHALL (*De Trevignac*); LUCILLE WATSON (*Mother Superior*); HENRY BRANDON (*Hadj*); HELEN JEROME EDDY (*a nun*); CHARLES WALDRON (*the Abbé*); JOHN BRYAN (*Brother Gregory*); NIGEL DE BRULIER (*the Lector*); PEDRO DE CORDOBA (*gardener*); FERDINAND GOTTSCHALK (*hotel clerk*); ADRIAN ROSELY (*Mustapha*); "CORKY" (*Bous-Bous*); ROBERT FRAZER (*Smain*); DAVID SCOTT (*Larby*); ANDREW McKENNA (*Mueddin*); BONITA GRANVILLE, MARCIA MAE JONES, BETTY JANE GRAHAM and ANN GILLIS (*children in convent*); MARION SAYERS, BETTY VAN AUKEN, EDNA HARRIS and FRANCES TURNHAM (*oasis girls*); LEONID KINSKY (*voluble Arab*); LOUIS ALDEZ (*blind singer*); BARRY DOWNING (*Little Boris*); JANE KERR (*Ouled Nails madam*); RUSSELL POWELL (*Ouled Nails proprietor*); ERIC ALDEN (*Anteoni's lieutenant*); MICHAEL MARK (*coachman*) HARLAN BRIGGS (*American tourist*); IRENE FRANKLIN (*wife*); LOUIS MERCIER, MARCEL DE LA BROSSE and ROBERT STEVENSON (*De Trevignac's patrol*).

CREDITS: RICHARD BOLESLAWSKI (*Director*); DAVID O. SELZNICK (*Producer*); W. P. LIPSCOMB, LYNN RIGGS (*Scenarists*); W. HOWARD GREENE (*Photographer*) HAROLD ROSSON (*Photographic Advisor*); MAX STEINER (*Musical Score*); LANSING C. HOLDEN (*Production Designer*); STURGES CARNE, LYLE WHEELER and EDWARD BOYLE (*Art Directors*); ERNST DRYDEN (*Costumer*); HAL C. KERN, ANSON STEVENSON (*Editors*); WILLIS GOLDBECK (*Producer's Assistant*); EARL A. WOLCOTT (*Sound Recorder*); JACK COSGROVE (*Special Effects*); ERIC STACEY (*Assistant Director*); NATALIE KALMUS (*Color Supervisor*); From the novel by ROBERT HICHENS.

SYNOPSIS: After the death of her father, Domini Enfilden (Marlene Dietrich), who had spent her formative years nursing him, decides to embark on a new life and is encouraged by her friend and confidant Mother Josephine (Lucille Watson) to seek peace in the Algerian desert.

With C. Aubrey Smith, Charles Boyer, Henry Brandon, and Joseph Schildkraut

With Charles Boyer

On the train that brings her to the desert city of Beni-Mora, Domini meets the brooding Boris Androvsky (Charles Boyer), who is actually Brother Antoine, a monk from the Trappist monastery of El Lagarni near Tunis. He has fled his order, thus breaking his vows to the horror of his fellow monks and a young French officer Captain de Trevignac (Alan Marshall) visiting the monastery at the time.

Although Boris is rude to Domini on the train, in Beni-Mora, the parish of the Mother Superior's friend Father Roubier (C. Aubrey Smith), their paths cross again. Domini senses in his behavior a great sorrow.

Domini hires a guide, Batouch (Joseph Schild-

With John Carradine and Basil Rathbone

kraut), and he and his brother Hadj (Henry Brandon) take her to see the Ouled-Nail dancing girls. One of the dancers, the fiery Irena (Tilly Losch), tries to stab Hadj and in the riot that ensues, Boris, also there for an evening's entertainment, rescues Domini. From this moment on, a bond is formed between them which develops into friendship and then love.

A friend, Count Anteoni (Basil Rathbone), takes Domini to the bazaar where a sand diviner (John Carradine) predicts a trip, a great happiness—and then suddenly stops and will not continue.

Soon after this evil omen, Father Roubier performs the wedding ceremony uniting Domini and Boris, and off into the desert the couple go on their honeymoon.

With Alan Marshal

With Charles Boyer

With Charles Boyer

At their honeymoon encampment a small group of soldiers on patrol, led by Captain de Trevignac, who have lost their way, happen upon them. It doesn't take long for the young officer to remember Boris. Eventually Domini learns of her husband's strange secret, which has acted like a barrier between them from the start.

Together the lovers decide that he must make his sin right with God. Sadly, Domini leaves him at the gate of the monastery and departs forever.

NOTES: Dietrich returned to the desert in *The Garden of Allah,* and she did so in the perfected three-color Technicolor process. Her beauty was accentuated by the white of her garments contrasting with the browns and plain colors of the desert locales. Vivid colors in the form of scarfs, veils, and other accessories provided accent notes. Producer David O. Selznick pulled the stopper out of the budget and moved his entire company to the Mohave desert, with headquarters in Yuma, Arizona.

W. Howard Greene and Harold Rosson won Academy Awards for their exquisite color photography, while composer Max Steiner and assistant director Eric Stacey received Academy Award nominations.

One would think that the 1904 novel by Robert Hichens (which had been adapted for the stage in 1911 and filmed by Metro-Goldwyn-Mayer in 1927 with Alice Terry) would be out of date, but the script by W. P. Lipscomb and Lynn Riggs held prewar audiences fascinated by its fatalism. And there was excitement, grandeur, and beauty—with a splendid musical score by Max Steiner to set the mood.

John McManus in *The New York Times* found *The Garden of Allah* "a distinguished motion picture rich in pictorial splendor . . . engrossingly acted."

One critic complained that Dietrich was still just a monosyllabic clothes-horse," while the *Herald Tribune* thought "the tale itself remains one in which romantic and religious fervor are substitutes for dramatic urgency, but it is acted sensitively and at times brilliantly by Marlene Dietrich, Charles Boyer, and an able supporting company."

The *Literary Digest* called it "the cinema's most astute and tasteful use of natural color photography to date," while *Newsweek* happily reported that "Dietrich and Boyer achieve the finest performances of their careers. . . . Color is written into the picture with the same care as the dialogue."

With Austin Trevor

Knight Without Armour

An Alexander Korda-London Films Presentation

Released through United Artists—1937

CAST: MARLENE DIETRICH (*Alexandra*); ROBERT DONAT (*A. J. Fotheringill*); IRENE VANBURGH (*Duchess*); HERBERT LOMAS (*Vladinoff*); AUSTIN TREVOR (*Colonel Adraxine*); BASIL GILL (*Axelstein*); DAVID TREE (*Maronin*); JOHN CLEMENTS (*Poushkoff*); FREDERICK CULLEY (*Stanfield*); LAWRENCE HANRAY (*Forrester*); DORICE FORDRED (*maid*); FRANKLIN KELSEY (*Tomsky*); LAWRENCE KINGSTON (*commissar*); HAY PETRIE (*station master*); MILES MALLESON (*drunken Red soldier*); LYN HARDING (*bargeman*); RAYMOND HUNTLEY (*White officer*); PETER EVAN THOMAS (*General Andreyevitch*).

CREDITS: JACQUES FEYDER (*Director*); ALEXANDER KORDA (*Producer*); LAJOS BIRO, ARTHUR WIMPERIS (*Scenarists*); FRANCES MARION (*Adaptation*); HARRY STRADLING (*Photographer*); JACK CARDIFF (*Camera Operator*); LAZARE MEERSON (*Settings*); GEORGE BENDA (*Costumer*); MIKLOS ROSZA (*Musical Score*); MUIR MATHESON (*Musical Director*); NED MANN (*Special Effects*); FRANCIS LYON (*Editor*); A. W. WATKINS (*Recording Director*); ROMAN GOUL (*Technical Adviser*); IMLAY WATTS (*Assistant Director*); From *Without Armour* by JAMES HILTON.

SYNOPSIS: A. J. Fotheringill (Robert Donat), a young Englishman living in pre-war St. Petersburg

With Dorice Fordred

as a translator, writes an article which offends the Imperial system and is given forty-eight hours to leave the country. He asks advice of a close friend (Frederick Culley) and learns that his friend is actually a British Secret Service agent. He is then commissioned by him to take the identity of Peter Ouranov and contact members of the revolutionary movement in a bookshop owned by a man named Axelstein (Basil Gill).

The Englishman mingles with various revolutionaries. One of them is wounded while attempting an assassination plot on the Minister of the Interior (Herbert Lomas) en route to the wedding of his daughter, Countess Alexandra (Marlene Dietrich), and Colonel Adraxine (Austin Trevor). The young revolutionary dies in Fotheringill's apartment and with Axelstein he is exiled to Siberia.

Meanwhile, the Revolution begins, and the Red

With Robert Donat

Army overcomes the Imperial household. Countess Alexandra, soon a widow, leaves for her summer palace at Khalinsk.

A year of bloody revolution ensues, and finally the Reds deliver Fotheringill and Axelstein from exile, and elect Axelstein the Commissar of Khalinsk. He makes Fotheringill his assistant. Khalinsk now under Red control, forces Axelstein to have the Countess placed under arrest and sent to Petrograd for examination, with Fotheringill accompanying her as escort. Disguised as peasants, they arrive at the village of Saratursk, which has been recaptured by the White Army. Fotheringill leaves Alexandra there with friends. However, soon the Red Army has again captured it back. Fotheringill, now in command of

prisoners, helps Alexandra escape to the woods, disguised as a Red soldier. Here they discover their love for each other, and the following day they endeavor to get to the border together.

They are taken off the train at Kazan, where Alexandra is suspected. She is saved by a former servant's loyalty in refusing to identify her. Alexandra is temporarily released, pending further examination at Samara.

The couple then board a train for Samara under the escort of a young Red named Poushkoff (John Clements), who quickly falls in love with the Countess, but shoots himself rather than give her up to the Reds, once he discovers her identity.

In the excitement, Fotheringill and Alexandra

With John Clements (official) and Robert Donat

134

escape and make their way to the river, where an old bargeman agrees to take them to Saratov. At Saratov, Alexandra is near collapse. Fotheringill seeks a doctor, but, during his absence, White soldiers happen along, accompanied by doctors from the American Hospital, and take Alexandra to the hospital. Upon his return, the Englishman finds her gone and rushes back to town. Here he is arrested by White soldiers but escapes to the neutral zone of the American Hospital. He learns that Alexandra is on a train about to depart for the border. In the film's closing moments, he boards the train as it pulls out of the station.

NOTES: This ambitious Alexander Korda picture beautifully depicted the chaotic period in Russia during the 1917 Revolution. The various political intrigues and rapid changes of power provided many dramatic flights for the stars of this film to take. There were tragic war sequences, exemplifying its utter futility, and while episodic in form and slowly paced and overlong, *Knight Without Armour* was exceedingly well directed by Jacques Feyder. The *New York World-Telegram's* critic noticed: "Not only has Miss Dietrich never looked more beautiful, but she makes the Countess a real and understandable human being."

Life, however, pointed out that "for taking . . . two baths, revealing her beautiful legs, and shedding a hollow-cheeked glamour through 9,000 feet of British film, she got $450,000. This makes her, on a job basis, the highest paid woman in the world." Quite a change for the young actress who, ten years earlier, had worked under Korda's direction in *Eine DuBarry von Heute* and *Madame Wünscht Keine Kinder.*

With Robert Donat

Filming had only begun on *Knight Without Armour* when co-star Robert Donat was stricken with a serious asthmatic attack, and Korda informed Dietrich that the actor would not be able to work for at least a month. He suggested that his role be minimized and re-cast with a lesser-known British actor, with Miss Dietrich assuming single star billing. She refused. Shooting continued for that month with every scene that didn't require Donat's presence. This was a smart move on Dietrich's part, as well as a humane one, since the chemistry between her and Donat was extraordinary.

With Robert Donat

Angel

A Paramount Picture—1937

CAST: MARLENE DIETRICH (*Maria Barker*); HERBERT MARSHALL (*Sir Frederick Barker*); MELVYN DOUGLAS (*Anthony Halton*); EDWARD EVERETT HORTON (*Graham*); ERNEST COSSART (*Walton*); LAURA HOPE CREWS (*Grand Duchess Anna Dmitrievna*); HERBERT MUNDIN (*Greenwood*); IVAN LEBEDEFF (*Prince Vladimir Gregorovitch*); DENNIE MOORE (*Emma*); LIONEL PAPE (*Lord Davington*); PHILLIS COGHLAN (*maid, the Barker home*); LEONARD CAREY (*first footman*); ERIC WILTON (*English chauffeur*); GERALD HAMER (*second footman*); HERBERT EVANS (*butler*); MICHAEL S. VISAROFF (*Russian butler*); OLAF HYTTEN (*photographer*); GWENDOLYN LOGAN (*woman with Maria*); JAMES FINLAYSON (*second butler*); GEORGE DAVIS (*taxi driver*); ARTHUR HURNI (*taxi driver*); JOSEPH ROMANTINI (*headwaiter*); DUCI KEREKJARTO (*prima violinist*); SUZANNE KAAREN (*girl who gambles*); LOUISE CARTER (*flower woman*).

CREDITS: ERNST LUBITSCH (*Director and Producer*); SAMSON RAPHAELSON (*Scenarist*); CHARLES LANG (*Photographer*); TRAVIS BANTON (*Costumer*); FARCIOT EDOUART (*Special Effects*); FREDERICK HOLLANDER (*Musical Score*); BORIS MORROS (*Musical Director*);

With Ernest Cossart and Herbert Marshall

With Melvyn Douglas

HANS DREIER, ROBERT USHER (*Art Directors*); WILLIAM SHEA (*Editor*); HARRY MILLS, LOUIS MESENKOP (*Sound*); JOSEPH LEFERT (*Assistant Director*); Based on a play by MELCHIOR LENGYEL; English play adaptation by GUY BOLTON, RUSSELL MEDCRAFT.
SONG: *By* FREDERICK HOLLANDER and LEO ROBIN; "Angel."

SYNOPSIS: Maria Barker (Marlene Dietrich), the neglected wife of a titled Englishman, Sir Frederick Barker (Herbert Marshall), goes on a secret trip to Paris for an adventure. When there, she visits her friend from the old days, the Grand Duchess Anna Dmitrievna (Laura Hope Crews), who runs a high-class haven for sophisticates.

Also visiting the Duchess' establishment for the first time is a young American named Anthony Halton (Melvyn Douglas), who spots Maria in one of the private sitting rooms and immediately be-

With Melvyn Douglas and Joseph Romantini

comes interested in her. Maria, out for a good time, agrees to his advances and together they see Paris and have an intimate dinner together. Maria refuses to give Halton her name, so he dubs her "Angel." Theirs is a happy time together, perhaps too happy; for like Cinderella, Maria disappears completely when she feels their relationship becoming too serious, and journeys home.

A few weeks later Maria and Sir Frederick, who is a delegate to the League of Nations, attend the races at Epsom Downs, where Maria nearly runs into Anthony Halton but flees before he sees her. Halton, still unaware of her identity, spots Sir Frederick almost at the same moment, and he approaches. It seems they were in the war together and have many old memories to discuss.

Sir Frederick invites his "old buddy" to dine with him and meet his wife. Suddenly Halton is face-to-face with his "Angel."

Later Sir Frederick finds out about her secret trip to Paris. When she takes another, he follows her. There she has a rendezvous with Halton. Now Maria must make a decision between her husband, who loves her deeply, and is suddenly aroused because of the ardent lover, and Halton, who says he too loves her. She returns to her husband.

NOTES: Ernst Lubitsch's particular brand of sophisticated humor and polish made this a stunning production *visually,* but not even his "touches" could speed up the tempo of this old potboiler. This is probably Dietrich's worst picture of the thirties. Her performance was adequate, but her leading men were too similar—sophisticated gentlemen of grace, breeding and polish. One of them should have been the rugged, ordinary type that always seemed to bring out the best in Marlene!

The best feature of *Angel* is the musical score by Frederick Hollander. His title song set the mood and freed the audience, if only temporarily, from a very dull script. The settings of Hans Dreier added lustre, as did the acting of Laura Hope Crews as a high-class madam. Dietrich's scenes with her were supercharged and crisply played.

Variety noted that "Miss Dietrich is glamour in double dress. This time she is wearing eyelashes you could hang your hat on, and every now and then the star flicks 'em as though a dust storm was getting in her way." *Time* said, "Ernst Lubitsch has sustained a romantic mood, a subdued shimmery elegance of playing. . . . with Dietrich beautiful in clothes nobody else would dare to wear."

The *Literary Digest,* on the other hand, found

With Herbert Marshall and Melvyn Douglas

Angel "very sophisticated, very subtle, very chic, vastly polished and entertaining."

Frank Nugent in *The New York Times* had nothing good to say, but was explicit just the same. "Unfortunately, Miss Dietrich is at the root of its [*Angel's*] evils. She still is a lovely lady, glamorously gowned, but she has the unhappy gift of absorbing the camera's attention to the exclusion of the other members of her company. Of the narrative itself, the film comes to a full stop every time she raises or lowers the artificially elongated Dietrich eyelids—and she hoists them up and down at one-minute intervals like the strong man handling a 1,000-pound weight in a sideshow. And, after looking deeply and frequently into the liquid hollows of her eyes, we begin to agree with Schopenhauer that women are sphinxes without riddles."

Howard Barnes in the *New York Herald Tribune* mentioned that "The production is performed with studied deliberation. Miss Dietrich is as hauntingly beautiful as ever . . . but . . . there is scarcely a sequence in which one is not conscious that she is more aware of camera angles than the vitalizing of an intriguing character."

With director Ernst Lubitsch

Destry Rides Again

A Universal Picture—1939

CAST: MARLENE DIETRICH (*Frenchy*); JAMES STEWART (*Tom Destry*); CHARLES WINNINGER (*Wash Dimsdale*); MISCHA AUER (*Boris Callahan*); BRIAN DONLEVY (*Kent*); IRENE HERVEY (*Janice Tyndall*); UNA MERKEL (*Lilybelle Callahan*); ALLEN JENKINS (*Bugs Watson*); WARREN HYMER (*Gyp Watson*); SAMUEL S. HINDS (*Hiram J. Slade*); JACK CARSON (*Jack Tyndall*); LILLIAN YARBO (*Clara*); TOM FADDEN (*Lem Claggett*); DICKIE JONES (*Eli Whitney Claggett*); VIRGINIA BRISSAC (*Ma Claggett*); JOE KING (*Sheriff Keogh*).

CREDITS: GEORGE MARSHALL (*Director*); JOE PASTERNAK (*Producer*); FELIX JACKSON, HENRY MEYERS and GERTRUDE PURCELL (*Scenarists*); HAL MOHR (*Photographer*); VERA WEST (*Miss Dietrich's Costumes*); JACK OTTERSON (*Art Director*); CHARLES PREVIN (*Musical Director*); FRANK SKINNER (*Musical Score*); MILTON CARRUTH (*Editor*); BERNARD B. BROWN (*Sound Supervisor*); VERNON KEAYS (*Assistant Director*); Based on the novel by MAX BRAND.

SONGS: *By* FREDERICK HOLLANDER and FRANK LOESSER, "Little Joe the Wrangler," "You've Got That Look (That Leaves Me Weak)," "The Boys in the Back Room."

SYNOPSIS: A suave gambler named Kent (Brian

With Allen Jenkins, Samuel S. Hinds, Warren Hymer, Charles Winninger, and Brian Donlevy

Donlevy) runs the lawless frontier town of Bottle Neck, utilizing the services of his barroom entertainer, Frenchy (Marlene Dietrich), to cheat suckers like Lem Claggett (Tom Fadden) out of their ranches so that he can collect a tariff on all cattle driven through.

When Sheriff Keogh (Joe King) learns that Claggett has been cheated at cards, he tries to enforce the law but is shot, and in the commotion the Mayor of Bottle Neck, Hiram J. Slade (Samuel S. Hinds), informs the patrons of the Last Chance Saloon that

With James Stewart

With Una Merkel

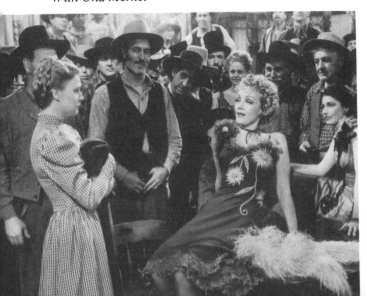

the sheriff has gone out of town. He and Kent appoint Wash Dimsdale (Charles Winninger), the town drunk, as the new sheriff. Wash, once deputy to the famous lawman Thomas Jefferson Destry, suddenly reforms and sends for his old pal's son Tom (James Stewart) to come to Bottle Neck as his deputy.

The mild-mannered Mr. Destry arrives by stagecoach with Janice Tyndall (Irene Hervey) and her headstrong brother Jack (Jack Carson), a cattleman. Wash introduces Tom to the townsfolk in the Last Chance Saloon, and when Kent tries to take Tom's guns away from him, they learn that he

141

Frenchy grabs a gun and begins firing, finally chasing Destry out of the saloon.

The town thinks Destry is too mild a deputy to be a threat to Kent's gang, but he nevertheless attempts to clean up Bottle Neck by looking for Sheriff Keogh's body. He swears in Boris Callahan (Mischa Auer), Lilybelle's husband, to find the late sheriff's body, and Destry tricks one of Kent's men, Bugs Watson (Allen Jenkins), into showing Boris where the body is. Meanwhile, Kent and his men break Bugs out of jail and Sheriff Dimsdale is killed.

Destry lines up the good townspeople to fight the gang, and Frenchy, now on Destry's side, organizes the women to help save their men from being shot to death as they march down the middle of the street into the saloon. Kent goes after Destry in the crowded saloon and fires at him, but Frenchy, seeing him about to fire, blocks the bullet with her body and slumps to the floor and dies. Destry then kills Kent.

With the town cleaned up and new settlers arriving daily, Tom Destry can look toward a bright future with pretty Janice Tyndall.

NOTES: "Westerns," director George Marshall once said, "have more elements of audience appeal than any other type of motion picture." How very true!

doesn't carry any. Frenchy hands the new deputy a mop and pail to help clean up Bottle Neck.

Suddenly, Lilybelle Callahan (Una Merkel) bursts into the saloon, demanding back her husband's pants, which Frenchy had won playing cards. A slam-bang fight ensues, with both ladies pulling hair and kicking each other, until Destry, still holding the pail in his hands, pours water over both of them.

With James Stewart and Una Merkel

For in *Destry Rides Again* Marshall gave us a rowdy western saga with plenty of blood-and-thunder punctuated by slapstick comedy, giving an overall "true spirit of the old west." At times the storyline was a serious narrative; at others a burlesque of the period. There was music, comedy, drama, and melodrama to suit every taste, and the action never flagged.

After *Angel,* exhibitors around the country had labelled Dietrich "box office poison." She left for Europe, and in 1938 was to appear in *The Image* for Julian Duvivier in Paris, but nothing came of this venture. Then she got the transatlantic call from Joe Pasternak seeking her services for a *western!* Her salary was a mere $75,000, but this film did more for her career than her last five pictures put together!

Variety, in 1939, revealed that Dietrich had replaced Paulette Goddard, Universal's first choice as Frenchy!

Destry Rides Again was turning point No. 2 in the career of Marlene Dietrich. Her hard-boiled dance hall girl (with a heart of gold) allowed her for the first time to display great flair and comic verve. Her Frenchy was tempestuous, wild, vivacious, wicked, wonderful!

There was one censorship problem and that was eliminated after the preview showings. In the poker sequence Dietrich takes some gold coins and drops them down her dress, and one of the men says, "There's gold in them thar hills!" The action remained, but the line was cut!

Casting James Stewart opposite her was sheer genius, as was the care that went into selecting the

With James Stewart

supporting cast. All were superb in their assignments. Although filmed before (by Tom Mix) and since (by Audie Murphy), this is the classic *Destry* of all time. And Dietrich was again on top of the heap!

With James Stewart

With Mischa Auer and Broderick Crawford

Seven Sinners

A Universal Picture—1940

CAST: MARLENE DIETRICH (*Bijou*); JOHN WAYNE (*Bruce*); BRODERICK CRAWFORD (*Little Ned*); MISCHA AUER (*Sasha*); ALBERT DEKKER (*Dr. Martin*); BILLY GILBERT (*Tony*); OSCAR HOMOLKA (*Antro*); ANNA LEE (*Dorothy*); SAMUEL S. HINDS (*Governor*); REGINALD DENNY (*Captain Church*); VINCE BARNETT (*bartender*); HERBERT RAWLINSON (*first mate*); JAMES CRAIG (*ensign*); WILLIAM BAKEWELL (*ensign*); ANTONIO MORENO (*Rubio*); RUSSELL HICKS (*first governor*); WILLIAM DAVIDSON (*police chief*); RICHARD CARLE (*district officer*); WILLIE FUNG (*shopkeeper*).

CREDITS: TAY GARNETT (*Director*); JOE PASTERNAK (*Producer*); JOHN MEEHAN, HARRY TUGEND (*Scenarists*); RUDOLPH MATE (*Photographer*); JACK OTTERSON (*Art Director*); *Miss Dietrich's costumes by* IRENE; VERA WEST (*Costumer*); FRANK SKINNER (*Musical Score*); CHARLES PREVIN (*Musical Director*); BERNARD B. BROWN (*Sound Supervisor*); Based on a story by LADISLAUS FODOR and LAZLO VADNAL.

SONGS: *By* FREDERICK HOLLANDER and FRANK LOESSER; "I've Been in Love Before," "I Fall Overboard," "The Man's in the Navy."

144

SYNOPSIS: Bijou (Marlene Dietrich), the toast of every gin-joint in the South Seas, is a torch singer who breeds trouble wherever she goes. The cabaret she has just sung in has been completely demolished by its patrons, and now she is being deported by a highly nervous Governor (Russell Hicks). With her are her constant companions, who always seem to suffer the same fate at the same time—Little Ned (Broderick Crawford) a lovable, empty-headed ex-sailor who has yearned for the Navy ever since he missed his ship in Singapore, and Sascha (Mischa Auer), a part-time magician, part-time pickpocket who can't keep his hands off other people's goods.

This trio boards the first lugger to leave the island. The ship's doctor, Dr. Martin (Albert Dekker) falls for Bijou in a big way, but his drinking habit reminds her of unpleasant days and she ignores him. In the hold of the ship Bijou, sitting with Little Ned and Sascha among crates of chickens, sings "I've Been in Love Before" as the first-class passengers watch from above. One of them, a young lady named Dorothy Henderson (Anna Lee), throws a coin down in appreciation of the song. Bijou is offended and stops.

Later, Bijou is checking a map of the South Sea islands, looking for one she hasn't been thrown off

With Albert Dekker

(with no success), when Dr. Martin tells her that Dorothy Henderson didn't mean to insult her. He tells her that she is the daughter of the *new* Governor (Samuel S. Hinds) of Boni-Komba, where the lugger is heading first! Bijou is elated, since it was three years ago that she was deported by Boni-Komba, and it would be great fun singing at Tony's 7 Sinners Café again.

Arriving at Boni-Komba, Bijou meets Bruce, a handsome naval officer (John Wayne), who helps her over a herd of sheep and then proceeds to meet Dorothy and escort her to the Naval Base for a tour, and then on to the Governor's mansion.

Bijou, with Little Ned and Sascha, arrives at the 7 Sinners Café and talks Tony (Billy Gilbert) into hiring her again, although he knows what will happen the minute he does. One person Bijou doesn't count on meeting on Boni-Komba is Antro (Oscar Homolka), an unpleasant reminder of shady dealings in the past.

At the official reception for Dorothy that evening, every ensign makes a fast exit, and finally Dorothy asks Bruce why he too doesn't go to the 7 Sinners Café to attend Bijou's opening.

At the café, Bruce bursts in and begins dressing down the junior officers for leaving the reception, before he realizes that he is interrupting Bijou's sen-

With William Davidson and Oscar Homolka

sational number, "The Man's in the Navy." She continues the song, clad in a U. S. Navy uniform, to the delight of the boys. Bruce falls for Bijou and arranges for her to be invited to sing at a party the men of his ship are throwing the following week. Governor Henderson asks Tony, unofficially, to take Bijou off the entertainment list, but Tony is again wrapped around Bijou's finger and she appears anyway.

The officers and men are in seventh heaven with Bijou's number but the ladies are most distressed. Governor Henderson asks Captain Church (Reginold Denny) to see that she leaves the ship. The captain tells Bruce to take Bijou home. After spending an evening with her, Bruce has almost decided to quit the Navy. Governor Henderson, meanwhile, informs Bijou that Bruce loves her and asks her to leave him alone. He threatens deportation. Little Ned hears that Bruce may leave the Navy for Bijou and slaps her around, telling her how horrible it is for a Navy man to be on land. Bijou is convinced and decides to leave the island—but not before she sings another song. The place is jammed, and a tremendous fight breaks out. In the confusion Tony is stabbed by Antro, who was aiming for Bruce.

Little Ned is back in the Navy, thanks to Bruce, and Bijou and Sascha are off to another island.

When boarding, Dr. Martin warmly greets her. Bijou notices that he has stopped his drinking, and as the ship pulls out of the harbor, the future looks bright for them both.

NOTES: Universal, having created a "new Dietrich" with *Destry Rides Again,* was prepared to cash in on a good thing. What they hadn't counted on was giving Dietrich a role that was to become one of her best! *Seven Sinners,* an action-packed, two-fisted melodrama, had wide appeal, and Dietrich's Bijou Blanche is a gorgeous satire on the Sadie Thompsons of the world.

Irene designed some of the wildest creations ever put on a woman's back. But since Marlene was never known to conform to any set pattern of feminine garb, these dresses and accessories had a life all their own. The black-and-white patchwork quilt get-up was a riot of bad taste, to say nothing of her rings, bracelets, cigarette holder (loaded with jewels), and the inevitable feathers! The most simple outfit was the shapeless Navy ensign's uniform, which Dietrich filled out in all the wrong places, giving it another dimension indeed!

John Wayne and the entire supporting cast played with verve. The production values were typical Universal—excellent sets, photography and musical score (by Frank Skinner, later to be used for the *Don Winslow of the Navy* serial).

Seven Sinners was also a stuntman's paradise. The stunt work in the opening fight over which the credits are shown contained some of the best work in that little-known field. Stuntman David Sharpe

With John Wayne

escape and make their way to the river, where an old bargeman agrees to take them to Saratov. At Saratov, Alexandra is near collapse. Fotheringill seeks a doctor, but, during his absence, White soldiers happen along, accompanied by doctors from the American Hospital, and take Alexandra to the hospital. Upon his return, the Englishman finds her gone and rushes back to town. Here he is arrested by White soldiers but escapes to the neutral zone of the American Hospital. He learns that Alexandra is on a train about to depart for the border. In the film's closing moments, he boards the train as it pulls out of the station.

NOTES: This ambitious Alexander Korda picture beautifully depicted the chaotic period in Russia during the 1917 Revolution. The various political intrigues and rapid changes of power provided many dramatic flights for the stars of this film to take. There were tragic war sequences, exemplifying its utter futility, and while episodic in form and slowly paced and overlong, *Knight Without Armour* was exceedingly well directed by Jacques Feyder. The *New York World-Telegram's* critic noticed: "Not only has Miss Dietrich never looked more beautiful, but she makes the Countess a real and understandable human being."

Life, however, pointed out that "for taking . . . two baths, revealing her beautiful legs, and shedding a hollow-cheeked glamour through 9,000 feet of British film, she got $450,000. This makes her, on a job basis, the highest paid woman in the world." Quite a change for the young actress who, ten years earlier, had worked under Korda's direction in *Eine DuBarry von Heute* and *Madame Wünscht Keine Kinder.*

With Robert Donat

Filming had only begun on *Knight Without Armour* when co-star Robert Donat was stricken with a serious asthmatic attack, and Korda informed Dietrich that the actor would not be able to work for at least a month. He suggested that his role be minimized and re-cast with a lesser-known British actor, with Miss Dietrich assuming single star billing. She refused. Shooting continued for that month with every scene that didn't require Donat's presence. This was a smart move on Dietrich's part, as well as a humane one, since the chemistry between her and Donat was extraordinary.

With Robert Donat

135

Angel

A Paramount Picture—1937

CAST: MARLENE DIETRICH (*Maria Barker*); HERBERT MARSHALL (*Sir Frederick Barker*); MELVYN DOUGLAS (*Anthony Halton*); EDWARD EVERETT HORTON (*Graham*); ERNEST COSSART (*Walton*); LAURA HOPE CREWS (*Grand Duchess Anna Dmitrievna*); HERBERT MUNDIN (*Greenwood*); IVAN LEBEDEFF (*Prince Vladimir Gregorovitch*); DENNIE MOORE (*Emma*); LIONEL PAPE (*Lord Davington*); PHILLIS COGHLAN (*maid, the Barker home*); LEONARD CAREY (*first footman*); ERIC WILTON (*English chauffeur*); GERALD HAMER (*second footman*); HERBERT EVANS (*butler*); MICHAEL S. VISAROFF (*Russian butler*); OLAF HYTTEN (*photographer*); GWENDOLYN LOGAN (*woman with Maria*); JAMES FINLAYSON (*second butler*); GEORGE DAVIS (*taxi driver*); ARTHUR HURNI (*taxi driver*); JOSEPH ROMANTINI (*headwaiter*); DUCI KEREKJARTO (*prima violinist*); SUZANNE KAAREN (*girl who gambles*); LOUISE CARTER (*flower woman*).

CREDITS: ERNST LUBITSCH (*Director and Producer*); SAMSON RAPHAELSON (*Scenarist*); CHARLES LANG (*Photographer*); TRAVIS BANTON (*Costumer*); FARCIOT EDOUART (*Special Effects*); FREDERICK HOLLANDER (*Musical Score*); BORIS MORROS (*Musical Director*);

With Ernest Cossart and Herbert Marshall

was chiefly responsible for the superior work in the six-minute fight which climaxed Bijou's existence on Boni-Komba. For sheer fun this film can be enjoyed over and over again.

The Frederick Hollander-Frank Loesser songs were top-notch too. "I've Been In Love Before (Haven't You?)" has been recorded often by Dietrich and is today a standard with disc jockeys around the country. The marvelous "The Man's in the Navy" has to be seen and heard to be appreciated. Dietrich's throaty voice gave it just the interpretation it needed.

Bosley Crowther in *The New York Times* said, "Miss Dietrich's Frenchy in *Destry* was an Arno sketch of countless sultry barroom belles; her Bijou Blanche in *Seven Sinners* is a delightfully subtle spoof of all the Sadie Thompsons and Singapore Sals that have stirred the hot blood of cool customers south and east of Manila Bay. If Miss Dietrich and her comedies were just both a little broader, Mae West would be in the shade."

Howard Barnes in the *New York Herald Tribune* stated, "Marlene Dietrich comes into her own again in *Seven Sinners*. . . . Here you will find the tough, glamorous, eloquent demi-mondaine of *The Blue Angel*. If anything, she is even better than she was in that original triumph. Forgetting all the svelte mannerisms which made her one of the screen's most wooden actresses for a number of years, she cuts loose in *Seven Sinners* with a perfect impersonation of a high-class slattern. It's a fine performance in a stunning romantic melodrama of the South Seas and the Navy."

With Billy Gilbert

The Flame of New Orleans

A Universal Picture—1941

CAST: Marlene Dietrich (*Claire Ledeux*); Bruce Cabot (*Robert Latour*); Roland Young (*Charles Giraud*); Mischa Auer (*Zolotov*); Andy Devine (*first sailor*); Frank Jenks (*second sailor*); Eddie Quillan (*third sailor*); Laura Hope Crews (*Auntie*); Franklin Pangborn (*Bellows*); Theresa Harris (*Clementine*); Clarence Muse (*Samuel*); Melville Cooper (*brother-in-law*); Anne Revere (*sister*); Bob Evans (*Williams*); Emily Fitzroy, Virginia Sale, and Dorothy Adams (*cousins*); Anthony Marlowe (*opera singer*); Gitta Alpar (*opera singer*); with Gus Schilling, Bess Flowers and Reed Hadley.

CREDITS: Rene Clair (*Director*); Joe Pasternak (*Producer*); Norman Krasna (*Scenarist*); Rudolph Mate (*Photographer*); Frank Skinner (*Musical Score*); Charles Previn (*Musical Director*); Jack Otterson, Martin Obzina and Russell A. Gausman (*Art Directors*); Rene Hubert (*Costumer*); Frank Gross (*Editor*); Bernard B. Brown (*Sound Supervisor*).

SONGS: *By* Charles Previn and Sam Lerner; "Sweet as the Blush of May" (sung by Dietrich), "Salt O'the Sea" (sung by the ship's crew), "Oh, Joyous Day" (sung by chorus during wedding ceremony).

SYNOPSIS: Floating down the Mississippi is a magnificent wedding dress, and we soon discover through narrative flashback the story of what happened to Claire Ledeux (Marlene Dietrich), who disappeared mysteriously on her wedding day.

Claire Ledeux, an adventuress from Europe, seeks to improve her fortunes by a favorable marriage in the colonial town of New Orleans in 1841. She impersonates a sheltered countess in order to accomplish her aims. At the opera one evening, she faints in the box next to Charles Giraud (Roland Young), once she is sure of his attention. He springs to her aid!

When the opera is over, Giraud has his man Samuel (Clarence Muse) follow Claire's maid Clem-

With Bruce Cabot

entine (Theresa Harris), and he discovers that the "countess" will be riding through the park the next afternoon. Clementine, meanwhile, has informed her mistress of the planned trip by carriage through the park.

Riding through the park, Claire is stopped by a handsome young seaman, whose pet monkey has wrapped his tail around the lower section of her carriage. She, thinking it is part of the plot with Giraud, tells the driver to continue. The young man overturns the carriage, retrieves the monkey, and is off! On her way home again, Claire sees Giraud and another man and realizes the whole mix-up.

Giraud, one of the biggest bankers in New Orleans, comes to call and while waiting for the countess he overhears her "gold-digging" remarks,

With Laura Hope Crews, Theresa Harris, Emily Fitzroy, Dorothy Adams, Virginia Sale, and Anne Revere

Assuming her "cousin" role again, Claire convinces Giraud that the look-alike woman is indeed *bad!* Clementine tells Giraud where he and his brother-in-law (Melville Cooper) might find this woman: the Oyster Bed Café on the waterfront. In the dimly-lit dive, Claire not only convinces these two gentlemen, but Zolotov and his friend Bellows (Franklyn Pangborn) as well. About to leave, Claire runs into Latour at the bar, who notices at once the resemblance between this tart and the beautiful countess.

Once the "cousin" has left the Oyster Bed Café, Giraud and Latour follow the woman. She leads them to the home of the countess. Climbing up to the second floor, Latour discovers that the "cousin" and the "countess" are in fact one. Giraud later makes a deal with young Latour, if he'll take the "cousin" away from New Orleans on his boat. The seaman accepts the offer.

Claire joins him that evening on his boat and as she is about to leave—in the morning hours—he tells her the next time he looks at her, she must come with him, regardless! At the wedding ceremony, when Claire and Giraud are about to take their vows, Latour appears. Claire faints and later disappears. A search cannot locate her anywhere. Latour's boat, meanwhile, chugs off to the Caribbean, leaving in its wake the exquisite wedding dress floating down the Mississippi.

so Clementine pretends that the woman he has heard is actually the countess's cousin. Soon Giraud asks Claire to a party, where she sees the seaman and his monkey. The young man, Robert Latour (Bruce Cabot), becomes very interested in the countess, but soon she has accepted Giraud's proposal of marriage. But his family, headed by his old aunt (Laura Hope Crews), must approve his choice. At a posh reception, at which Claire sings "Sweet as the Blush of May" for the guests, there appears Zolotov (Mischa Auer), a Russian from her past, and soon stories begin to circulate about the notorious woman of St. Petersburg.

With Eddie Quillan, Bruce Cabot,
Frank Jenks, and Andy Devine

150

With Clarence Muse (extreme left), Theresa Harris, Gus Schilling, and Bess Flowers

NOTES: This delightful story offered Dietrich some marvelous bits of satire. Working with the great French director René Clair certainly was advantageous. He brought out many of Marlene's subleties of expression. She was beautifully photographed and sumptuously gowned. Much of the lush photography was reminiscent of the von Sternberg period. Clair had much trouble with American censors, and some of his flair vanished as a result.

While most critics agreed that it was not a typically Clair picture, his touches were everywhere: the disgruntled flower girls at the wedding; the wedding gown inexplicably floating on the river; dowager Laura Hope Crews telling innocent Dietrich the facts of life on the eve of her wedding.

Archer Winsten in the *New York Post* commented, "It is always a pleasure to experience the light touch which is laid on without a trowel."

With Roland Young

151

Manpower

A Warner Bros.-First National Picture—1941

CAST: EDWARD G. ROBINSON (*Hank McHenry*); MARLENE DIETRICH (*Fay Duval*); GEORGE RAFT (*Johnny Marshall*); ALAN HALE (*Jumbo Wells*); FRANK MCHUGH (*Omaha*); EVE ARDEN (*Dolly*); BARTON MACLANE (*Smiley Quinn*); WALTER CATLETT (*Sidney Whipple*); JOYCE COMPTON (*Scarlett*); LUCIA CARROLL (*Flo*); WARD BOND (*Eddie Adams*); EGON BRECHER (*Pop Duval*); CLIFF CLARK (*Cully*); JOSEPH CREHAN (*Sweeney*); BEN WELDEN (*Al Hurst*); CARL HARBAUGH (*Noisy Nash*); BARBARA LAND (*Marilyn*); BARBARA PEPPER (*Polly*); DOROTHY APPLEBY (*Wilma*); ISABEL WITHERS (*floor nurse*); FAYE EMERSON (*nurse*); JAMES FLAVIN (*orderly*); CHESTER CLUTE (*clerk*); NELLA WALKER (*floorlady*); HARRY HOLMAN (*Justice of the Peace*); BEAL WONG (*Chinese singer*); MURRAY

With Frederick Hollander

ALPER (*lineman*); DICK WESSEL (*lineman*); JANE RANDOLPH (*hat check girl*); with Lynn Baggett.

CREDITS: RAOUL WALSH (*Director*); MARK HELLINGER (*Producer*); HAL B. WALLIS (*Executive Producer*); ERNEST HALLER (*Photographer*); ADOLPH DEUTSCH (*Musical Score*); MAX PARKER (*Art Director*); MILO ANDERSON (*Costumer*); LEO F. FORBSTEIN (*Musical Director*); RALPH DAWSON (*Editor*); DOLPH THOMAS (*Sound Recorder*); BYRON HASKIN, H. F. KOENEKAMP (*Special Effects*) PERC WESTMORE (*Makeup Artist*); Original Screenplay by RICHARD MACAULAY and JERRY WALD.

SONGS: *By* FREDERICK HOLLANDER and FRANK LOESSER, "I'm in No Mood for Music Tonight," "He Lied and I Listened."

SYNOPSIS: The men of the Pacific Power and Light Company are relaxing in a cheap but happy dive in Los Angeles. Outside, a storm is raging and soon the men are summoned by phone to repair the power lines. Hank McHenry (Edward G. Robinson) saves his pal Johnny Marshall (George Raft) from the hot wires but gets a load of electricity in one leg. Later, one of their crew isn't so lucky—"Pop" Duval is killed, and Hank and Johnny have to break the news to his daughter Fay (Marlene Dietrich), a hostess in a cheap clip joint. Johnny dislikes the kind of gal Fay is, since he had once gone with "Pop" to meet his daughter when she was released from a local jail. Hank, however, is fascinated by her, thinking she's merely a victim of circumstances.

With George Raft and Edward G. Robinson

Hank and Johnny room together and share each other's confidences. Hank speaks longingly of Fay and how he'd like to help her out, since she obviously has no money. Johnny tries everything in his power, but his friend won't change his mind. Hank begins to frequent the club where Fay sings and gets customers to buy her drinks. She likes this mild-mannered guy and tries to tell him that the club is just a clip-joint and that he's too nice a fellow to

With George Raft, Beal Wong, Frank McHugh, and Edward G. Robinson

With William Royle, Eve Arden, and Barton MacLane

get the "treatment." Hank continues to visit the club and see Fay. Finally one evening he proposes marriage. Knowing that she doesn't love him (but not realizing that she does love his buddy Johnny), Hank awaits her decision. Fay, thinking what it would be like to be away from this kind of life, finally accepts.

Soon after they set up housekeeping, Johnny is injured on the job, and Hank insists that he recuperate at their new house, where Fay can look after him. Fay takes this opportunity to inform Johnny of her love for him, but his friendship for Hank is too great to let anything develop.

Unhappy about life with Hank, Fay decides to leave town, but visits the club once more before leaving. Chatting with her friends Dolly (Eve Arden), Scarlett (Joyce Compton) and the other girls makes Fay realize that she'll never be able to shake this type of establishment. Just then, Smiley Quinn (Barton MacLane), her former boss, comes up to the table and tells her to contact a friend of his in Chicago about a job, when suddenly the joint is raided and Fay is taken to the police station with the others.

Johnny learns of Fay's arrest, and realizing what this news will do to his pal Hank, rushes to the jail

With Lucia Carroll, Eve Arden, director Raoul Walsh, Lynn Baggot, and Joyce Compton

and bails her out. She again reminds him of her love, but Johnny only slaps her around to remind her that she's Hank's wife.

Fay then goes out to where Hank is working on a job in the pouring rain and Johnny joins the crew fixing the wires. During a break Hank comes in the shed to find Fay. She tells him of her love for Johnny, and Hank assumes that his pal has been unfaithful with his wife. He races out into the storm and the two men have a terrific fight, during which Hank is accidentally killed.

NOTES: Continuing the "sexy babe" image that Universal started, Warner Bros. borrowed Dietrich and cast her between Edward G. Robinson and George Raft, long personal friends of Marlene's.

She was given slinky gowns and two Frederick Hollander-Frank Loesser songs to bellow, and she got slapped around in typical fashion. The supporting cast was exceedingly good, as was the nimble direction of Raoul Walsh. In short, it was basically a man's picture—rip-roaring melodrama with plenty of action, excitement, and women. *Life* said, "As the clip-joint babe, Marlene Dietrich sings a husky song, crosses a pair of nifty legs, bakes a batch of biscuits and, as has become customary in recent successes, gets slapped around."

Howard Barnes in reviewing *Manpower* for the *New York Herald Tribune* noted, "The human drama, which finds Robinson, Raft, and Dietrich forming a romantic triangle is never credible. The stars work hard to make you care whether or not Robinson marries Dietrich or Raft finally wins her, but most of their efforts look pretentious with the material they have at hand."

In *The New York Times,* Bosley Crowther commented. "The principal participants in the drama are Edward G. Robinson and George Raft. And the inevitable lady in the case, over whom the solid buddies dispute, is none other than Marlene Dietrich, sporting every danger signal save a 'high voltage' sign. . . . She does what she has to do well, but she's in to make trouble—and that's all."

With George Raft

With Edward G. Robinson

The Lady Is Willing

A Charles K. Feldman Group Production

A Columbia Picture—1942

CAST: MARLENE DIETRICH (*Elizabeth Madden*); FRED MACMURRAY (*Dr. Corey McBain*); ALINE MACMAHON (*Buddy*); STANLEY RIDGES (*Kenneth Hanline*); ARLINE JUDGE (*Frances*); ROGER CLARK (*Victor*); MARIETTA CANTY (*Mary Lou*); DAVID JAMES (*Baby Corey*); RUTH FORD (*Myrtle*); STERLING HOLLOWAY (*Arthur Miggle*); HARVEY STEPHENS (*Dr. Golding*); HARRY SHANNON (*Detective Sergeant Barnes*); ELISABETH RISDON (*Mrs. Cummings*); CHARLES LANE (*K. K. Miller*); MURRAY ALPER (*Joe Quig*); KITTY KELLY (*Nellie Quig*); CHESTER CLUTE (*income tax man*); ROBERT EMMETT KEANE (*hotel manager*); EDDIE ACUFF (*Murphy*); NEIL HAMILTON (*Charlie*); JIMMY CONLIN (*bum*); CHARLES HALTON (*Dr. Jones*); HELEN AINSWORTH (*interior decorator*); MYRTLE ANDERSON (*maid*).

CREDITS: MITCHELL LEISEN (*Director* and *Producer*); JAMES EDWARD GRANT, ALBERT MCCLEERY (*Scenarists*); TED TETZLAFF (*Photographer*); W. FRANKE HARLING (*Musical Score*); LIONEL BANKS (*Supervising Art Director*); RUDOLPH STERNAD (*Art Director*); EDA WARREN (*Editor*); LODGE CUNNINGHAM (*Sound Recorder*); DOUGLAS DEAN (*Dance Director*); MORRIS STOLOFF (*Musical Director*); For Miss Dietrich; *Gowns by* IRENE; *Hats by* JOHN FREDERICS; *Jewels by* PAUL FLATO; Based on an Original Story by JAMES EDWARD GRANT.

SONG: *By* JACK KING and GORDON CLIFFORD; "Strange Thing (And I Find You)."

SYNOPSIS: Elizabeth Madden (Marlene Dietrich), a celebrated musical comedy star, finds an abandoned baby and declares to her associates that she will raise the child. To show how much this lady knows about children, Elizabeth thinks the child is a girl, when it is actually a boy. The first time the

*With Eddie Acuff, Aline Mc-
Mahon, and Harry Shannon*

baby cries, she thinks "she" is dying and begins calling doctors. She nearly drives her secretary Buddy (Aline MacMahon) and her business manager Kenneth Hanline (Stanley Ridges) crazy before they get in touch with Dr. Corey McBain (Fred MacMurray), a pediatrician with a yen to do research on pneumonia.

The doctor is intrigued by a woman as celebrated as Miss Madden who can't even tell the sex of a child. He explains that the child is a boy, and he was crying merely because he was hungry. She promptly names the baby Corey. When she is told that she cannot adopt the child because she is not married, she makes the doctor an offer. He can give up his practice and devote all of his time to research with rabbits, if he will marry her so she can adopt Baby Corey.

Agreeing to this "arrangement," the doctor moves into another wing of her vast apartment and Elizabeth continues her musical comedy career as well as

*With Sterling Holloway and Davy
Joseph James*

157

becoming a devoted "mother." During this marriage-of-convenience, however, one thing happens that neither of them count on: they fall in love with each other. This brings about complications—especially when the doctor's ex-wife, Frances (Arline Judge), pops in and causes a misunderstanding between Elizabeth and Corey.

Elizabeth, angry over the whole mess, takes Baby Corey with her on tour but he suddenly develops mastoiditis and has to be operated on at once. Corey McBain flys in to perform the delicate operation and saves the baby's life. Meanwhile, the love between them deepens.

NOTES: A welcome change of pace for Marlene Dietrich was in store for her in *The Lady Is Willing*. It was a totally sympathetic role. Elizabeth Madden was vain, stubborn, and majestic—but she did elicit a sympathetic response·from the audience. What a pity the script couldn't have been better! It was directed with certain flair by Mitchell Leisen and the snappy dialogue tended to uplift the sagging script at times, but not often enough.

Columbia went all out and assigned Dietrich a trio of magic-makers who whipped up her gowns,

With Arline Judge, Fred MacMurray, and Davy Joseph James

With Roger Clark and ensemble

hats, and jewels with great care. Only Dietrich could wear such bizarre creations and appear anything other than *mad*. But it was her acting which won the plaudits.

As Herbert Cohn in the *Brooklyn Daily Eagle* told his readers, "A versatile actress, Miss Dietrich, a likable personality and an effective player makes her Liza Madden a credible figure." While Kate Cameron in the *New York Daily News* noted, "She [Dietrich] is, if possible, more breathtakingly beautiful than ever, in a sympathetic role that permits her a little wider range of acting than her other vehicles. She moves from light comedy to pathos a little awkwardly, but this is less her fault than that of the scenarists, who ring too quick a change from comedy to tragedy, disregarding the effect of the emotional switch on director, actors, and audience."

During the filming of this comedy-drama, Dietrich was carrying little David James around the set when she tripped on a light cable and went crashing to the floor. She twisted her body quickly so the child would be protected and in doing so suffered a severe sprain. This is no doubt what anyone would have done in the circumstances, but Dietrich with a cast on one of her famous gams, caused quite a sensation.

With Fred MacMurray

With Fred MacMurray

With Marietta Canty

The Spoilers

A Universal Picture—1942

CAST: MARLENE DIETRICH (*Cherry Mallotte*); RANDOLPH SCOTT (*Alex McNamara*); JOHN WAYNE (*Roy Glennister*); MARGARET LINDSAY (*Helen Chester*); HARRY CAREY (*Dextry*); RICHARD BARTHELMESS (*Bronco Kid*); GEORGE CLEVELAND (*Banty*); SAMUEL S. HINDS (*Judge Stillman*); RUSSELL SIMPSON (*Flapjack*); WILLIAM FARNUM (*Wheaton*); MARIETTA CANTY (*Idabelle*); JACK NORTON (*Mr. Skinner*); RAY BENNETT (*Clark*); FORREST TAYLOR (*Bennett*); CHARLES HALTON (*Struve*); BUD OSBORNE (*Marshall*); DREW DEMAREST (*Galloway*); ROBERT W. SERVICE (*the poet*); CHARLES MCMURPHY, ART MILES, and WILLIAM HAADE (*deputies*); ROBERT HOMANS (*sea captain*).

CREDITS: RAY ENRIGHT (*Director*); FRANK LLOYD (*Producer*); LAWRENCE HAZARD, TOM REED (*Scenarists*); MILTON KRASNER (*Photographer*); CLARENCE KOLSTER (*Editor*); HANS J. SALTER (*Musical Score*); CHARLES PREVIN (*Musical Director*); VERA WEST (*Costumer*); JACK OTTERSON, JOHN B. GOODMAN (*Art Directors*); RUSSELL A. GAUSMAN, EDWARD R. ROBINSON (*Set Decorators*); BERNARD B. BROWN (*Sound Supervisor*); LEE MARCUS (*Associate Producer*); From the novel by REX BEACH.

SYNOPSIS: In Nome, Alaska, in 1900 two miners (Russell Simpson and George Cleveland) storm into town with the story that they have been claim-jumped. Cherry Mallotte (Marlene Dietrich), owner of Nome's most glittering gin palace, decides to meet the newly-arrived gold commissioner, Alex McNamara (Randolph Scott). He becomes interested in Cherry, but her heart belongs to Roy Glennister (John Wayne), who is a partner with Al Dextry (Harry Carey) in the fabulous Midas mine.

Glennister, meanwhile, arrives from Seattle on the boat and when Cherry meets him at the shore, he seems more than interested in a young filly named Helen Chester (Margaret Lindsay), a niece of Judge Stillman (Samuel S. Hinds), who has come to Nome to set up the first United States Court.

Even though Cherry has prepared Roy's favorite dishes—brandy and hard-boiled eggs—she is angered

With Russell Simpson and George Cleveland

by his attentions to the judge's niece and throws him out of her apartment.

Soon the gold commissioner and the judge arrive at the Midas mine with a court order so they can properly assess who is the legal owner of the mine, thus shutting it down for a few weeks until court convenes. Dextry smells a rat and refuses to budge, but Glennister, upon the advice of Helen, agrees to shut down the mine. This action causes a split between Roy and Dextry.

When the judge postpones the date of the hearing 90 days (while keeping all of their assets locked up in a safe) Roy realizes something is amiss. He is sure now that Helen is in with the judge and the gold commissioner.

Roy, Cherry, and Dextry, decide to send their lawyer (William Farnum) to Seattle to appeal the case.

The Bronco Kid (Richard Barthelmess), Cherry's chief Faro dealer, frustrated by unrequited love for her, tries to kill Roy when he robs the bank's safe, which has his money inside. He misses, however, and mortally wounds the Marshall. McNamara, arrests Glennister for the crime, but Roy is later helped to escape by a reformed Bronco Kid, Cherry, and Mr. Skinner (Jack Norton) after Cherry discovers from Helen that the judge and McNamara plan to kill Roy while attempting to escape.

In order to gain full control of the mine (which the crooks have been mining), Roy and the Bronco

With Randolph Scott

161

With John Wayne and Marietta Canty

Kid fire up the train and with a large group of men ram the barricade which the court put up around it. The Bronco Kid is killed in the crash. Back in town Roy and Alex McNamara have a tremendous fight over Cherry and the crooked dealings Alex has been mixed up in.

Roy beats Alex and the crooks are taken to jail. And Roy gets the best prize of all—Cherry!

NOTES: This was the fourth filmed version of the famous Rex Beach classic saga of Alaska of five that have thus far been made. Jammed full of excitement, climaxed by a brawling fist-fight between the principal male stars, a terrific blend of close-ups of John Wayne and Randolph Scott together with long shots of similar-looking stuntmen.

William Farnum, the original Roy Glennister of the 1914 silent version, played Wheaton the lawyer in this version. He enjoyed his assignment, although he admitted, "movies have changed a good deal since my day."

This was the first time in this story's history that a female star was top-billed, and they didn't even provide Marlene with a song (a serious omission since there was ample opportunity for one). They did play the song "Little Joe the Wrangler" from *Destry Rides Again,* however, as background music in the saloon.

The art direction and set decoration were so good

With Randolph Scott

they warranted Academy Award nominations for the four men heading those departments.

The New York Times noticed, "As Cherry Mallotte, a lady saloonkeeper, Miss Dietrich carries on in the roughcut diamond tradition of Mae West and wears beruffled costumes about as concealing as the fins on a fish. . . . Sprinkled with double-entendres nearly as frankly cut as Miss Dietrich's gowns, the author and producer have kept their tongues firmly in their cheeks, even when stout Mr. Wayne and Mr. Scott begin tearing up the set. It's a lovely brawl."

A "SPOILERS" CHRONOLOGY

1913-14—(Selig)—Tom Santschi–William Farnum–Katherine Williams
1923—(Goldwyn)—Milton Sills–Noah Berry–Anna Q. Nilsson
1930—(Paramount)—Gary Cooper–Betty Compson–William (stage) Boyd
1942—(Universal)—Marlene Dietrich–John Wayne–Randolph Scott
1955—(Univ-Int'l)—Rory Calhoun–Anne Baxter–Jeff Chandler

With Randolph Scott and John Wayne

Pittsburgh

A Universal Picture—1942

CAST: MARLENE DIETRICH (*Josie Winters*); RANDOLPH SCOTT (*Cash Evans*); JOHN WAYNE (*Pittsburgh Markham*); FRANK CRAVEN (*Doc Powers*); LOUISE ALLBRITTON (*Shannon Prentiss*); SHEMP HOWARD (*Shorty*); THOMAS GOMEZ (*Joe Malneck*); LUDWIG STOSSEL (*Dr. Grazlich*); SAMUEL S. HINDS (*Morgan Prentiss*); PAUL FIX (*mine operator*); WILLIAM HAADE (*Johnny*); DOUGLAS FOWLEY (*Mort Brawley*) SAMMY STEIN (*Killer Kane*); HARRY SEYMOUR (*theatre manager*); CHARLES COLEMAN (*butler*); NESTOR PAIVA (*Barney*); HOBART CAVANAUGH (*derelict*); VIRGINIA SALE (*Mrs. Bercovici*); WADE BOTELER (*mine superintendent*); MIRA MCKINNEY (*Tilda*); ALPHONSE MARTELL (*Carlos*); CHARLES SHERLOCK (*chauffeur*); BESS FLOWERS (*woman*).

CREDITS: LEWIS SEILER (*Director*) CHARLES K. FELDMAN (*Producer*); ROBERT FELLOWS (*Associate Producer*); KENNETH GAMET, TOM REED (*Scenarists*); JOHN TWIST (*Additional Dialogue*); ROBERT DE GRASSE (*Photographer*); FRANK SKINNER, HANS J. SALTER (*Musical Score*); VERA WEST (*Costumer*); JOHN B. GOODMAN (*Art Director*); RUSSELL A. GAUSMAN, IRA S. WEBB (*Set Decorators*); CHARLES PREVIN (*Musical Director*); PAUL LANDRES (*Editor*); JOHN P. FULTON (*Special Effects*); CHARLES GOULD (*Assistant Director*); Based on an Original Story by GEORGE OWEN and TOM REED.

SYNOPSIS: Josie Winters (Marlene Dietrich) is left alone by the death of her coal-miner father and tries to shake the coal dust from her hair and get rid of the old nickname "hunky"—a person brought up in the coal-mining communities. She gets herself involved with a crooked fight promoter, Mort Brawley (Douglas Fowley), who keeps her in swell clothes and a chauffeur-driven limousine.

At a local theatre in Coal Town one evening, Brawley has staged a prizefighter named Killer Kane (Sammy Stein) to fight anyone in the place. A cash prize is offered to the man who can stay in the ring for the full fifteen rounds. Into the theatre struts Pittsburgh Markham (John Wayne), who tricks his close buddy Cash Evans (Randolph Scott) into going for the prize. In the front row of the audience

With Randolph Scott and John Wayne

Pittsburgh notices the lovely Josie Winters, and he directs a few well-chosen remarks in her direction.

Once it becomes apparent that the fight is "fixed," the boys begin tearing up the joint and the audience becomes one big fight ring. Escaping to the sidewalk with only a few scratches, the boys learn that there has been a cave-in at the mine and that their close friend, Doc Powers (Frank Craven), is trapped below. They jump into the nearest car available, which happens to be Josie's. They're off and running before she makes her presence in the back seat known.

It is at the mine that the boys discover that this

With Randolph Scott, Thomas Gomez, and Frank Craven

165

With John Wayne

flashy babe is really a "hunky" girl at heart. She pitches in and goes down in the mine with them. She, too, is a friend of Doc's. Doc Powers gets away with only a broken leg and Josie stays on to nurse Doc. The boys continue to pop in on Doc every day to see how he's doing and, naturally, to catch a glimpse of Josie. She makes it perfectly clear to these two roughneck miners that she wants nothing to do with coal and coal miners.

Since both men are madly in love with Josie by this time, this bit of news only stimulates their desire

to start their own company. Through a clever bit of business, the boys put over a big deal with a steel tycoon named Morgan Prentiss (Samuel S. Hinds), and soon Pittsburgh has gone highbrow by marrying the boss's daughter Shannon (Louise Allbritton). Josie is crushed, for she has fallen for Pittsburgh even though Cash has proposed marriage to her.

Soon the coal and steel companies merge. Pittsburgh heads the combine and becomes power-mad. His lack of concern for his workers is highlighted when their spokesman, Joe Malneck (Thomas Gomez), is refused a look at the company's books. The workers strike. Soon Pittsburgh has no company, no wife (she's divorced him), and few friends. His power-seeking ways have forced Cash to go into business with Doc Powers. He has also lost Josie, the one person he's really loved all along, for she has married Cash.

For a long time Pittsburgh disappears from view. Cash's company is now turning out war materials for our country's defense and Josie, Doc, and Joe Malneck are working as a team to keep America fit and strong and ever-ready. One day Cash hears of a fellow in one of his shops who might be better utilized on an executive level. The man is Pittsburgh Markham, who has humbly worked for base pay just to do a fine job. The former partners are reunited, and Josie now has two men to look after.

NOTES: Essentially, this is a tale of Pittsburgh's part in the all-out war effort. The two parallel stories are tied together by Frank Craven's narration. The rise of two coal miners; their struggles; their successes; their failures; and the woman who inspires them and loves them throughout all their adventures. The second portion dealt with the rise of the great city of Pittsburgh itself from coal mining town to coal and steel eminence and its vital contributions

With Randolph Scott

With John Wayne and Randolph Scott

to the United States economy. This was accomplished with documentary footage of Pittsburgh's giant factories, mines, companies, etc., interwoven into the storyline.

Marlene Dietrich was again pitted between two husky men who both loved her and fought over her. She was a woman who had known sorrow, poverty, sickness, and death. And she was a gal who was striving to rise above such a background. She cared enough about the two miners to urge them on in their endeavors and stick by them through thick and thin. Hers was a down-to-earth reality which displayed more guts than you were prepared for—and more love and affection poured forth too.

There were action aplenty and superb fights to keep the men interested. Some spicy outfits on Marlene gave the women their due. The supporting cast was first-rate—Louise Allbritton, in one of her first important roles, was excellent as Shannon, the unloved wife of success-driven Pittsburgh Markham.

Pittsburgh made money for Universal, but Dietrich was growing weary of the type of "dame" she had come to portray. She soon was to forsake picture-making for a number of years while she entertained our troops throughout Europe.

G. E. Blackford in the *New York Journal-American* happily told his readers, "She [Dietrich] provides the spark that makes the whole thing tick, and few could provide it better."

The *New York Herald Tribune* said, "The acting is the best feature of the film. Miss Dietrich, as Hunky, the ex-coal miner's daughter, appears fetchingly seductive whether garbed in evening clothes or covered with coal dust."

Follow the Boys

A Universal Picture—1944

CAST: GEORGE RAFT (*Tony West*); VERA ZORINA (*Gloria Vance*); GRACE MCDONALD (*Kitty West*); CHARLEY GRAPEWIN (*Nick West*); CHARLES BUTTERWORTH (*Louie Fairweather*); RAMSAY AMES (*Laura*); ELIZABETH PATTERSON (*Annie*); REGIS TOOMEY (*Dr. Henderson*); GEORGE MACREADY (*Walter Bruce*); FRANK JENKS (*Chic Doyle*); ALLISON RICHARDS (*McDermott*); EMMETT VOGAN (*Harkness*); CYRIL RING (*Laughton*); THEODORE VON ELTZ (*William Barrett*); MARTHA O'DRISCOLL (*herself*); MAXIE ROSENBLOOM (*himself*); SPOOKS (*Junior*). Guest Stars Appearing as Themselves: Jeanette MacDonald, Orson Welles' Mercury Wonder Show, Marlene Dietrich, Dinah Shore, Donald O'Connor, Peggy Ryan, W. C. Fields, The Andrew Sisters, Artur Rubinstein, Carmen Amaya and her Company, Sophie Tucker, The Delta Rhythm Boys, Leonard Gautier's dog-act "The Bricklayers," Ted Lewis and his Band, Freddie Slach and his Orchestra, Charlie Spivak and his Orchestra, Louis Jordan and his Orchestra. In the Hollywood Victory Committee Sequence: Maria Montez, Susanna Foster, Louise Allbritton, Robert Paige, Alan Curtis, Lon Chaney, Jr., Gloria Jean, Andy Devine, Turhan Bey, Evelyn Ankers, Noah Beery, Jr., Samuel S. Hinds, Louise Beavers, Clarence Muse, Gale Sondergaard, Peter Coe, Nigel Bruce and Thomas Gomez.

CREDITS: EDDIE SUTHERLAND (*Director*); CHARLES K. FELDMAN (*Producer*); ALBERT L. ROCKETT (*Associate Producer*); HOWARD CHRISTIE (*Assistant Director*); DAVID ABEL (*Photographer*); GEORGE HALE (*Dance Creator and Director*); JOHN B. GOODMAN, HAROLD H. MACARTHUR (*Art Directors*); LEIGH HARLINE (*Musical Director*); FRED R. REITSHAUS, JR. (*Film Editor*); VERA WEST (*Gowns*); BERNARD B. BROWN (*Sound Supervisor*); ROBERT PRITCHARD (*Sound Technician*); Original Screenplay, LOU BRESLOW and GERTRUDE PURCELL.

SONGS: "The Bigger the Army and Navy"; "I'll Get By"; "Mad About Him Blues"; "I'll Walk Alone"; "I'll See You In My Dreams"; "Beyond the Blue Horizon"; "Good Night"; "Furlough Fling"; "Shoo Shoo, Baby"; "Swing Low, Sweet Chariot"; "Merriment"; "Besame Mucho"; "Sweet Georgia Brown"; "Is You Is, or Is You Ain't"; "Tonight"; "I Feel a Song Coming On"; "The House I Live In"; "A Better Day is Comin'"; "Andrews Sisters' Medley"; "Kittens with Their Mittens Laced"; "Some of These Days."

NOTES: Originally entitled *Three Cheers for the Boys,* this all-star musical package was Hollywood's tribute to the hundreds of entertainers from all branches of show business who were giving of themselves freely so American servicemen and servicewomen everywhere would find their burden a little easier to carry.

On the set

Naturally this type of entertainment didn't need a plotline, but Universal gave it a "lead-in" which lent credibility to the enormous lineup of talent that was to follow.

An ex-vaudevillian hoofer (George Raft) goes to Hollywood in the 1930's. Work is aplenty and he rises from a bit player to star in an amazingly short span of time (mainly through partnership with the lovely Gloria Vance (Zorina). When our base at Pearl Harbor is attacked, our boy Georgie tries to enlist but is rejected. Following a lengthy period of self-reproach he gets a brainstorm and forms a Hollywood Victory Committee which later merges with the USO, whose sole purpose it is to bring cheer into the lives of our fighting forces wherever they are. The idea is great and meets with success. His life is again full and useful.

Dietrich joined Orson Welles' Mercury Wonder Show and in a delightful sketch is sawed in half ('tis magic!) much to the astonishment of a couple of GI's. Of course trick photography did add to the fun, which all went to prove, if nothing else, that even half a Dietrich is better than none!

Other highlights included pianist Artur Rubinstein playing the haunting "Liebestraum"; Dinah Shore's delicious rendition of "Mad About Him Blues"; Raft doing a Charleston to "Sweet Georgia Brown" in a half-ton truck; the incomparable Andrew Sisters with "Shoo Shoo Baby"; Jeanette MacDonald taking us back with "Beyond the Blue Horizon"; the Delta Rhythm Boys giving special meaning to the lovely "The House I Live In" and the

With Orson Welles

wonderful comic nonsense of Donald O'Connor and Peggy Ryan—two of Universal's most gifted youngsters during those years.

The Jule Styne-Sammy Cahn song "I'll Walk Alone" was nominated for an Academy Award. It was a big hit with the wartime public and today is a standard.

With Orson Welles

169

Kismet

A Metro-Goldwyn-Mayer Picture in Technicolor—1944

CAST: RONALD COLMAN (*Hafiz*); MARLENE DIETRICH (*Jamilla*); JAMES CRAIG (*Caliph*); EDWARD ARNOLD (*Mansur, the Grand Vizier*); HUGH HERBERT (*Feisal*); JOY ANN PAGE (*Marsinah*); FLORENCE BATES (*Karsha*); HARRY DAVENPORT (*Agha*); HOBART CAVANAUGH (*Moolah*); ROBERT WARWICK (*Alfife*); BEATRICE and EVELYNE KRAFT (*court dancers*); BARRY MACOLLUM (*Amu*); VICTOR KILLIAN (*Jehan*); CHARLES MIDDLETON (*the miser*); HARRY HUMPHREY (*gardener*); NESTOR PAIVA (*captain of police*); EVE WHITNEY (*café girl*); MINERVA URECAL (*retainer*); CY KENDALL (*herald*); DAN SEYMOUR (*fat Turk*); DALE VAN SICKLE (*assassin*); PEDRO deCORDOBA (*Meuzin*).

CREDITS: WILLIAM DIETERLE (*Director*); EVERETT RISKIN (*Producer*); JOHN MEEHAN (*Scenarist*); CHARLES ROSHER (*Photographer*); HERBERT STOTHART (*Musical Score*); CEDRIC GIBBONS, DANIEL B. CATHCART (*Art Directors*); EDWIN B. WILLIS, RICHARD PEFFERLE (*Set Decorators*); DOUGLAS SHEARER (*Sound Recorder*); BEN LEWIS (*Editor*); MARVIN STUART (*Assistant Director*); Costume Supervision by IRENE; Costume Execution by KARINSKA; A. ARNOLD GILLESPIE, WARREN NEWCOMBE (*Special Effects*); From the play by EDWARD KNOBLOCH.

SONGS: *By* HAROLD ARLEN and E. Y. HARBURG; "Willow in the Wind," "Tell Me, Tell Me, Evening Star."

SYNOPSIS: Hafiz (Ronald Colman), a beggar-magician who is also a scoundrel aspires to make his lovely daughter, Marsinah (Joy Ann Page) the bride of a prince. Unknown to Hafiz, Marsinah has been having a romance with a gardener's son (James Craig), who in reality is the Caliph of Bagdad in disguise. Hafiz, posing as the "Prince of Hassir," ruler of a fictitious province, has been carrying on a clandestine romance with Jamilla (Marlene Dietrich), queen of the castle of the Grand Vizier (Edward Arnold), who has incurred the Caliph's wrath because of his excessive taxation of the people.

To have Jamilla to himself, and at the same time fulfill his boast to his daughter, Hafiz steals expensive garments from a bazaar and visits the Vizier as the "Prince of Hassir." He persuades him to consider

With Ronald Colman

making Marsinah his new queen. But before he can present Marsinah, Hafiz is arrested for the robbery and brought before the Vizier. The latter decrees that his hands be lopped off. Thinking quickly, Hafiz, offers to kill the young Caliph if the Vizier would set him free and marry his daughter. The Vizier agrees.

Performing tricks of magic before the Caliph, Hafiz fails in an attempt to stab the young ruler. He eludes the guards and, to keep Marsinah from being involved in the assassination plot, rushes to the Vizier's castle to take her away. There, he kills several guards and finally kills the Vizier himself, just

as the Caliph's soldiers apprehend him. When the Caliph learns that Marsinah is Hafiz's daughter, he pardons the rascal and makes him a real prince, with the understanding that he must leave Bagdad forever. Pleased by his daughter's forthcoming marriage to the Caliph, Hafiz, accompanied by Jamilla, leaves Bagdad for another land, always to be together.

NOTES: Based on the celebrated play by Edward Knobloch, this film was just another version in a long line of cinemazations. Otis Skinner first appeared in *Kismet* in 1911 and for years thereafter

With Edward Arnold and Joy Page

toured the country with it. His name became synonymous with *Kismet* and vice-versa, much the same as Alfred Drake's has become with the musical version, which has been playing since 1953 somewhere in the country.

Skinner first filmed *Kismet* in 1920 for Robertson-Cole; his daughter, Cornelia Otis Skinner, had a small part in it. With the advent of sound, he remade it for First National. The production was opulent and among the settings (which resembled Douglas Fairbanks' for *Robin Hood*), one could find Loretta Young, David Manners, and Mary Duncan as Jamilla! That same year, in Germany, Wilhelm (later William in Hollywood) Dieterle filmed a version which proved highly successful throughout Europe. Now it was Dieterle's turn again. He must have reasoned that this old chestnut would carry the ball itself, for his direction was slow-paced and undistinguished. But his knack for spectacle was quite successful with the audiences of 1944.

With Ronald Colman and Joy Page

However, when one considers that Maria Montez and Jon Hall (over at Universal) were doing the same type of thing better, Colman and Dietrich seem strange choices for an adventure of this kind.

It took M-G-M to paint the legendary Dietrich legs the public had come to know so well. So, under four coats of gold paint, Dietrich and her legs did a fantastic dance á la Isadora Duncan, which added immeasurably to the picture's pure escapist value. Ronald Colman may have lacked the devil-may-care qualities of a Douglas Fairbanks or an Errol Flynn, but his innate charm and voice were his chief assets and served him well. It was Marlene, however, in a smaller role, who had a field day slithering in and out from behind pillars and reclining on silken divans. Her role was really too brief.

Louis Kronenberger in *PM* stated: "After *Kismet*, God had better give up trying to compete with M-G-M." The production did cost over $3,000,000— a tidy sum when one considers the wartime restrictions placed on film budgets. It is also interesting to note that this was the first time Dietrich ever played a *dancer,* giving her a perfect opportunity to display the legs she had hitherto made so noticeable.

The photography of Charles Rosher; the art direc-

tion of Cedric Gibbons and Daniel B. Cathcart; the set decorations of Edwin B. Willis and Richard Pefferle; and the sound recording supervised by Douglas Shearer were all nominated for Academy Awards.

Cue magazine remarked, "The picture is escapist, amusing, merry and bubbling with good humor, sparkling with gay good spirits." *The New Yorker* felt, "Apart from one interesting dance in the court of the Grand Vizier of Bagdad, to whom she is attached in a remote and slightly confusing way, Miss Dietrich does not even take a deep breath, which speaks well for the sense of proportion of one who has just been touring the Mediterranean war theatre by jeep and plane with a musical saw."

The New York Times noticed that "Miss Dietrich has three major and one or two minor scenes in the picture, all of which add up to a pleasing job, but undoubtedly her chief contribution is the rather lavish display of Dietrich in general and the highly publicized Dietrich legs in particular."

Kismet can be seen on television these days as *Oriental Dream,* retitled so as not to confuse viewers with the 1955 musical version filmed with Ann Blyth by M-G-M.

Martin Roumagnac

Released in the United States by Lopert Films, Inc., as The Room Upstairs—1948

An Alcina Production—1946

CAST: MARLENE DIETRICH (*Blanche Ferrand*); JEAN GABIN (*Martin Roumagnac*); MARGO LION (*Martin's sister*); MARCEL HERRAND (*the consul*); JEAN D'YD (*Blanche's uncle*); DANIEL GELIN (*the lover*); JEAN DARCANTE (*the lawyer*); HENRI POUPON (*Gargame*); MARCEL ANDRE (*judge*); PAULOT (*Perez*); CHARLES LEMONTIER (*Bonnemain*); with Michel Ardan, Paul Faivre, Marcelle Geniat and Lucien Nat.

CREDITS: GEORGES LACOMBE (*Director*); MARC LE PELLETIER (*Producer*); PIERRE VERY (*Scenarist*);

With Jean Gabin

With Jean Gabin

ROGER HUBERT (*Photographer*); GEORGE WAKHEVITCH (*Art Director*); Music by MARCEL MIROUZE; Based on the novel by PIERRE-RENE WOLF.

SYNOPSIS: Martin Roumagnac (Jean Gabin), a construction engineer, is engaged by Blanche Ferrand (Marlene Dietrich) who wishes a house built in the small French provincial town of Clairval. Mlle. Ferrand, who has spent many years in Australia, pays quite a bit of attention to the handsome M. Roumagnac. Soon the pair are inseparable and spend many happy moments together. Martin is beside himself with love for this attractive woman-of-the-world.

When he learns of Blanche's side-line career as a high-class prostitute, he kills her in a mad rage. At

With Jean Gabin

his murder trial, however, it is brought out that she really did love him. Circumstantial evidence acquits him, but one of Blanche's rejected suitors (Daniel Gelin) sees that justice is carried out by killing Roumagnac.

NOTES: There were high hopes for this turgid melodrama when it was first announced that Marlene Dietrich would remain in France, where she had been entertaining troops in 1945, to film *Martin Roumagnac* with France's great favorite, Jean Gabin. They had been constant companions during his brief career in Hollywood after the fall of France.

At best this ponderous film of passion is second-rate Dietrich and below-average Gabin. When it was first screened in the United States in late 1946 for possible release in this country, the censors had a fit at the blatant way in which prostitution was played.

To get by the powerful Catholic Legion of Decency, thirty minutes had to be cut, and then, in order to get audiences to see the film, the title was changed to *The Room Upstairs*. The original French version (with spice included) ran 115 minutes, but the scissored American version ran a mere 88 minutes. It was not a success by any stretch of the imagination!

With Jean Gabin

Golden Earrings

A Paramount Picture—1947

CAST: RAY MILLAND (*Col. Ralph Denistoun*); MAR-
LENE DIETRICH (*Lydia*); MURVYN VYE (*Zoltan*);
BRUCE LESTER (*Byrd*); DENNIS HOEY (*Hoff*); QUEN-
TIN REYNOLDS (*himself*); REINHOLD SCHUNZEL (*Pro-
fessor Krosigk*); IVAN TRIESAULT (*Major Reimann*);
HERMINE STERLER (*Greta Krosigk*); ERIC FELDARY
(*Zweig*); GISELA WERBISECK (*dowager*); LARRY SIMMS
(*page boy*); HANS VON MORHART (*S. S. trooper*); MME.
LOUISE COLOMBET (*flower woman*); ROBERT VAL and
GORDON ARNOLD (*gypsy boys*); MARTHA BAMATTRE
(*wise old woman*); ANTONIA MORALES (*gypsy dancer*);
JACK WILSON (*Hitler Youth leader*).

CREDITS: MITCHELL LEISEN (*Director*); HARRY
TUGEND (*Producer*); ABRAHAM POLONSKY, FRANK
BUTLER and HELEN DEUTSCH (*Scenarists*); DANIEL L.
FAPP (*Photographer*); HANS DREIER, JOHN MEEHAN
(*Art Directors*); GORDON JENNINGS (*Special Photo-
graphic Effects*); FARCIOT EDOUART (*Process Photogra-
phy*); SAM COMER, GRACE GREGORY (*Set Directors*);
JOHNNY COONAN (*Assistant Director*); VICTOR YOUNG

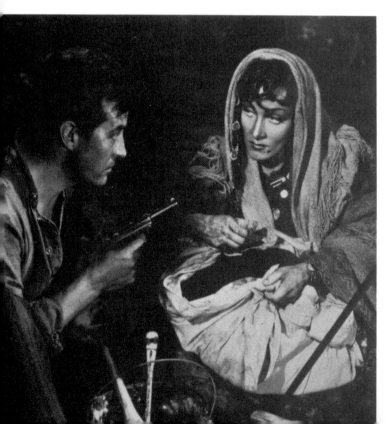

With Ray Milland

(*Musical Score*); ALMA MACRORIE (*Editor*); MARY
KAY DODSON (*Costumer*) PHIL BOUTELJE (*Music As-
sociate*); Dances staged by BILLY DANIELS; WALLY
WESTMORE (*Makeup Supervision*); DON MCKAY,
WALTER OBERST (*Sound Recorders*); LEO SHUKEN,
SIDNEY CUTNER (*Orchestrations*); From a novel by
YOLANDA FOLDES.

SONG: *By* VICTOR YOUNG, JAY LIVINGSTON and RAY
EVANS; "Golden Earrings."

SYNOPSIS: In post-war London, Major General
Ralph Denistoun (Ray Milland) receives a box at
his hotel. It contains a pair of golden earrings. He
takes the first Paris-bound plane available. With him
on the flight is war correspondent Quentin Reynolds,
who has noticed Dennistoun's pierced ears. The general then relates the story, which began six years
earlier, before England officially got into the war,
when he and a young officer named Byrd (Bruce
Lester), members of British Intelligence, were being
held incommunicado by some Nazis in a farmhouse.
They plan to question their prisoners about a poison-gas formula which the brilliant Professor Krosigk (Reinhold Schunzel) has discovered.

Denistoun and Byrd overpower Gestapo official
Hoff (Dennis Hoey) and his aides, escaping in
Nazi uniforms, and decide to split up and see which
one of them can reach the professor first. They
arrange a meeting place near Stuttgart. Denistoun
takes to the Black Forest, and when he begins to
bury the Nazi uniform, he hears a gypsy singing.
She is cooking a fish stew in a great pot. This is his
first encounter with Lydia (Marlene Dietrich), a
gypsy who lives away from her band, travelling the
back roads.

With Ray Milland and Murvyn Vye

Her uncanny knowledge of the Black Forest and
of roads seldom travelled by Nazis give Denistoun a
perfect opportunity to journey forth to his meeting
place with Byrd and/or Professor Krosigk. Lydia
helps him and gives him a perfect disguise. She
colors his skin with a dark stain, pierces his ears,
and gives him a glistening pair of golden earrings
and a handsome gypsy jacket. She also teaches him
how to tell fortunes, which he picks up quickly.

Catching up eventually with the band of gypsies
Lydia usually travels with, Denistoun must fight
Zoltan (Murvyn Vye) the leader, not only because
the handsome jacket he wears belongs to Zoltan, but
Lydia wants to have her man prove himself before
the others. Denistoun wins the fight and the respect
of Zoltan. He now is one of the gypsies.

Soon they are camped near the signpost where he
and young Byrd are to meet. The main road is
choked with Nazi vehicles and men, which prevents
him from getting into Stuttgart to see Professor
Krosigk. Soon Byrd, dressed in knickerbockers and
a Tyrolean hat, arrives at the signpost. When Denistoun appears, Byrd doesn't recognize him at first.
They discover that neither has had an opportunity
to meet with the professor. Just then a band of Hitler
Youth passes by and Denistoun pretends he's read-
ing Byrd's palm. He is shocked to see there the sign

With Ray Milland

177

With Gordon Arnold and Robert Val

of death. After Byrd rides off to see the professor, Lydia tells Denistoun that there is nothing he can do. Fate rules the destiny of man.

Sure enough, Byrd is killed, but before he dies he tells Denistoun that he was unsuccessful in his attempt to get the poison-gas formula. Denistoun then sets about the task, but Professor Krosigk does not believe him until a Nazi official and his aides arrive to denounce the scientist as a traitor to the Reich.

It is then that the professor, with nothing to lose now, hands the gypsy "fortune-teller" a five-mark note upon which is written the secret formula.

Lydia takes Denistoun to the Rhine, where he leaves her, but he vows to return to her after the war. This concludes Denistoun's story.

Denistoun returns to Germany and scales the same mountain Lydia led him to six years before. There he finds her waiting. They are together again, and they ride away in her wagon.

NOTES: Returning to Hollywood after a three-year absence, Dietrich plunged into the role of Lydia, the tattered Hungarian gypsy, with renewed vigor. Her playing of this role made even the eating of greasy fish stew seem glamorous. Dietrich donned a dark wig, dark make-up, torn and dirty gypsy garments, and sang bits of Hungarian gypsy songs. She was giving the public their first taste of neo-realism, although they didn't know it at the time.

Her Lydia was both alternatively seductive and humorous and as one critic pointed out, was "a sharp reminder of what glamour really is."

Ray Milland, still riding high on the prestige of *The Lost Weekend,* released a year earlier, was top-billed. He played Denistoun with great polish and

With Ray Milland

With Bruce Lester and Ray Milland

considerable charm. Broadway actor Murvyn Vye, fresh from his appearance in *Carousel,* sang the title song (in English) while Marlene merely dabbled with the same melody in Hungarian, humming a few bars to herself.

There were censorship problems because Lydia and Denistoun were living together but were not married. The "condemned" notice tacked on *Golden Earrings* by the Catholic Legion of Decency only stimulated the box-office receipts.

Otis L. Guernsey, Jr. in the *New York Herald Tribune* said, "Miss Dietrich has a new Dietrich look in dark makeup and long-skirted gypsy rags, in which her legs are never seen. The love scenes between them contain exactly what one would expect in movie dalliance between a colonel and a wild gypsy lass. . . ."

In his *New York Times* review, Bosley Crowther pointed out that "The fabulous legs of Marlene Dietrich and that lady's distinguished charms, which have not been seen in movies since *Kismet* of three years back, are still rather miserably hidden beneath some bear-grease and a lot of gypsy rags in Para- mount's *Golden Earrings.* . . . For some strange suicidal instinct has apparently inspired that studio to do everything to Miss Dietrich that would submerge her special assets in this film and make a greasy ragamuffin of her, which we doubt that the public cares to see."

With Ray Milland

A Foreign Affair

A Paramount Picture—1948

CAST: JEAN ARTHUR (*Phoebe Frost*); MARLENE DIETRICH (*Erika von Schluetow*); JOHN LUND (*Captain John Pringle*); MILLARD MITCHELL (*Col. Rufus J. Plummer*); PETER VON ZERNECK (*Hans Otto Birgel*); STANLEY PRAGER (*Mike*); BILL MURPHY (*Joe*); GORDON JONES (*First M.P.*); FREDDIE STEELE (*Second M.P.*); RAYMOND BOND (*Pennecott*); BOYD DAVIS (*Giffin*); ROBERT MALCOLM (*Kraus*); BOBBY WATSON (*Adolf Hitler in film clip*); CHARLES MEREDITH (*Yandell*); MICHAEL RAFFETTO (*Salvatore*); JAMES LARMORE (*Lieutenant Hornby*); DAMIEN O'FLYNN (*Lieutenant Colonel*).

CREDITS: BILLY WILDER (*Director*); CHARLES BRACKETT (*Producer*); CHARLES BRACKETT, BILLY WILDER and RICHARD L. BREEN (*Scenarists*); ROBERT HARARI (*Adaptation*); CHARLES B. LANG, JR. (*Photographer*); FARCIOT EDOUART, DEWEY WRIGLEY (*Process Photographers*); GORDON JENNINGS (*Special Effects*); DOANE HARRISON (*Editor*); FREDERICK HOLLANDER (*Musical Score*); EDITH HEAD (*Costumer*); From an Original Story by DAVID SHAW.

SONGS: *By* FREDERICK HOLLANDER; "Black Market," "Illusions," "Ruins of Berlin."

SYNOPSIS: Prim, efficient Congresswoman Phoebe Frost (Jean Arthur) flies to Berlin with a committee whose sole purpose it is to investigate the morale of U. S. troops in Germany. At Tempelhof Airport, Phoebe brushes aside the official greeting of Colonel Plummer (Millard Mitchell) and at her request is introduced to Captain John Pringle (John Lund). It seems she has brought him a birthday cake from a long-lost girl-friend, the daughter of one of her constituents.

When the committee is taken to the hotel, Pringle takes the cake to the Brandenburg Gate

With John Lund

With Jean Arthur and John Lund

barter market, where he exchanges the cake for a mattress. He takes the mattress to the apartment of his girl Erika von Schluetow (Marlene Dietrich). After two M.P.'s crash into the apartment, it is established that Erika, an ex-Nazi, has been sentenced to a labor camp, but Pringle has secretly doc-tored her papers so that she can continue, instead, as a popular singer in a basement night club.

Meanwhile, Phoebe and her committee are touring Berlin. Soon she leaves them to go about on her own. She lets two GI's, who think she's a German girl, pick her up, and eventually the trio arrive at the Lorelei, the black market night club where Erika entertains.

As Erika begins singing, the GI's tell Phoebe of the rumors about Erika, which concern her political past and her officer-protected present. Captain Pringle, having spotted Phoebe, hides behind some water pipes. At that very moment Phoebe spots the birthday cake on one of the tables. Pringle inter-cedes just as Phoebe begins to cause a fuss and in-forms her that the cake was stolen from his jeep. Phoebe, however, is still determined to investigate the Lorelei—and Erika!

At a conference the next day, Phoebe accuses Colonel Plummer of hiding the true conditions that exist in Berlin. She cites the incidents of the previous day and shows the colonel some old German news-reels showing Erika at the opera with Hans Otto Birgel (Peter von Zerneck), a big Nazi leader, being greeted warmly by Hitler (Bobby Watson). She tells him that she intends to find the officer protecting Erika and innocently asks Pringle to help her.

After blocking her path every time she gets close to the truth, Pringle realizes the jig is up when he spots Erika's file (which he had previously hidden) on the Colonel's desk. The colonel, however, informs

With Frederick Hollander

Pringle that Hans Otto Birgel is still alive, not dead as the records showed, and that he wants him to continue seeing Erika in public.

Pringle takes Phoebe to the Lorelei the next evening and Erika joins them at the table. Pringle is ordered to report to the colonel and Phoebe is left alone at the club. Soon the place is raided by American MP's and the German police. At the police station Erika tells the officer that Phoebe is her country cousin and they are released. Erika takes Phoebe to her apartment and tells her that Pringle is merely stringing her along. Soon a jeep's horn is sounded and Phoebe learns from Erika that this is Pringle's usual signal that he wants to come up. Phoebe throws the keys to the apartment out of the window and in comes Pringle. He kisses Erika and Phoebe flees.

Phoebe and the committee are about to leave by plane when the fog-bound airfield is closed until further notice. Coming back into town, the colonel explains the difficulty in capturing ex-Nazis and explains Pringle's assignment. Meanwhile, Hans Otto Birgel has appeared at the Lorelei and tries to shoot Pringle, but is himself killed. The colonel and Phoebe arrive at this moment and Pringle hides under a sheet. Phoebe, thinking him dead, faints. Erika is turned over to the MP's and Phoebe, hardly a prim spinster now, kisses the very much alive Pringle.

NOTES: Billy Wilder, in the summer of 1947, took a small crew to Berlin and photographed the half-dozen "establishing" exterior shots which gave the effect that the entire picture was shot there. It was generally agreed that, with this role, Dietrich came back into the front ranks of the glamorous ladies on the screen. Erika contains much of the old Dietrich magic which first appeared in the early thirties.

With Jean Arthur

182

With Jean Arthur

Here was a role that gave her glamour, realism, dramatic scenes, humorous moments, and some haunting songs.

Frederick Hollander was on hand to write for her three new songs and for the first time he wrote his own English lyrics. Hollander himself appeared as her accompanist during the numbers. He performed this same task in *The Blue Angel* (at the wedding dinner sequence) and as accompanist in *Manpower*.

The scenarists, Charles Brackett, Billy Wilder, and Richard L. Breen, were all nominated for Academy Awards for their script, and Charles B. Lang, Jr., was also so honored for his excellent photography in a black-and-white picture.

Because Erika had been a Nazi, Dietrich didn't want to do the role. But Billy Wilder persuaded her how good a part it was when he showed her June Havoc's test for the same part.

Life said, "As a singer in the nightclub, Marlene Dietrich enjoys a triumphant return to the same sexy role that made her famous eighteen years ago in the German film *The Blue Angel*—the heartless siren who lures men to degradation and goes on singing." Henry Hart in the *National Board of Review Magazine* commented, "For such a diaphanous rag, well-proportioned bone, and luminous hank of hair as Marlene Dietrich, almost any script is an adequate vehicle. One-hoss shays have been hastily baled together for her in Hollywood for fifteen years, yet the custom has not staled her infinite witchery. She remains our day's most convincing portrayer of the fly-catching flower that blooms in the night."

Costumer Edith Head said at this time, "You don't design clothes for Dietrich. You design them *with* her."

With director Billy Wilder

With Betty Harper, Franchot Tone, Henry Fonda,
and director-writer Fletcher Markle

Jigsaw

A Tower Pictures Production, Released through
United Artists—1949

CAST: FRANCHOT TONE (*Howard Malloy*); JEAN
WALLACE (*Barbara Whitfield*); MYRON McCORMICK
(*Charles Riggs*); MARC LAWRENCE (*Angelo Agostini*);
WINIFRID LENIHAN (*Mrs. Hartley*); BETTY HARPER
(*Caroline Riggs*); HEDLEY RAINNIE (*Sigmund Kos-
terich*); WALTER VAUGHN (*District Attorney Walker*);
GEORGE BREEN (*Knuckles*); ROBERT GIST (*Tommy
Quigley*); HESTER SONDERGAARD (*Mrs. Borg*); LUELLA
GEAR (*pet shop owner*); ALEXANDER CAMPBELL (*Pem-
berton*); ROBERT NOE (*Waldron*); ALEXANDER LOCK-
WOOD (*Nichols*); KEN SMITH (*Wylie*); ALAN MACATEER
(*museum guard*); MANUEL APARICIO (*warehouse
guard*); BRAINARD DUFFIELD (*butler*); with Unbilled
Guest Appearances: MARLENE DIETRICH (*night club
patron*); FLETCHER MARKLE (*night club patron*);
HENRY FONDA (*night club waiter*); JOHN GARFIELD
(*street loiterer*); MARSHA HUNT (*secretary-reception-
ist*); LEONARD LYONS (*columnist*); BURGESS MEREDITH
(*bartender*).

CREDITS: FLETCHER MARKLE (*Director*); EDWARD
J. DANZIGER, HARRY LEE DANZIGER (*Producers*);
FLETCHER MARKLE, VINCENT McCONNOR (*Scenarists*);
DON MALKAMES (*Photographer*); ROBERT W. STRINGER
(*Musical Score*); ROBERT MATTHEWS (*Editor*); WIL-
LIAM L. NEMETH (*Special Effects*); DAVID M. POLAK
(*Sound Recorder*); FRED RYLE (*Makeup*); SAL J.
SCOPPA, JR. (*Assistant Director*); Original Story by
JOHN ROEBURT.

NOTES: This independent film shot in New York
City with a $400,000 budget was largely financed
by the producers and its star, Franchot Tone. The
idea was indeed an interesting one. An earnest assistant District Attorney (Franchot Tone), while
investigating two murders, uncovers a vicious "hate
group." Other than the bizarre climax in a modern
art museum, the film's depth was questionable. *Variety* looked at it this way. "Carrying on the cine-
matic attack against race and religious intolerance,
Jigsaw is a well-intentioned but lightweight film. . . ."

The plot took Mr. Tone, at one point, into the
famous Blue Angel nitery. And who would best ex-
emplify a smartly dressed habitué but Marlene Dietrich? The only glimpse of her focuses on Dietrich's
departure with her escort (played by writer-director
Markle), to whom she says, "No, no, no, I'm not
interested. Some time later perhaps."

With Richard Todd

Stage Fright

With Jane Wyman (far right)

A Warner Bros.-First National Picture—1950

CAST: JANE WYMAN (*Eve Gill*); MARLENE DIETRICH (*Charlotte Inwood*); MICHAEL WILDING (*Smith*); RICHARD TODD (*Jonathan Cooper*); ALISTAIR SIM (*Commodore Gill*); KAY WALSH (*Nellie*); DAME SYBIL THORNDIKE (*Mrs. Gill*); MILES MALLESON (*bibulous gent*); HECTOR MACGREGOR (*Freddie*); JOYCE GRENFELL (*shooting gallery attendant*); ANDRE MORELL (*Inspector Byard*); PATRICIA HITCHCOCK (*Chubby*); with Irene Handel, Arthur Howard, Everley Gregg, Helen Goss, Cyril Chamberlain and ALFRED HITCHCOCK as a nameless passerby.

CREDITS: ALFRED HITCHCOCK (*Director and Producer*); WHITFIELD COOK (*Scenarist*); ALMA REVILLE (*Adaptation*); JAMES BRIDIE (*Additional Dialogue*); WILKIE COOPER (*Photographer*); EDWARD JARVIS (*Editor*); TERENCE VERITY (*Art Director*); LEIGHTON LUCAS (*Musical Score*); LOUIS LEVY (*Musical Director*); Miss Wyman's Wardrobe, MILO ANDERSON; Miss Dietrich's Wardrobe, CHRISTIAN DIOR; HAROLD KING (*Sound*); FRED AHERN (*Production Supervisor*); COLIN GUARDE (*Makeup Artist*); From the novel "Man Running" by SELWYN JEPSON.

Singing "The Laziest Gal in Town"

SONG: *By* COLE PORTER; "The Laziest Gal in Town."

SYNOPSIS: Jonathan Cooper (Richard Todd) is suspected of murdering the husband of the woman he loves, musical comedy star Charlotte Inwood (Marlene Dietrich). He goes to a girl friend for help. She is Eve Gill (Jane Wyman), a student of acting at the Royal Academy of Dramatic Arts. He explains to Eve how he got involved with Miss Inwood and how one evening she appeared at his apartment in a bloodstained dress and asked him to go to her apartment and get her a fresh dress. In doing so, he was seen by the maid Nellie (Kay Walsh), who had already discovered the body.

Eve takes him to the seacoast and begs her father, Commodore Gill (Alistair Sim), to take him on a sea voyage. Later, when Eve and her father suggest to Cooper that the actress was probably only *using* him, Cooper flies into a rage and throws the bloodstained dress into the fireplace, thus destroying his only claim to innocence.

Eve, meanwhile, has thought up a plan to help Cooper, and early in the morning returns to the city. At the Inwood residence Eve hides herself in the crowd that has gathered and watches as Detective

With Andre Morell and Michael Wilding

Inspector Smith (Michael Wilding) departs, says a few words to a colleague, then walks across the street and into a pub. Eve, playing detective, goes into the pub and takes a corner table. To attract Smith's attention she feigns a coughing spell, which brings the Detective Inspector to her table posthaste. She coyly gets certain facts of the Inwood murder case out of

With Jane Wyman

the inspector, during which time the maid Nellie comes into the pub and speaks quite loudly of her mistress and the murder. Smith sees Eve home and she invites him to tea the following afternoon, at her mother's home.

Continuing her plot, Eve persuades the maid Nellie to let her pose as her "cousin" for a few days. Nellie, thinking Eve is a reporter, gets paid handsomely for the favor.

At the Inwood residence, Eve meets Charlotte Inwood and her producer Freddie Williams (Hector MacGregor) and immediately distrusts them both. While waiting in another room for Miss Inwood, Eve hears Detective Inspector Smith in the next room. He's come to ask more questions of Charlotte. He leaves with his colleague Inspector Byard (Andre Morell) without ever seeing Eve in her maid's disguise! Eve is informed by Charlotte that she must also act as a dresser at the theatre and to report to her that evening.

That afternoon Smith arrives for tea and is charmed by Mrs. Gill (Dame Sybil Thorndike), Eve's mother, a slightly forgetful matron. Eve arrives soon afterwards, still in her disguise, and meets her father in the hallway. She changes quickly and they enter the living room. Her father tells her at this time that "Johnny" has left their cottage by the sea; meaning, of course, that Cooper has returned to the city.

At the theatre that evening, while Charlotte is singing "The Laziest Gal in Town" on stage, Eve spots Cooper roaming backstage. He doesn't know that Eve is posing as Charlotte's maid's cousin. Eve hides in the passageway until Cooper goes into Charlotte's dressing room. Then when the two are together, Eve listens at the door. Cooper tells the star that he still has the bloodstained dress, but now realizes she doesn't love him at all.

The next afternoon, at a theatrical garden party, Charlotte is singing "La Vie en Rose" when a small boy walks up to her with a doll whose dress is bloodstained. This was Commodore Gill's way of forcing her to confess! She stops her song and is carried off. Eve discovers, in the meanwhile, that she loves Detective Inspector Smith, and the feeling is mutual. However, it soon becomes apparent to Smith that his curious friend Eve is actually the new maid when Freddie calls Eve to the stage to help Charlotte. At the theatre that evening, after the performance, Eve gets Charlotte in an empty dressing room to make her talk. A "live" mike is broadcasting every word they speak over a speaker system in the now deserted theatre. Soon Cooper arrives and, when seen by the police, begins a merry chase, hiding in a prop room beneath the stage. Eve, accompanying him to his hiding place, soon learns some strange facts about her friend!

NOTES: While it was far from superb Alfred Hitchcock, this film does contain some of his best touches. The scene of the hidden microphone broadcasting the conversation between the inquisitive maid and

187

Singing "La Vie en Rose"

Dietrich had a new song too. Cole Porter wrote "The Laziest Gal in Town" especially for her. The number was given a lush background and she gave it a sexy rendition.

Howard Barnes in the *New York Herald Tribune* wisely commented, "It is Miss Dietrich, though, who dominates *Stage Fright*. She sings sultry songs and charms all her gentlemen callers throughout the work. It is only a pity that she and Hitchcock could not have found a more substantial frame for her didoes."

Alfred Hitchcock said, "Miss Dietrich has that spark that transmits itself visually. It's rare."

With director Alfred Hitchcock

the reticent star all over the empty theatre is pure Hitchcock. The tension was well formulated, although the director deceives his audience from beginning to end. The finale was not given above for those who haven't seen the film—and those who have forgotten it.

Marlene Dietrich was most effective as Charlotte Inwood, in some stunning gowns by Dior and with fresh, razor-sharp dialogue to utter. At one point when a frightened Jane Wyman (as Doris Dimsdale, the "cousin" maid) speaks of a murderer in the theatre, Charlotte calmly replies, "The only murderer here is the orchestra leader."

Although she sang the standard "La Vie en Rose,"

No Highway

Released in the United States as No Highway in the Sky.

A 20th Century-Fox Picture—1951

CAST: JAMES STEWART (*Mr. Honey*); MARLENE DIETRICH (*Monica Teasdale*); GLYNIS JOHNS (*Marjorie Corder*); JACK HAWKINS (*Dennis Scott*); RONALD SQUIRE (*Sir John*); JANETTE SCOTT (*Elspeth Honey*); NIALL McGINNIS (*Captain Samuelson*); ELIZABETH ALLAN (*Shirley Scott*); KENNETH MORE (*Dobson*); DAVID HUTCHESON (*Penworthy*); BEN WILLIAMS (*guard*); MAURICE DENHAM (*Major Pease*); WILFRID HYDE WHITE (*Fisher*); HECTOR MacGREGOR (*1st engineer*); BASIL APPLEBY (*2nd engineer*); MICHAEL KINGSLEY (*navigator*); PETER MURRAY (*radio operator*); DORA BRYAN (*Rosie*).

CREDITS: HENRY KOSTER (*Director*); LOUIS D. LIGHTON (*Producer*); R. C. SHERRIFF, OSCAR MILLARD and ALEC COPPEL (*Scenarists*); GEORGES PERINAL (*Photographer*); MANUEL DEL CAMPO (*Editor*); C. P. NORMAN (*Art Director*); BUSTER AMBLER (*Sound Recorder*); BLUEY HILL (*Assistant Director*); Miss Dietrich's Wardrobe by CHRISTIAN DIOR; Based on the Novel by NEVIL SHUTE.

SYNOPSIS: Mr. Honey (James Stewart), a gangling absent-minded scientist, is convinced that the tail-plane of a new type of aircraft will snap off after 1,440 hours of flying time. His company is sending him from England to Labrador to investigate an air crash, when he discovers the plane he is flying on has already done 1420 hours.

He tells the pilot he must turn back, but the pilot refuses, thinking Honey's explanations preposterous. His deep concern for the safety of all of the passengers is noticed by musical comedy star Monica Teasdale (Marlene Dietrich) who, not understanding any of the technical jargon he speaks, begins to believe in this man, whose sincerity is overwhelming. Honey is the type of man thoroughly engrossed in his work and his dedication shows through to such a degree that Monica sides with him when the going gets rough.

Besides the famed actress, Honey has also elicited the sympathy of stewardess Marjorie Corder (Glynis Johns), who is likewise convinced that this man knows what he's talking about and that something will happen if steps aren't taken to prevent it.

The plane reaches Gander without difficulty and because of his insistence is thoroughly checked. The ground crew, looking for visible signs of wear and tear, naturally find nothing and give the plane the "okay" to take off. Honey, fearing more loss of life, pulls the undercarriage lever and wrecks the plane's chances of takeoff.

With Glynis Johns

Back in England, Honey tries to explain to his superiors, Dennis Scott (Jack Hawkins), and the owner of the aircraft company, Sir John (Ronald Squire), that "energy caused by vibration must be absorbed by the metal itself" and wants to begin extensive tests to prove his theory. The executives,

With Glynis Johns, Janette Scott, and Elizabeth Allan

190

With James Stewart

however, consider Honey to be out of his mind and almost turn his plan down until Monica Teasdale visits them and explains why she believes in this man and his reasoning. Giving the matter more serious thought, they decide to give Mr. Honey the go-ahead on his project.

Meanwhile, both Monica and Miss Corder become interested in this man's personal life, of which there is little except for a young daughter, Elspeth (Janette Scott). It seems with the death of his wife, Honey submerged himself in his job, neglecting his daughter. Both women pitch in and become friends with Elspeth and have many happy times together while her father is struggling against all odds to prove his theory.

Finally, after weeks of intense testing, Honey's theory proves 100% correct. Not only is he vindicated, but many lives will be saved in the future of aviation by his doggedness.

NOTES: Dietrich returned to England again to work with James Stewart, her co-star of *Destry Rides Again*. Although in a subordinate role, she appeared to considerable advantage in smartly-tailored suits, crisp veils, and lush furs. Dior had a field day. Her role was sympathetic and Dietrich gave a clearly-wrought performance, sustaining a sketchy role with her usual aplomb.

Otis L. Guernsey, Jr. in the *New York Herald Tribune* said, "Playing a movie star who comes to believe Mr. Honey's dire predictions of doom, Miss Dietrich appears in the type of throaty glamour role she knows best, and it is good to see her on the screen. *Variety* noted, "Miss Dietrich, as a noted film actress, stands out in a very sympathetic part."

With Jack Hawkins and Ronald Squire

191

With Arthur Kennedy

Rancho Notorious

A Fidelity Pictures Production in Technicolor

Distributed by RKO-Radio Pictures—1952

CAST: MARLENE DIETRICH (*Altar Keane*); ARTHUR KENNEDY (*Vern Haskell*); MEL FERRER (*Frenchy Fairmont*); LLOYD GOUGH (*Kinch*); GLORIA HENRY (*Beth*); WILLIAM FRAWLEY (*Baldy Gunder*); LISA FERRADAY (*Maxine*); JOHN RAVEN (*chuck-a-luck dealer*); JACK ELAM (*Geary*); GEORGE REEVES (*Wilson*); FRANK FERGUSON (*Preacher*); FRANCIS MCDONALD (*Harbin*); DAN SEYMOUR (*Comanche Paul*); JOHN KELLOGG (*Factor*); RODRIC REDWING (*Rio*); STUART RANDALL (*Starr*); ROGER ANDERSON (*Red*); CHARLES GONZALES (*Hevia*); FELIPE TURICH (*Sanchez*); JOSE DOMINGUEZ (*Gonzales*); STAN JOLLEY (*Deputy Warren*); JOHN DOUCETTE (*Whitey*); CHARLITA (*Mexican girl in bar*); RALPH SANFORD (*politician*); LANE

With Lloyd Gough, Frank Ferguson, Jack Elam, and George Reeves

With Lloyd Gough, Frank Ferguson, Charles Gonzales, Felipe Turich, and Roger Anderson

CHANDLER (*Sheriff Hardy*); FUZZY KNIGHT (*barber*); FRED GRAHAM (*Ace Maguire*); DICK WESSEL (*deputy*); DICK ELIOT (*storyteller*); WILLIAM HAADE (*Sheriff Bullock*).

CREDITS: FRITZ LANG (*Director*); HOWARD WELSCH (*Producer*); DANIEL TARADASH (*Scenarist*); HAL MOHR (*Photographer*); BEN HERSH (*Production Supervisor*); OTTO LUDWIG (*Editor*); WIARD IHNEN (*Production Designer*); ROBERT PRIESTLEY (*Set Decorator*); Miss Dietrich's Costumes by DON LOPER; JOE KING (*Wardrobe*); EMIL NEWMAN (*Musical Score*); RICHARD MUELLER (*Technicolor Color Consultant*); HUGH McDOWELL, MAC DALGLEISH (*Sound Recorders*); EMMETT EMERSON (*Assistant Director*); FRANK WESTMORE (*Makeup Artist*); Miss Dietrich's Hair Stylist, NELLIEMARIE MANLEY; From a story by SYLVIA RICHARDS.

SONGS: *By* KEN DARBY; sung by Miss Dietrich: "Gypsy Davey," "Get Away, Young Man"; sung by William Lee: "Legend of Chuck-a-Luck."

SYNOPSIS: In a little Wyoming town, in the 1870's, Vern Haskell's (Arthur Kennedy) fiancée Beth (Gloria Henry) is brutally molested and killed during a holdup of her father's general store. Vern, the sheriff, and a posse ride out after the two killers. When the men reach the boundary line, the sheriff turns back. Vern, with vengeance in his heart, tracks them alone.

Coming upon the murderer's accomplice, Whitey (John Doucette), who has been left for dead, Vern hears the man murmur the word "Chuck-a-Luck" before dying. With this as his only clue, Vern begins to hunt for Beth's killer.

By sheer hit-and-miss questioning in a dozen towns, Vern finally learns that "Chuck-a-Luck" is somehow connected with a legendary figure named

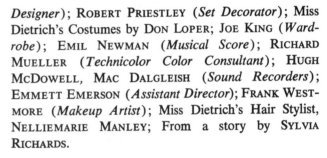

With Arthur Kennedy and Mel Ferrer

With Mel Ferrer

Altar Keane (Marlene Dietrich), whose romantic escapades as a fabulous saloon entertainer are recalled by a number of men. Vern also learns that Altar's closest companion is a man called Frenchy Fairmont (Mel Ferrer) who has the reputation as the fastest gun in the west, and who once rescued Altar from a cheap gambling casino after she had managed to win a large sum of money—also with his help—in a game of chuck-a-luck.

His first break comes when he discovers that Frenchy has been arrested in a neighboring town, and he proceeds to get himself jailed in the same cell with the notorious outlaw. After winning Frenchy's confidence, Vern joins him in a jail break, displaying great ingenuity. Together the men ride out of town.

The pair arrive at a hidden valley near the border, and there, far below, is the "Chuck-a-Luck" Vern has long been searching for. This is the name of a refuge for outlaws and bandits of every description. Chatelaine of this rancho notoriqus is the beautiful Altar Keane, who runs a successful horse ranch, from all outward appearances!

Somewhere among these men, Vern knows, is Beth's killer. He stays on as a hand but learns nothing, for the credo of "Chuck-a-Luck" is *no questions asked* of anyone residing there.

Vern's next course of action is a pretended romantic interest in Altar, but she ignores his advances and remains loyal to Frenchy. Then one evening Vern notices Altar wearing the large brooch he had given Beth the day she was killed. He assumes that Frenchy gave it to her, but cannot get her to reveal the donor. The unexpected arrival of the Marshall and his deputies changes his plans.

Returning a few days later from a bank holdup ahead of the others, Vern cajoles Altar into telling him who gave her that brooch. When she tells him it was her "cut" from a job Kinch (Lloyd Gough)

With Stuart Randall, Arthur Kennedy, Francis McDonald, and Jack Elam

194

pulled, Vern flies into a rage, explaining the origin of the brooch.

In town Vern confronts Kinch with his crime and bids him to draw. Kinch, knowing that Vern has picked up every trick of Frenchy's prowess with firearms, refuses. The sheriff interrupts them, and Vern tells the sheriff the story. Kinch is arrested. The other outlaws, however, rescue Kinch and ride back to "Chuck-a-Luck" convinced that Altar has betrayed them.

In the gun battle that ensues, Kinch is killed and Altar is mortally wounded shielding Frenchy from a bullet. Vern and Frenchy then ride out of the valley for the last time.

NOTES: *Rancho Notorious*, originally called *Chuck-a-Luck*, is at best a poor man's *Destry Rides Again*. When not at its best, it's much more fun. Without being too critical, the viewer can have a marvelous time in the old West with Marlene Dietrich in glorious color. Her co-stars were Arthur Kennedy, a fine actor—one of Hollywood's really unappreciated talents—and Mel Ferrer, who was most ill-at-ease in a western role. He struggled valiantly, but the odds were too great. One never really believed that he was "the fastest gun in the west."

The title credits and end-credits failed to list Lloyd Gough as "Kinch" at all, yet his role was the pivotal one. After all, Arthur Kennedy spends an entire movie chasing him—he could at least get billing! Dietrich was re-united with Francis McDonald (as Harbin), who played Gary Cooper's sidekick in *Morocco*.

This was Marlene Dietrich's first professional encounter with famous director Fritz Lang, a close friend for many years. Unfortunately, Lang was not at his best directing a western; his forte was sociological dramas. The story, however, did move along at a good pace and there was plenty of excitement, tension, and bold, bawdy humor, especially in Dietrich's flashback scenes showing her as various men remembered her in days gone by. And the color photography (by Hal Mohr) was extremely good and made one wish for more Dietrich color films, but it made the limited budget painfully noticeable. There were painted backdrops, cheap interiors, etc.

Don Loper's costumes gave Dietrich a lasting western glamour and properly exposed those supreme gams in earlier sequences while covering them completely later in men's trousers. Ken Darby's songs were routine.

Bosley Crowther in *The New York Times* noted that Dietrich had little to do. "One scene, introduced as a reflection of her youth as a dance-hall girl, wherein she and several other floozies ride gentlemen piggy-back across a barroom floor, gives promise of something on the order of her cut-ups in *Destry Rides Again*, but that is the only demonstration of rowdy behavior that she gives. And one song number, 'Get Away, Young Man,' brings but an echo of La Dietrich of yore."

195

Around the World in 80 Days

A Michael Todd Company, Inc. Production

Released Through United Artists—1956

CAST: David Niven (*Phileas Fogg*); Cantinflas (*Passepartout*); Robert Newton (*Mr. Fix*); Shirley MacLaine (*Aouda*); with the following stars in cameo parts: Charles Boyer, Joe E. Brown, Martine Carol, John Carradine, Charles Coburn, Ronald Colman, Melville Cooper, Noël Coward, Finlay Currie, Reginald Denny, Andy Devine, Marlene Dietrich, Luis Miguel Dominguin, Fernandel, Sir John Gielgud, Hermione Gingold, Jose Greco, Sir Cedric Hardwicke, Trevor Howard, Glynis Johns, Buster Keaton, Evelyn Keyes, Beatrice Lillie, Peter Lorre, Edmund Lowe, Victor McLaglen, Col. Tim McCoy, A. E. Matthews, Mike Mazurki, John Mills, Alan Mowbray, Robert Morley, Edward R. Murrow, Jack Oakie, George Raft, Gilbert Roland, Cesar Romero, Frank Sinatra, Red Skelton, Ronald Squire, Basil Sydney, Richard Wattis and Harcourt Williams.

CREDITS: Michael Anderson (*Director*); Michael Todd (*Producer*); William Cameron Menzies (*Associate Producer*); S. J. Perelman, James Poe, and John Farrow (*Scenarists*); Victor Young (*Musical Score*); Miles White (*Costumer*); Lionel Lindon (*Photographer*); Gene Ruggiero, Paul Weatherwax (*Editors*); James W. Sullivan, Ken Adams (*Art Directors*); Based on the novel by Jules Verne.

SYNOPSIS: In 1872, Phileas Fogg (David Niven), an English gentleman, and Passepartout (Cantinflas), his valet, depart London on the boat train to Paris in order to win a bet of £20,000. They are attempting to go around the world in the incredibly fast time of 80 days.

An avalanche blocks the railroad tunnel to Marseilles, so Fogg buys a balloon and the pair fly south. High winds, however, blow them off course and they land in Spain. There, in return for Passepartout's session in the bull ring, a wealthy sheik rushes them to Marseilles by boat just in time to catch a connecting steamer to India.

At Suez, Scotland Yard detective Mr. Fix (Robert Newton) is convinced that Fogg has just robbed the Bank of England and while awaiting orders to arrest him, follows the two to India. While travelling through India, Fogg and his valet rescue a young Indian princess, Aouda (Shirley MacLaine), from being burned alive in a suttee ceremony, and she

With David Niven and Frank Sinatra

joins them on their journey. In Calcutta, Fix has Fogg arrested for causing a disturbance. Jumping bail, Fogg and his friends sail to Hong Kong. Fix, however, gets Passepartout drunk and "shanghaied" aboard a ship sailing for Japan. Fogg resourcefully hires a junk and arrives at Yokohama and finds his valet before his ship leaves for America.

Arriving in San Francisco, their party visits a saloon and there a dance hall queen (Marlene Dietrich) entertains them. From San Francisco they set out for New York. Crossing the plains, they are attacked by Indians, and Passepartout is captured. The time lost in rescueing him is costly, for they arrive in New York too late to catch the boat to Liverpool.

Boarding a trading schooner bound for South America, Fogg bribes the captain to change course for England. When the fuel runs out, Fogg buys the vessel and burns everything he can to keep up steam. They arrive in Liverpool and race to the railroad station, but Fogg is arrested by Fix. Several hours later Fogg is released, having been cleared of the bank robbery charge. The bet has apparently been lost, for they arrive in London five minutes too late.

With Cantinflas, David Niven, and Frank Sinatra

With Red Skelton and Cantinflas

Aouda and Fogg, meanwhile, have decided to get married, and Passepartout is sent to make all the necessary arrangements. While doing so, he learns that Fogg has gained a day's time by travelling from east to west, having crossed the International date-line.

Fogg and his friends rush into his club just as the clock is striking quarter to nine, the very moment Fogg is due. His triumph is clouded by the fact that a woman has entered the sacred precincts of the club. Fogg then invites the members to the curb to meet the future Mrs. Fogg.

NOTES: Miles White provided Marlene with an attractive wig and a fetching gown for her cameo role as the dance hall queen in San Francisco. Frank Sinatra, Red Skelton, and George Raft were in the same sequence.

The picture won the Best Picture Oscar. The scenarists also won Academy Awards for their nimble and witty script; Victor Young, who died before the awards were made, finally won an Oscar; Lionel Lindon's photography earned him an Oscar. Editors Gene Ruggiero and Paul Weatherwax won Oscars. Michael Anderson, Miles White, and James W. Sullivan and Ken Adams were nominated.

In his review in *Films in Review,* Henry Hart said, "This is a producer's triumph—not a director's, nor an actor's (though there are fine performances), nor a writer's. *Around the World in 80 Days* is what a motion picture should be because Todd made, or was prevailed upon to make, so many showmanlike decisions—to film the Verne story, get Perelman to liven it up, cast Niven and Cantinflas, have stars play bit parts, make Victor Young supply pleasing music, let director Michael Anderson have his head."

The Monte Carlo Story

A Titanus Production in Technicolor

Released through United Artists—1957

CAST: MARLENE DIETRICH (*Marquise Maria de Crevecoeur*); VITTORIO DE SICA (*Count Dino della Fiaba*); ARTHUR O'CONNELL (*Mr. Hinkley*); NATALIE TRUNDY (*Jane Hinkley*); JANE ROSE (*Mrs. Freeman*); CLELIA MATANIA (*Sophia*); ALBERTO RABAGLIATI (*Albert*); MISCHA AUER (*Hector*); RENATO RASCEL (*Duval*); CARLO RIZZO (*Henri*); TRUMAN SMITH (*Mr. Freeman*); MIMO BILLI (*Roland*); MARCO TULLI (*Francoise*); GUIDO MARTUFI (*Paul*); JEAN COMBAL (*hotel managing director*); VERA GARRETTO (*Caroline*); YANNICK GEFFROY (*Gabriel*); BETTY PHILIPPSEN (*Zizi*); FRANK COLSON (*Walter—1st American*); SERGE FLIEGERS (*Harry—2nd American*); FRANK ELLIOTT (*Mr. Ewing*); BETTY CARTER (*Mrs. Ewing*); GERLAINE FOURNIER (*the German lady*); SIMONEMARIE ROSE (*the lady in magenta*); CLARA BECK (*American oil heiress*).

CREDITS: SAMUEL A. TAYLOR (*Director*); MARCELLO GIROSI (*Producer*); SAMUEL A. TAYLOR (*Scenarist*); GIUSEPPE ROTUNNO (*Photographer*); NINO MISIANO (*Production Manager*); GASTONE MEDIN (*Art Director*); LUISA ALESSANDRI, ROBERTO MONTEMURRO and MARIA RUSSO (*Assistant Directors*); KURT DOBRAWSKY (*Sound Recorder*); ELIO COSTANZI (*Wardrobe*); Miss Dietrich's Gowns by JEAN LOUIS; From an Original Story by MARCELLO GIROSI and DINO RISI.

SONGS: "Les Jeux Sont Faits" (by MICHAEL EMER); "Rien ne Va Plus," "Back Home in Indiana."

SYNOPSIS: Count Dino della Fiaba (Vittorio de Sica), a handsome nobleman of extraordinary charm, having abandoned his native Naples, now resides in Monte Carlo to be near the great gambling salon at the Casino of Monte Carlo. Five years earlier he had lost his entire fortune at the roulette table and since that time his former servants, now employed in the principality's leading luxury hotel, have been loaning him a few thousand francs every night to play at the Casino. The Count, however, confines his activity to *baccarat* and *trente et quarante*.

With Mischa Auer and Vittorio De Sica

Meanwhile, Dino has been working on an infallible system to beat the roulette wheel and repay his good friends with a premium besides. Unfortunately, the count's debit has reached the $10,000 mark and his "backers" meet and agree to exploit the Count's considerable charm in finding him a suitable "wealthy" mate. An array of nuptial candidates are presented to the count in the lobby of the hotel, but none of them please him until he sees the Marquise Maria de Crevecoeur (Marlene Dietrich).

What the count doesn't know, however, is that Maria is a born gambler like himself and is in a similar fix, having gambled away the money the late Marquis had left her. She has come to Monte Carlo to find a wealthy suitor to underwrite her passion for the gambling tables.

Soon the Count begins an ardent courtship and before long they discover they have much in common, namely gambling day and night. Then, deeply in love, they decide to marry, and at that moment

With Vittorio De Sica and Renato Rascel

they learn of each other's utter poverty. They sadly decide to go their separate ways.

Moments later, Mr. Homer Hinkley (Arthur O'Connell), an American widower trying out his first yacht, *The Hoosier*, arrives in Monte Carlo and smashes into Count Dino's *Speranza*. While repairs are being made on the damaged *Speranza*, the count and his "sister," the Marquise, become guests aboard *The Hoosier*.

Hinkley soon discovers he loves Maria. His teenage daughter Jane (Natalie Trundy) worships Count Dino. Hinkley timidly but persistently asks Maria to marry him. She makes a full confession about being an adventuress and an inveterate gambler, but Hinkley is only the more insistent. She finally accepts.

Jane comforts Dino in his grief at losing Maria, and she "proposes" to him. When he protests that he is much too old for her, she argues that mathematically they are getting *closer* in age as each gets older and that now she is nineteen. Suddenly, the Count realizes that this is the number combination he has searched for to beat the roulette table.

Soon all of Monte Carlo learns that "Count Dino is back at the roulette table" and winning a fortune. Nothing can stop this winning streak until Hinkley appears and learns from his daughter of her part in

With Arthur O'Connell

the count's good fortune. Then he reminds Jane that she is not nineteen yet, but only eighteen. The count checks his system. The new number combination will not work. Soon he begins to lose, but before all is gone his former chauffeur gently taps him on the head with a small monkey wrench. He is carried

With Arthur O'Connell (seated, right)

away from the table and his friends collect the remaining chips.

His debts paid, the count says he is finished with gambling forever and decides to return to Naples. Maria, at the same time, is leaving on Hinkley's yacht when she sees the count standing alone on the deck of his yacht. She tells Hinkley that the count is not her "brother" and that she loves him. He pulls along side and Maria boards the *Speranza*. Together they head back toward Monte Carlo and the gambling tables.

NOTES: Dietrich's only Italian-made picture was, despite the teaming with the popular Vittorio De Sica, an undistinguished film. And to add to the somewhat dreary script and uneven acting, Dietrich was badly photographed by Giuseppe Rotunno, whose principal forte is lush scenery—not beautiful women! A typical example of Rotunno's gorgeous visuals is John Huston's *The Bible* ('66) which did much to establish the mood of that epic, but fell short of its mark when concentration was directed to a star like Ava Gardner. *The Monte Carlo Story* did boast terrific color photography of the Riviera but little else!

This situation left *The New York Times* critic little to say, except, ". . . the story is familiar indeed—the one about two aristocratic adventurers out to fleece some rich visitors. The wordly prowlers are, of course, perfectly realized in Miss Dietrich's bland beauty and Mr. De Sica's gentleness."

202

With Charles Laughton and John Williams

Witness for the Prosecution

An Edward Small-Arthur Hornblow Production

Released through United Artists—1958

CAST: TYRONE POWER (*Leonard Vole*); MARLENE DIETRICH (*Christine Vole*); CHARLES LAUGHTON (*Sir Wilfrid Robarts*); ELSA LANCHESTER (*Miss Plimsoll*); JOHN WILLIAMS (*Brogan-Moore*); HENRY DANIELL (*Mayhew*); IAN WOLFE (*Carter*); UNA O'CONNOR (*Janet MacKenzie*); TORIN THATCHER (*Mr. Meyers*); FRANCIS COMPTON (*Judge*); NORMA VARDEN (*Mrs. French*); PHILIP TONGE (*Inspector Hearne*); RUTA LEE (*Diana*); MOLLY RODEN (*Miss McHugh*); OTTOLA NESMITH (*Miss Johnson*); MARJORIE EATON (*Miss O'Brien*).

CREDITS: BILLY WILDER (*Director*); ARTHUR HORNBLOW, JR. (*Producer*); BILLY WILDER, HARRY KURNITZ (*Scenarists*); LARRY MARCUS (*Adaptation*); RUSSELL HARLAN (*Photographer*); EMMETT EMERSON (*Assistant Director*); EDITH HEAD (*Miss Dietrich's Costumes*); JOSEPH KING (*Costumer*); RAY SEBASTIAN, HARRY RAY and GUSTAF NORIN (*Makeup*); DANIEL MANDELL (*Editor*); HOWARD BRISTOL (*Set Decorator*); ALEXANDRE TRAUNER (*Art Director*); MATTY MALNECK (*Musical Score*); LEONID RAAB (*Music Arranger*); ERNEST GOLD (*Music Conductor*); FRED LAU and SAMUEL GOLDWYN SOUND DEPARTMENT (*Sound Recorder*); From the stage play by AGATHA CHRISTIE.

SONG: *By* RALPH ARTHUR ROBERTS and JACK BROOKS; "I May Never Go Home Anymore."

SYNOPSIS: Recovering from a heart attack, famous barrister Sir Wilfrid Robarts (Charles Laughton) returns from the hospital with an over-solicitous nurse, Miss Plimsoll (Elsa Lanchester), always at his side. His attitude is anything but cheery, since his doctor has forbidden him to handle any more courtroom criminal trials, which have been his life's work.

Before getting settled in his offices, a solicitor,

With Tyrone Power

Mr. Mayhew (Henry Daniell), brings a client, Leonard Vole (Tyrone Power), to see him. Mayhew hopes that Sir Wilfrid will take an interest in his client's case. In his private office, Sir Wilfrid trades a forbidden cigar for his legal advice. Slowly, as Vole relates his story, the barrister's interest grows.

Vole describes the many jobs he has held and his slight acquaintance with Mrs. Emily French (Norma Varden), a wealthy widow whose murdered body was recently discovered in her home. Vole describes his chance meeting with Mrs. French and explains that he continued seeing her to interest her in backing his new all-purpose eggbeater. Vole also tells Sir Wilfrid that the only witness with him at the exact time of Mrs. French's murder was his wife Christine.

Brogan-Moore (John Williams), Sir Wilfrid's junior partner, enters the room with a newspaper which states that the murdered woman's will has been probated, leaving £80,000 to Leonard Vole. Sir Wilfrid turns the case over to Brogan-Moore as Inspector Hearne (Philip Tonge) arrives to arrest Mr. Vole for the crime.

As Sir Wilfrid prepares to go upstairs to his private chambers, he is stopped by the arresting presence of Christine Vole (Marlene Dietrich), who has come to see him. She tells him that she does not believe in her husband's innocence even though she consents to "alibi" for him on the stand.

After Mrs. Vole leaves, Brogan-Moore feels the case is hopeless, but Sir Wilfrid decides to take the case himself against doctors orders.

At the prison the next day Sir Wilfrid, to better understand the relationship between the Voles, lis-

tens as Vole describes his first meeting with Christine, a singer in a German café during the war. After a riot in the bombed-out cabaret where Christine sings, they escape to Christine's flat. After their eventual marriage they returned to England after the war. Sir Wilfrid then tells Vole that he can't put Christine on the stand. Vole is shaken since his wife is his only chance.

The trial opens at Old Bailey amidst interested crowds, when the attorney for the Crown, Mr. Myers (Torin Thatcher), opens the trial with a series of witnesses. There is great intensity as Sir Wilfrid cross-examines, and tension mounts. Proceedings are occasionally interrupted so Sir Wilfrid can have his blood-pressure checked by his doctor and Miss Plimsoll.

Mr. Myers then calls his last witness for the prosecution—Christine Vole! The courtroom is shocked and amazed. On the stand, she says she is not legally married to Vole, but is the wife of Otto Ludwig Helm in Germany and therefore can testify against Vole. She calmly states that Vole told her he had murdered the rich widow.

Sir Wilfrid, in cross-examination, tears into Christine's testimony, making her admit her lies, her violations of the marriage vow, and the fact that she

As the Cockney girl

*Same scene without the Cockney
girl makeup*

lied to the police originally. In a desperate move, Sir Wilfrid then puts Leonard Vole on the stand, feeling that his simple account of the facts will set things straight. Mr. Myers is unable to shake the honest and sincere testimony of Vole in cross-examination.

Court is adjourned. Vole is shocked at his wife's treachery. Sir Wilfrid retreats to his offices for a

With Charles Laughton and Henry Daniell

rest. There, he receives an anonymous call from a woman who summons him to Euston Station to get the "lowdown on that German trollop." Sir Wilfrid and Mayhew visit the station, where a Cockney slut sells them a packet of love letters written by Christine to another man and then disappears into the fog.

The men examine the letters, which say Christine deliberately lied about Vole in order to frame him and thus set herself free to be with another man.

Next day, Sir Wilfrid triumphantly produces these letters in court and Christine is then put back on the stand. Finally she admits the letters are hers. The jury goes out and soon brings back a verdict of "Not Guilty" for Leonard Vole.

But this is only the first "ending" to this picture. There is yet another twist to the plot, and in a moment's time everything is cleared up.

NOTES: This marked the first time that Marlene Dietrich, *as an actress,* became totally involved in a characterization. Her belief in Christine Vole was complete. The audience knew everything about this woman that they were supposed to. When they felt any doubt, it was because Dietrich was deliberately holding something from them. She was, in short, totally believeable and thoroughly exciting.

In adapting this celebrated stage thriller to the screen, Billy Wilder and Harry Kurnitz (working with Larry Marcus' adaptation) took liberties that proved to be nothing short of brilliant: the addition of Elsa Lanchester's fluttering, coddling nurse was sheer genius (and she performed with great inventiveness); adding necessary flashback sequences, which help take the action out of the stage-setting format, gave Dietrich not only a chance to remind audiences of her long-haired svelte beauty (in a tight black dress slit up the side to display those still beautiful legs), but enabled her to sing the song "I May Never Go Home Anymore"; giving the widow role to Norma Varden, an underrated actress who is always believeable; and bringing Una O'Con-

With Tyrone Power (head in hands)

nor back to the screen after a long absence as her maid, Janet MacKenzie. The rest of the supporting cast, headed by John Williams and Henry Daniell, were first-rate.

The role of Christine Vole, on the stage, was a pure tour-de-force, since the actress playing Mrs. Vole also played the cockney tart. Whether Dietrich, on the screen, actually played this second part is open for debate. There are many conflicting stories. One says that Wilder filmed the phone booth scene in Euston Station twice. Once Dietrich was in full makeup as the Cockney woman—wig, false teeth, scar on the face, and makeup on her hands. She made the call to Laughton. Then Wilder had her change back into Christine Vole and make the same call using the identical Cockney accent. He used the former because preview audiences were totally convinced by her performance and, consequently, the suspense was heightened. The latter version (although pictured on these pages) was never used.

Another story has it that Wilder filmed the scenes at the Euston Station once with Dietrich and another time with another actress in identical makeup and dress and that the final footage used was that of the other actress. At any rate, it was a well-kept secret—so well kept that Marlene Dietrich missed getting an Academy Award nomination because the knowledge of her playing two roles had to be suppressed for plot reasons.

Charles Laughton, giving one of his most brilliant performances, was nominated for an Academy Award, as was his wife Elsa Lanchester, for "best supporting actress." Billy Wilder won a nomination for his direction and the Samuel Goldwyn Sound Department, Fred Lau, Sound Recorder, also was nominated. The reason Russell Harlan's outstanding black-and-white photography didn't get a nomination is that during the late fifties, the photography award was merged (color and black-and-white became one), and naturally all of the pictures nominated were in color. This ridiculous situation was eventually changed, and now color and black-and-white are separate categories.

Robert Downing summed things up beautifully in *Films in Review*: "Almost everyone who has seen both play and movie thinks the latter is the better. There are several reasons: Producer Hornblow engaged a magnificent cast; the screenplay by Billy Wilder and Harry Kurnitz is superior to Agatha

Christie's play; Wilder's direction is rich with touches and devices that enliven and amuse; and Russell Harlan's black-and-white photography is never static, despite the fact that much of the action occurs in London's Old Bailey, or, rather, in an excellent reconstruction thereof.

"Marlene Dietrich proves in *Witness for the Prosecution* that she is a dramatic actress as well as a still glamorous chanteuse. . . . Her husband, an opportunistic weakling accused of murder, is played by Tyrone Power with such skillful ambivalence the audience is never certain of his guilt or innocence. . . . Charles Laughton . . . has been given a cardiac condition so the part of a bossy nurse could be written in for Elsa Lanchester. Not since *The Beachcomber* has this husband-and-wife team performed so fortuitously."

The *New York Herald Tribune* commented, "Miss Dietrich is a sultry siren, so inscrutable that even Laughton asks, 'What's the woman up to? What's her game?' Well might he ask. Whatever it is, she plays it with fire and finesse."

Touch of Evil

A Universal-International Picture—1958

CAST: CHARLTON HESTON (*Ramon Miguel Vargas*); JANET LEIGH (*Susan Vargas*); ORSON WELLES (*Hank Quinlan*); JOSEPH CALLEIA (*Pete Menzies*); AKIM TAMIROFF (*"Uncle" Joe Grandi*); JOANNA MOORE (*Marcia Linnekar*); RAY COLLINS (*Adair*); DENNIS WEAVER (*the night man*); VALENTIN DE VARGAS (*Pancho*); MORT MILLS (*Schwartz*); VICTOR MILAN (*Manuelo Sanchez*); LALO RIOS (*Risto*); MICHAEL SARGENT (*"Pretty Boy"*); with Guest Appearances by Marlene Dietrich, Zsa Zsa Gabor, Mercedes McCambridge, Joseph Cotten.

CREDITS: ORSON WELLES (*Director and Scenarist*); ALBERT ZUGSMITH (*Producer*); BILL THOMAS (*Gowns*); HENRY MANCINI (*Musical Score*); PHIL BOWLES (*Assistant Director*); RUSSELL METTY (*Photographer*); Based on the novel *Badge of Evil* by WHIT MASTERSON.

SYNOPSIS: As a conscientious young narcotics investigator from Mexico, Ramon Miguel Vargas (Charlton Heston), and his wife Susan (Janet Leigh), cross the border into the United States, his car blows up, and soon he is after a young Mexican he thinks planted the bomb.

He runs into the fanatical Hank Quinlan (Orson Welles), the psychopathic cop who runs this Texas border town, and appeals to him for aid. Hank is not finicky when dealing with crime and even plants evidence to back up his intuitions. Soon he frames a Mexican youth for murder, but doesn't count on Vargas, who sets out to expose the detectives unethical methods.

Meanwhile, a vengeful narcotics gang menaces Vargas' young wife Susan, which puts Vargas face to face with Hank. Fighting this "big man about town" single-handed is not an easy job, but Vargas wins in the end as the final disintegration of the powerful Hank Quinlan becomes painfully apparent.

NOTES: Marlene Dietrich "guest starred" in this film but had four or five large sequences. All were with Welles. She played, in dark wig and smoking a

With Orson Welles

cigar, Welles' long-time mistress, a madame in a bordello under the constant protection of Welles and his staff.

Dietrich's characterization was unusually good and her dialogue was brittle. At one point, she looks at the grossly fat Welles and quips, "Lay off the candy bars."

This story of brutality and lawlessness had as its theme good versus evil, but Welles achieved only effect and not substance. However, any Welles picture is worth the price of admission, and since this one contains many of his personal touches, it's far above the norm.

Howard Thompson in *The New York Times* said, "Mr. Welles' is an obvious but brilliant bag of tricks. Using a superlative camera (manned by Russell Metty) like a black-snake whip, he lashes the action right into the spectator's eye."

Paul V. Beckley in the *New York Herald Tribune* thought, "To call his (Welles') touch Rembrandtesque may be a bit strong, but when he plays with

black-and-white film, as in this picture, Mr. Welles does revel in chiaroscuro, the play of light and shadow emphasizing not only the eminently melodramatic structure of the film but likewise its mood and meaty characterization." *Films in Review,* however, thought "the subject matter of *Touch of Evil* is so banal and its story-line is so confusing . . . but . . . Welles has furbished it with photographic, directorial, and acting 'touches' which compensate for the irrationality of the picture itself."

With Orson Welles

Judgment at Nuremberg

A Roxlom Production

Released through United Artists—1961

CAST: SPENCER TRACY (*Judge Dan Haywood*); BURT LANCASTER (*Ernst Janning*); RICHARD WIDMARK (*Colonel Tad Lawson*); MARLENE DIETRICH (*Mme. Bertholt*); MAXIMILIAN SCHELL (*Hans Rolfe*); JUDY GARLAND (*Irene Hoffman*); MONTGOMERY CLIFT (*Rudolf Peterson*); WILLIAM SHATNER (*Captain Byers*); EDWARD BINNS (*Senator Burkette*); KENNETH MAC- KENNA (*Judge Kenneth Norris*); WERNER KLEMPERER (*Emil Hahn*); ALAN BAXTER (*General Merrin*); LOR- BEN MEYER (*Werner Lammpe*); RAY TEAL (*Judge Curtiss Ives*); MARTIN BRANDT (*Friedrich Hofstetter*); VIRGINIA CHRISTINE (*Mrs. Halbestadt*); BEN WRIGHT (*Halbestadt*); JOSEPH BERNARD (*Major Abe Radnitz*); JOHN WENGRAF (*Dr. Wieck*); KARL SWENSON (*Dr.

With Spencer Tracy

With Virginia Christine and Spencer Tracy

Geuter); HOWARD CAINE (*Wallner*); OTTO WALDIS (*Pohl*); OLGA FABIAN (*Mrs. Lindnow*); SHEILIA BROMLEY (*Mrs. Ives*); BERNARD KATES (*Perkins*); JANA TAYLOR (*Elsa Scheffler*); PAUL BUSCH (*Schmidt*).

CREDITS: STANLEY KRAMER (*Director* and *Producer*); PHILIP LANGNER (*Associate Producer*); ABBY MANN (*Scenarist*); ERNEST LASZLIO (*Photographer*); FRED KNUDTSON (*Editor*); ERNEST GOLD (*Musical Score*); IVAN VOLKMAN (*Assistant Director*); RUDOLPH STERNAD (*Production Designer* and *Art Director*); JEAN LOUIS (*Gowns*); JOSEPH KING (*Wardrobe*); ART COLE (*Property Master*); CLEM BEAUCHAMP (*Production Manager*); GEORGE MILO (*Set Decorator*).

NOTES: Stanley Kramer's forceful drama of the post-war Nuremberg trials attacked a contemporary subject usually only hinted at in pictures. It was a big picture from every aspect. It contained superb photography, excellent acting, and fine blending of Hollywood-filmed interiors with the location shots done in Germany, giving a feeling of authenticity throughout.

Since there was so much brought out in these trials, director Kramer wisely selected four of the lesser-known members of the Nazi hierarchy for his film. Spencer Tracy as the presiding judge had the task of rendering one of the great decisions in history. His strong performance contained dignity, obvious compassion, and unique understanding of the elements involved. A considerably subdued Burt Lancaster played a war-time scholar and jurist with a fine intensity. Richard Widmark, as the prosecutor,

With Spencer Tracy

With Supreme Court Justice William O. Douglas and Spencer Tracy on the set of Judgment at Nuremberg

filled the courtroom with dramatic force, as did the counsel for the defense (Maximilian Schell). Montgomery Clift played a sterilized witness for the prosecution well. Judy Garland, as another vital witness, was excellent.

Marlene Dietrich played Mme. Bertholt, the widow of a German general, with great feeling and a quiet nobility. Her role had been written into the script to provide a break in the tension of the trials.

And to make it all plausible, Tracy lives in her home during his stay as leading judge. His conversations with her give him some of the feelings and thoughts of one side of the German people.

Kramer's use of big stars for his drama worked both for him and against him. His story's success was assured at the box-office with a top-flight cast, while, on the other hand, some of the character roles might have had more power had they been played by play-

ers of skill whose faces were not so familiar.

In the film's dramatic conclusion, as the guilty are handed out their sentences of life imprisonment, a grim reminder was put before the audience: ". . . of the 99 men sentenced to prison by the time the Nurenberg trials ended on July 14, 1949, not one of the guilty is still serving a sentence."

Paul V. Beckley in the *New York Herald Tribune* stated, "Miss Dietrich does remain herself as far as charm is concerned, but her performance is integral to the story. As a German aristocrat she has just the proper air of world-weariness, the veiled arrogance tempered with sensitivity."

Hollis Alpert in the *Saturday Review* noted, "The success of his more than three-hour-long motion picture is twofold: he has put on the screen an entirely absorbing story, and he has provided thoughtful insights into the nature of Nazism and its hold on the German people."

Maximilian Schell, repeating the role he originated on the television version of *Judgment,* won an Academy Award for his electric performance and Abby Mann won for his deft screenplay. *Judgment at Nuremberg* also received nominations for Best Picture, Best Actor (Spencer Tracy), Best Supporting Actor (Montgomery Clift), Best Supporting Actress (Judy Garland), Best Director (Stanley Kramer), Best Photographer (Ernest Laszlio), Best Editor (Fred Knudtson), Best Costumes (Jean Louis), and Best Art Direction (Rudolph Sternad and George Milo).

Black Fox

An Arthur Steloff-Image Production
Released by Heritage Films, Inc.

(A Documentary Feature)—1962

CREDITS: LOUIS CLYDE STOUMEN (*Director* and *Producer*); JACK LE VIEN (*Executive Producer*); LOUIS CLYDE STOUMEN (*Script*); MARLENE DIETRICH (*Narrator*); AL STAHL (*Animation Supervision*); RICHARD KAPLAN (*Production Supervisor*); KENN COLLINS, MARK WORTREICH (*Editors*); EZRA LADERMAN (*Musical Score*); Distributed by METRO-GOLDWYN-MAYER.

SYNOPSIS: This brilliant documentary made by Americans about the German dictator Adolf Hitler displayed new material and more perspective and insight than had previous films on the same subject.

Weaving the life of Hitler into a medieval tale about the cruel and cunning Reynard the Fox, Louis Clyde Stoumen converted history into a bitter allegory. Never before had the reality of the greed and euphoria of Nazi Germany been so profoundly displayed.

In addition to actual films of Hitler this documentary feature made use of Gustav Doré's illustrations for Dante's "Inferno" and the etching of Wilhelm von Kaulbach illustrating the legend of "Reynard the Fox." Goethe's adaptation of the old fable served as a frame for the entire film. All was heightened by contemporary drawings, the best of which were the caricatures of George Grosz. The pointedly juxtaposed film footage was effectively edited.

NOTES: *Black Fox* won an Academy Award as the best feature-length documentary in 1962. It was worthy of that honor.

Variety said, "Marlene Dietrich's mellifluous accented voice is a neat counterpart to the blending of fact and image and she also adds a note of drama and feeling without any false histrionics. It is all soberly and absorbingly executed."

The *Christian Science Monitor* had this to say: "Against the background of this collage of fact and fantasy images, Marlene Dietrich reads in a voice of deceptive languor the angrily ironic narration, which finds Mr. Stoumen profoundly disturbed, of course, by what happened, but even more outraged by why it happened."

In the *Los Angeles Herald-Examiner,* John G. Houser said, "Miss Marlene Dietrich, German born, and who witnessed the birth of Nazism before fleeing to become an American citizen, narrates the moving documentary without malice or evident emotion but with perceptivity and almost clinical analysis. At times there was spontaneous applause for comments coupled with the visual material."

Frank Mulcahy commented in the *Los Angeles Times,* "The narration is by Marlene Dietrich, whose purposely unemotional and seemingly matter-of-fact delivery is far more effective than the 'Voice-of-Doom' announcer commonly used in documentaries."

Perhaps the most moving segment concerned the extermination camp victims, with Dietrich saying, "And the children . . . they didn't even spare the children."

Paris When it Sizzles

A Paramount Picture in Technicolor—1964

CAST: WILLIAM HOLDEN (*Richard Benson*); AUDREY HEPBURN (*Gabrielle Simpson*); GREGOIRE ASLAN (*police inspector*); NOEL COWARD (*Alexander Mayerheimer*); RAMOND BUSSIERES (*gangster*); CHRISTIAN DUVALLEX (*maitre d'hotel*) and THOMAS MICHEL; with unbilled guest appearances by Marlene Dietrich, Tony Curtis, and Mel Ferrer, and the voices of Fred Astaire and Frank Sinatra.

CREDITS: RICHARD QUINE (*Director*); RICHARD QUINE, GEORGE AXELROD (*Producers*); GEORGE AXELROD (*Scenarist*); CHARLES LANG, JR. (*Photographer*); NELSON RIDDLE (*Musical Score*); JEAN D'EAUBOUNE (*Set Decorator*); HUBERT DE GIVENCHY (*Miss Hepburn's Gowns*); ARCHIE MARSHEK (*Editor*); PAUL FEYDER (*Assistant Director*); CHRISTIAN DIOR (*Miss Dietrich's Gowns*); Based on a story by JULIEN DUVIVIER and HENRI JEANSON.

SYNOPSIS: Richard Benson (William Holden), a vain, semi-drunk hack screenwriter residing in a lavish roof-top suite of a Paris hotel, has two or three days in which to whip up a cloak-and-dagger yarn for Mayerheimer Productions. He hires a young typist, Gabrielle Simpson (Audrey Hepburn), to work along with him on this project. She agrees to stay with him in the apartment-suite because of the short deadline.

On the set with director Richard Quine

Between them, they dream up fantastic plots, characters, and situations, envisioning themselves in the major parts as spies, lovers, gangsters, secret agents, etc. After such shenanigans, Benson has fallen for Gabrielle hook, line, and sinker.

NOTES: The obvious fault with this dreary film was its script. In short, it was a film having script troubles dealing with a scriptwriter having similar troubles. It was dull, ponderous, and witless entertainment. Much too much of the film was spent in wildly-decorated dream sequences as the two, Richard and Gabrielle, devise various plots for this screenplay.

Dietrich's appearance was an all-too-brief sight gag. Stepping out of a limousine and darting into the House of Dior in Paris, she was divinely clad in one of Dior's exquisite white creations with a hat to match.

Variety summed up their review in the words, "contrived, utterly preposterous and totally unmotivated," whereas *Newsweek* began theirs with "Audrey Hepburn and William Holden are not so much the stars as the captives of *Paris When It Sizzles.*" Most other reviewers merely paraphrased the final word of the title: *Paris When It Sizzles . . .* fizzles!

Schöner Gigolo—
Armer Gigolo
(Just a Gigolo)

A Leguan film Production—1979
Released in the U.S. by United Artists Classics—1981

CAST: DAVID BOWIE *(Paul von Przygodsky);* SYDNE ROME *(Cilly);* KIM NOVAK *(Helga);* DAVID HEMMINGS *(Capt. Hermann Kraft);* MARIA SCHELL *(Mutti);* CURT JURGENS *(Prince);* MARLENE DIETRICH *(Baroness von Semering);* ERIKA PLUHAR *(Eva);* RUDOLF SCHUNDLER *(Gustav, Paul's Father);* HILDE WEISSNER *(Aunt Hilda);* WERNER POCHATH *(Otto);* BELA ERNY *(Von Lipzig);* FRIEDHELM LEHMANN *(Maj. von Muller);* RAINER HUNOLD *(Lothar);* EVELYN KUN-NEKE *(Frau Aeckerle);* KARIN HARDT *(Frau Uexkull);* GUDRUN GENEST *(Frau von Putzdorf);* URSULA HEYER *(Greta);* CHRISTIANE MAYBACH *(Gilda);* MARTIN HIRTHE *(Director);* RENE KOLLDEHOFF *(Max, Cilly's Agent);* GUNTER MEISNER *(Drunken Worker);* PETER SCHLESINGER *(First Man in Bath).*

CREDITS: DAVID HEMMINGS *(Director);* ROLF THIELE *(Producer);* ENNIO DE CONCINI, JOSHUA SIN-CLAIR *(Scenarists);* CHARLY STEINBERGER *(Photographer);* GUNTER FISCHER *(Musical Score);* Songs: "Revolutionary Song" by David Bowie and Jack Fishman, performed by Sydne Rome; "Johnny" by Frederick Hollander and Jack Fishman, "I Kiss Your Hand, Madame" by Ralph Erwin, Fritz Rotter, Sam Lewis and Joe Young, and "Jealous Eyes" by Mihaly Erdeli and Jack Fishman, all performed by The Manhattan Transfer; "Salome" by Robert Stolz and Arthur Redner, "Charmaine" by Erno Rappe and Lew Pollack, "Black Bottom" by Ray Henderson, Buddy De Sylva and Nacio Herb Brown, all performed by The Pasadena Roof Orchestra; "Ragtime Dance" by Scott Joplin and A.S. Masters (arranged by Jack Fishman), "Easy Winners" by Scott Joplin (arranged by Jack Fishman), both performed by The Ragtimers; "Just a Gigolo" by L. Casucci and Irving Caesar,

performed by Marlene Dietrich; "Don't Let It Be Too Long" by Günther Fischer and David Hemmings, performed by Sydne Rome; PETER ROTHE *(Production Designer);* MAX MAGO, INGRID ZORE *(Costumes);* ALFRED SRP, SUSAN JAEGER, MAXINE JULIUS *(Editors);* HERBERT F. SCHUBERT *(Choreographer);* EVA MARIA SCHONECKER *(Assistant Director).*

SYNOPSIS: In wartime 1918 Germany, enthusiastic young Lt. Paul von Przygodsky (portrayed by the bland, inanimate David Bowie) reports at the front to Capt. Hermann Kraft (the film's director, David Hemmings), but is seriously injured by an exploding mine just as the armistice is announced. Two years later, after recuperating in a military hospital, Paul returns to the family that believed him dead: his father (Rudolf Schündler), literally paralyzed by German's defeat; and his mother (Maria Schell), who works in a Turkish bath. There's also a warm welcome from— Cilly (Sydne Rome), the housekeeper's rebellious, now-grown daughter, who wants to be an entertainer; and Eva (Erika Pluhar), his family's tenant, whose profession is entertaining men. There's mutual attraction between Paul and both women, as he finds employment as a sandwich-board man.

In 1924, Paul is reunited with Capt. Kraft, who shares quarters with his lover Otto (Werner Pochath) and works underground for the new Germany. Paul goes to work for the party, as well, until his alliance is disrupted by Otto's jealousy and the disapproval of Cilly, who has become a cabaret star. But before she can seduce Paul, she's offered a Hollywood movie and she leaves Germany. Thereafter, Paul meets and enters into an affair with the wealthy and glamorous widow Helga (Kim Novak), going on to join the stable of gigolos working under the auspices of the formidable Baroness von Semering (a subdued but characteristically enigmatic Marlene Dietrich) at Berlin's Eden Bar. Helga returns with a wealthy but elderly new husband, who wants to adopt Paul, but the latter declines when the old man wants them to make love in his presence. Cilly returns from Hollywood a film star, intent on marrying an elderly German Prince (Curt Jurgens). At the same time, she's amorous toward Paul, who informs her she'll have to pay for his time at the Eden. As the Baroness steps to the Bar's piano and croons "Just a Gigolo," Paul wanders outside, and is killed by a bullet fired in a street fight between Communists and Nazis. Using Paul as a martyr for his cause, Kraft attires the body as a Nazi and accords him a hero's funeral.

NOTES: Reputedly, this was Germany's most costly post-war film (at 12-million DM). Originally released there in 1979 at a length of 147 minutes, *Just a Gigolo* was negatively received by both press and public, and was subsequently cut by some forty-two minutes before eventually being shown in an English-language version in Britain and the U.S. Again, there was little excitement stirred up for the picture, outside of some general interest in its international cast, especially in the case of little-seen Kim Novak and, of course, Dietrich—then missing from American screens for seventeen years! For many, Marlene's cameo became the picture's sole attraction. How did she look? How did she sound? Was she photographed through gauze? Her screen credit reads "and with pride Marlene Dietrich," but her cameo consists of but two brief scenes in the movie's final half-hour, reportedly shot in Paris (although credits proudly announce "filmed entirely in Berlin"), and in neither of which does she share a frame with her vis-à-vis, David Bowie. Veiled but still visibly beautiful at seventy-six, Dietrich interviews him for her gigolo-stable, then returns to sing the film's title song, during which Paul leaves the Eden Bar to meet his fate. And yet, while she talk-sings (in a faint echo of her old style) the song's close, director David Hemmings's cameras actually *leave* her—without so much as a final close-up—to follow *Bowie*, as the familiar Dietrich baritone voice croons, "When the end comes, I know they'll say 'just a gigolo,' as life goes on...without me." It provides a quietly poignant moment, devoid of sentiment, yet hardly doing justice to a great screen legend's final appearance.

As the Baroness with her gigolos

Marlene

(A Documentary Feature)

An Oko-Filmproduktion/Karel Dirka Film—1984
Released in the U.S. by Alive Films—1986

CREDITS: MAXIMILIAN SCHELL *(Director);* PETER
GENÉE *(Producer);* NORBERT BITTMANN *(Co-Pro-
ducer);* MEIR DOHNAL, MAXIMILIAN SCHELL
(Script); IVAN SLAPETA, PAVEL HISPLER, HENRY
HAUCK *(Photographers);* MICHAEL KUNSDORFF,
BAVARIA TRICKTEAM *(Rostrum Photography);*
PAVEL VOSICKY, RUDOLF ROEMMELT *(Graphics);*
HEIDI GENÉE, DAGMAR HIRTZ *(Editors);* HEINZ
EICKMEIER, ZBYNEK HLOCH *(Art Directors);*
NICHOLAS EICKMEIER *(Costumes);* NICHOLAS
ECONOMOU *(Musical Score);* with ANNIE ALBERS,
BERNARD HALL, MARTA RAKOSNIK, PATRICIA
SCHELL, IVANA SPINNELL, WILLIAM VON STRANZ:
and the voices of MARLENE DIETRICH, MAXI-
MILIAN SCHELL. Film Clips—*Tragödie der Liebe*
(1923); *Ich Kusse Ihre Hand, Madame* (1929); *Der
Blaue Engel/The Blue Angel* (1930); *Morocco*
(1930); *Dishonored* (1931); *Blonde Venus* (1932);
The Scarlet Empress (1934); *The Devil Is a Woman*
(1935); *Desire* (1936); *Destry Rides Again* (1939);
Citizen Kane (1941); *Stage Fright* (1950); *Witness
for the Prosecution* (1957); *Touch of Evil* (1958);
Judgment at Nuremberg (1961); *Schöner Gigolo—
Armer Gigolo/Just a Gigolo* (1979). In subtitled
German, French, and English dialogue.

With Spencer Tracy in Judgment at Nuremberg *(1962)*

With Gary Cooper and John Halliday in Desire *(1936)*

With James Stewart in Destry Rides Again *(1939)*

With John Williams in Witness for the Prosecution *(1957)*

NOTES: Considering that its subject—then eighty-one-year-old movie legend Marlene Dietrich—was alive, well, and living (not yet in her eventual seclusion) in Paris, this is a unique and extraordinary documentary. Dietrich had contracted to submit to forty hours of interviews by actor/filmmaker Maximilian Schell—an Oscar-winning co-star of *Judgment at Nuremberg* in which the actress had her last substantial role. But she adamantly refused either to be photographed or even to allow her Paris apartment—in which all of the interviews were conducted—to appear on camera. Thus, director Schell and producer Peter Genée were forced to exercise their creative ingenuity. And so, following taping sessions in 1982 with the often-contentious actress, they reconstructed her living quarters in a movie studio, directing cameras over the area to help give viewers as close a look at her furnishings and possessions as could be approximated. And, while carefully edited excerpts from Dietrich's recorded answers to Schell's questions illuminate the reproduced Parisian interiors, a succession of well-chosen film clips offer a cursory survey of Marlene's glamorous screen career, from the German silent *Tragödie der Liebe* to her final motion picture cameo in the 1978-made *Just a Gigolo,* and concert footage, photographed in both color and monochrome.

In the audio portions here included, the legendary lady shows little interest in her career ("I was an actress. I made films. Period.") and no concern whatever for the glamorous mystique she once nurtured ("I wasn't contracted to be exciting."). Dietrich's husky speaking voice, as recorded in 1982, sounds perhaps even deeper in timbre than one might expect, and considerably aged: sometimes her tones are firm and definite, but at others, shaky and even a bit slurred. Frequently, she dismisses her movies and her career as "kitsch" and "rubbish," disclaiming any continued interest in them on her part. She harbors no nostalgia for *The Blue Angel,* her breakthrough film, dismissing co-star Emil Jannings as "hammy" and her own erotic Lola-Lola as merely "snotty." Asked why she persists in claiming *The Devil Is a Woman* (1935) to be her finest picture, she childishly snaps, "Because it's the best!"

Critical commentary on *Marlene* ranged from "hypnotic hodge-podge" to "a tartly funny, utterly fascinating film" and "Schell's moving, unconventional documentary." Unquestionably, it remains among the most unusual biographical documentary movies ever produced.

With Richard Todd in Stage Fright *(1950)*

With Rosa Valletti in Der Blaue Engel/The Blue Angel *(1930)*

Dietrich in World War II

At the Hollywood Canteen:

..............With actor Laird Cregar and servicemen

..............With Deanna Durbin, Sgt. Carl Bell (millionth serviceman to visit the Canteen), Lana Turner, and Eddie Cantor

..............With a group of sailors and marines

Inspecting a lineup of GI "gams" at Namur, Belgium

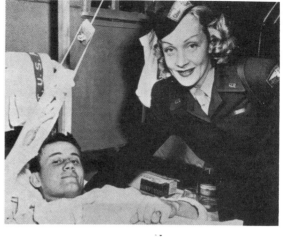

Visiting a wounded soldier in a hospital somewhere in Europe

At the first Inter-Allied Athletic Meet in Berlin's Olympic Stadium, 1945

Slogging through mud with a group of GI's in her native Germany

With Irving Berlin in Italy

Two previously unpublished photographs: Dietrich with Russian and American troops in Germany

The Lady Goes Legit

*An album of photographs of Marlene since her return to
the stage . . . in night clubs and theatres all over the world*